Just The facts101

Textbook Key Facts

Doing Business and Investing

in Kyrgyzstan Guide

by Cram101

Table of Contents

Just The Facts101

Exam Prep for

Doing Business and Investing in Kyrgyzstan Guide

Just The Facts101 Exam Prep is your link from
the textbook and lecture to your exams.

**Just The Facts101 Exam Preps are unauthorized and comprehensive reviews
of your textbooks.**

All material provided by CTI Publications (c) 2019

Textbook publishers and textbook authors do not participate in or contribute to these reviews.

Just The Facts101 Exam Prep

eAIN 444617

Foundations of Business

A business, also known as an enterprise, agency or a firm, is an entity involved in the provision of goods and/or services to consumers. Businesses are prevalent in capitalist economies, where most of them are privately owned and provide goods and services to customers in exchange for other goods, services, or money.

:: Critical thinking ::

In psychology, _____ is regarded as the cognitive process resulting in the selection of a belief or a course of action among several alternative possibilities. Every _____ process produces a final choice, which may or may not prompt action.

Exam Probability: **Low**

1. *Answer choices:*

(see index for correct answer)

- a. Decision-making
- b. Rigour
- c. Interpretive discussion
- d. Source credibility

Guidance: level 1

:: Export and import control ::

" _____ " means the Government Service which is responsible for the administration of _____ law and the collection of duties and taxes and which also has the responsibility for the application of other laws and regulations relating to the importation, exportation, movement or storage of goods.

Exam Probability: **Medium**

2. *Answer choices:*

(see index for correct answer)

- a. ATA Carnet
- b. Export of cryptography
- c. Customs
- d. GOST R Conformity Declaration

Guidance: level 1

:: Critical thinking ::

An _____ is a set of statements usually constructed to describe a set of facts which clarifies the causes, context, and consequences of those facts. This description of the facts et cetera may establish rules or laws, and may clarify the existing rules or laws in relation to any objects, or phenomena examined. The components of an _____ can be implicit, and interwoven with one another.

Exam Probability: **High**

3. *Answer choices:*

(see index for correct answer)

- a. Explanation
- b. Pseudophilosophy
- c. False equivalence
- d. Decidophobia

:: Fraud ::

> In law, _____ is intentional deception to secure unfair or unlawful gain, or to deprive a victim of a legal right. _____ can violate civil law , a criminal law , or it may cause no loss of money, property or legal right but still be an element of another civil or criminal wrong. The purpose of _____ may be monetary gain or other benefits, for example by obtaining a passport, travel document, or driver`s license, or mortgage _____ , where the perpetrator may attempt to qualify for a mortgage by way of false statements.

Exam Probability: **Medium**

4. *Answer choices:*

(see index for correct answer)

- a. Fraud
- b. Intrinsic fraud
- c. Identity theft
- d. Shell corporation

:: Marketing ::

_____ is the percentage of a market accounted for by a specific entity. In a survey of nearly 200 senior marketing managers, 67% responded that they found the revenue- "dollar _____" metric very useful, while 61% found "unit _____" very useful.

Exam Probability: **Medium**

5. *Answer choices:*

(see index for correct answer)

- a. Instant rebate
- b. Market share
- c. Experiential marketing
- d. Corporate anniversary

Guidance: level 1

:: Reputation management ::

_____ or image of a social entity is an opinion about that entity, typically as a result of social evaluation on a set of criteria.

Exam Probability: **Low**

6. *Answer choices:*

(see index for correct answer)

- a. Star
- b. Reputation
- c. Whuffie
- d. TrustedSource

Guidance: level 1

:: Business planning ::

_____ is an organization's process of defining its strategy, or direction, and making decisions on allocating its resources to pursue this strategy. It may also extend to control mechanisms for guiding the implementation of the strategy. _____ became prominent in corporations during the 1960s and remains an important aspect of strategic management. It is executed by strategic planners or strategists, who involve many parties and research sources in their analysis of the organization and its relationship to the environment in which it competes.

Exam Probability: **Medium**

7. *Answer choices:*
(see index for correct answer)

- a. Business war games
- b. Exit planning
- c. Strategic planning
- d. Community Futures

:: Meetings ::

An _____ is a group of people who participate in a show or encounter a work of art, literature , theatre, music , video games , or academics in any medium. _____ members participate in different ways in different kinds of art; some events invite overt _____ participation and others allowing only modest clapping and criticism and reception.

Exam Probability: **Low**

8. *Answer choices:*

(see index for correct answer)

- a. Salon
- b. Prayer meeting
- c. Representative town meeting
- d. Altenberg Workshops in Theoretical Biology

:: Real estate ::

_____ s serve several societal needs – primarily as shelter from weather, security, living space, privacy, to store belongings, and to comfortably live and work. A _____ as a shelter represents a physical division of the human habitat and the outside .

Exam Probability: **Low**

9. *Answer choices:*

(see index for correct answer)

- a. Premises liability
- b. Building
- c. Land agent
- d. Finca

Guidance: level 1

:: Casting (manufacturing) ::

A _____ is a regularity in the world, man-made design, or abstract ideas. As such, the elements of a _____ repeat in a predictable manner. A geometric _____ is a kind of _____ formed of geometric shapes and typically repeated like a wallpaper design.

Exam Probability: **Medium**

10. *Answer choices:*

(see index for correct answer)

- a. Entrainment defect
- b. Pattern
- c. Lost-foam casting
- d. Cope and drag

Guidance: level 1

:: Marketing ::

A _____ is a group of customers within a business's serviceable available market at which a business aims its marketing efforts and resources. A _____ is a subset of the total market for a product or service. The _____ typically consists of consumers who exhibit similar characteristics and are considered most likely to buy a business's market offerings or are likely to be the most profitable segments for the business to service.

Exam Probability: **High**

11. *Answer choices:*
(see index for correct answer)

- a. Editorial calendar
- b. Partnerized inventory management
- c. Product
- d. Business stature

:: ::

_____ is an abstract concept of management of complex systems according to a set of rules and trends. In systems theory, these types of rules exist in various fields of biology and society, but the term has slightly different meanings according to context. For example.

Exam Probability: **Medium**

12. *Answer choices:*

(see index for correct answer)

- a. levels of analysis
- b. Regulation
- c. process perspective
- d. similarity-attraction theory

:: Workplace ::

_____ is a systematic determination of a subject's merit, worth and significance, using criteria governed by a set of standards. It can assist an organization, program, design, project or any other intervention or initiative to assess any aim, realisable concept/proposal, or any alternative, to help in decision-making; or to ascertain the degree of achievement or value in regard to the aim and objectives and results of any such action that has been completed. The primary purpose of _____ , in addition to gaining insight into prior or existing initiatives, is to enable reflection and assist in the identification of future change.

Exam Probability: **Low**

13. *Answer choices:*

(see index for correct answer)

- a. Workplace aggression
- b. Workplace spirituality
- c. Emotions in the workplace
- d. Rat race

Guidance: level 1

:: Product management ::

A _____ , trade mark, or trade-mark is a recognizable sign, design, or expression which identifies products or services of a particular source from those of others, although _____ s used to identify services are usually called service marks. The _____ owner can be an individual, business organization, or any legal entity. A _____ may be located on a package, a label, a voucher, or on the product itself. For the sake of corporate identity, _____ s are often displayed on company buildings. It is legally recognized as a type of intellectual property.

Exam Probability: **Low**

14. *Answer choices:*

(see index for correct answer)

- a. Product manager
- b. Trademark
- c. Swing tag
- d. Technology acceptance model

Guidance: level 1

:: Industrial Revolution ::

The _____ , now also known as the First _____ , was the transition to new manufacturing processes in Europe and the US, in the period from about 1760 to sometime between 1820 and 1840. This transition included going from hand production methods to machines, new chemical manufacturing and iron production processes, the increasing use of steam power and water power, the development of machine tools and the rise of the mechanized factory system. The _____ also led to an unprecedented rise in the rate of population growth.

Exam Probability: **Medium**

15. *Answer choices:*

(see index for correct answer)

- a. Ironworks
- b. Haarlem Mill
- c. Weaving shed
- d. Bread and Roses

Guidance: level 1

:: Business ethics ::

_____ is a type of harassment technique that relates to a sexual nature and the unwelcome or inappropriate promise of rewards in exchange for sexual favors. _____ includes a range of actions from mild transgressions to sexual abuse or assault. Harassment can occur in many different social settings such as the workplace, the home, school, churches, etc. Harassers or victims may be of any gender.

Exam Probability: **Low**

16. *Answer choices:*

(see index for correct answer)

- a. Jewish business ethics
- b. Moral hazard
- c. United Nations Global Compact
- d. Corporate social entrepreneurship

Guidance: level 1

:: ::

_____ is the study and management of exchange relationships. _____ is the business process of creating relationships with and satisfying customers. With its focus on the customer, _____ is one of the premier components of business management.

Exam Probability: **Medium**

17. *Answer choices:*

(see index for correct answer)

- a. information systems assessment
- b. imperative
- c. similarity-attraction theory

- d. levels of analysis

Guidance: level 1

:: Monopoly (economics) ::

A _____ is a form of intellectual property that gives its owner the legal right to exclude others from making, using, selling, and importing an invention for a limited period of years, in exchange for publishing an enabling public disclosure of the invention. In most countries _____ rights fall under civil law and the _____ holder needs to sue someone infringing the _____ in order to enforce his or her rights. In some industries _____ s are an essential form of competitive advantage; in others they are irrelevant.

Exam Probability: **Medium**

18. *Answer choices:*
(see index for correct answer)

- a. Privatization
- b. Legal monopoly
- c. Private finance initiative
- d. Patent

Guidance: level 1

:: International relations ::

A _____ is any event that is going to lead to an unstable and dangerous situation affecting an individual, group, community, or whole society. Crises are deemed to be negative changes in the security, economic, political, societal, or environmental affairs, especially when they occur abruptly, with little or no warning. More loosely, it is a term meaning "a testing time" or an "emergency event".

Exam Probability: **High**

19. *Answer choices:*

(see index for correct answer)

- a. Crisis
- b. Freedom of the seas
- c. Foreign policy interest group
- d. Russian and Eurasian Security Network

Guidance: level 1

:: Financial statements ::

In financial accounting, a _____ or statement of financial position or statement of financial condition is a summary of the financial balances of an individual or organization, whether it be a sole proprietorship, a business partnership, a corporation, private limited company or other organization such as Government or not-for-profit entity. Assets, liabilities and ownership equity are listed as of a specific date, such as the end of its financial year. A _____ is often described as a "snapshot of a company's financial condition". Of the four basic financial statements, the _____ is the only statement which applies to a single point in time of a business' calendar year.

Exam Probability: **High**

20. *Answer choices:*

(see index for correct answer)

- a. Balance sheet
- b. Government financial statements
- c. Statement of retained earnings
- d. PnL Explained

Guidance: level 1

:: Elementary arithmetic ::

In mathematics, a _____ is a number or ratio expressed as a fraction of 100. It is often denoted using the percent sign, "%", or the abbreviations "pct.", "pct"; sometimes the abbreviation "pc" is also used. A _____ is a dimensionless number .

21. *Answer choices:*

(see index for correct answer)

- a. Arithmetic for Parents
- b. Equality
- c. Trailing zero
- d. Alligation

Guidance: level 1

:: ::

A _____ is any person who contracts to acquire an asset in return for some form of consideration.

22. *Answer choices:*

(see index for correct answer)

- a. surface-level diversity
- b. co-culture
- c. Sarbanes-Oxley act of 2002
- d. hierarchical

:: Human resource management ::

_____ are the people who make up the workforce of an organization, business sector, or economy. "Human capital" is sometimes used synonymously with " _____ ", although human capital typically refers to a narrower effect . Likewise, other terms sometimes used include manpower, talent, labor, personnel, or simply people.

Exam Probability: **Medium**

23. *Answer choices:*

(see index for correct answer)

- a. Service record
- b. At-will employment
- c. Potential analysis
- d. Human resources

:: Summary statistics ::

_____ is the number of occurrences of a repeating event per unit of time. It is also referred to as temporal _____ , which emphasizes the contrast to spatial _____ and angular _____ . The period is the duration of time of one cycle in a repeating event, so the period is the reciprocal of the _____ . For example: if a newborn baby's heart beats at a _____ of 120 times a minute, its period—the time interval between beats—is half a second . _____ is an important parameter used in science and engineering to specify the rate of oscillatory and vibratory phenomena, such as mechanical vibrations, audio signals , radio waves, and light.

Exam Probability: **Medium**

24. *Answer choices:*

(see index for correct answer)

- a. Frequency distribution
- b. Decile
- c. Percentile
- d. Frequency

Guidance: level 1

:: Organizational behavior ::

_____ is the state or fact of exclusive rights and control over property, which may be an object, land/real estate or intellectual property. _____ involves multiple rights, collectively referred to as title, which may be separated and held by different parties.

25. *Answer choices:*

- a. Organizational citizenship behavior
- b. Collaborative partnerships
- c. Counterproductive norms
- d. Ownership

Guidance: level 1

:: Industry ::

_____ describes various measures of the efficiency of production. Often , a _____ measure is expressed as the ratio of an aggregate output to a single input or an aggregate input used in a production process, i.e. output per unit of input. Most common example is the labour _____ measure, e.g., such as GDP per worker. There are many different definitions of _____ and the choice among them depends on the purpose of the _____ measurement and/or data availability. The key source of difference between various _____ measures is also usually related to how the outputs and the inputs are aggregated into scalars to obtain such a ratio-type measure of _____ .

26. *Answer choices:*

- a. Industrial robot
- b. Low carbon leakage
- c. Recommended exposure limit
- d. Productivity

Guidance: level 1

:: Graphic design ::

An _____ is an artifact that depicts visual perception, such as a photograph or other two-dimensional picture, that resembles a subject—usually a physical object—and thus provides a depiction of it. In the context of signal processing, an _____ is a distributed amplitude of color.

Exam Probability: **Low**

27. *Answer choices:*

(see index for correct answer)

- a. Stencil
- b. Adobe Creative Suite
- c. Rapid visualization
- d. Creative Review

Guidance: level 1

:: Information science ::

A _____ is a written, drawn, presented, or memorialized representation
of thought. a _____ is a form, or written piece that trains a line of
thought or as in history, a significant event. The word originates from the
Latin _____ um, which denotes a "teaching" or "lesson": the verb doceo
denotes "to teach". In the past, the word was usually used to denote a written
proof useful as evidence of a truth or fact. In the computer age, " _____ "
usually denotes a primarily textual computer file, including its structure and
format, e.g. fonts, colors, and images. Contemporarily, " _____ " is not
defined by its transmission medium, e.g., paper, given the existence of
electronic _____ s. " _____ ation" is distinct because it has more
denotations than " _____ ". _____ s are also distinguished from
"realia", which are three-dimensional objects that would otherwise satisfy the
definition of " _____ " because they memorialize or represent thought;
_____ s are considered more as 2 dimensional representations. While
_____ s are able to have large varieties of customization, all _____ s
are able to be shared freely, and have the right to do so, creativity can be
represented by _____ s, also. History, events, examples, opinion, etc. all
can be expressed in _____ s.

Exam Probability: **Medium**

28. *Answer choices:*

(see index for correct answer)

- a. Information flow
- b. Document
- c. Information centre
- d. Documentalist

Guidance: level 1

:: International trade ::

_____ or globalisation is the process of interaction and integration among people, companies, and governments worldwide. As a complex and multifaceted phenomenon, _____ is considered by some as a form of capitalist expansion which entails the integration of local and national economies into a global, unregulated market economy. _____ has grown due to advances in transportation and communication technology. With the increased global interactions comes the growth of international trade, ideas, and culture. _____ is primarily an economic process of interaction and integration that's associated with social and cultural aspects. However, conflicts and diplomacy are also large parts of the history of _____ , and modern _____ .

Exam Probability: **Low**

29. *Answer choices:*

(see index for correct answer)

- a. Balassa index
- b. Broad Economic Categories
- c. Regional integration
- d. Globalization

Guidance: level 1

:: Stock market ::

The _____ of a corporation is all of the shares into which ownership of the corporation is divided. In American English, the shares are commonly known as "_____ s". A single share of the _____ represents fractional ownership of the corporation in proportion to the total number of shares. This typically entitles the _____ holder to that fraction of the company's earnings, proceeds from liquidation of assets , or voting power, often dividing these up in proportion to the amount of money each _____ holder has invested. Not all _____ is necessarily equal, as certain classes of _____ may be issued for example without voting rights, with enhanced voting rights, or with a certain priority to receive profits or liquidation proceeds before or after other classes of shareholders.

Exam Probability: **High**

30. *Answer choices:*

(see index for correct answer)

- a. Stock
- b. Tech Buzz
- c. Stockjobber
- d. Intermarket sweep order

Guidance: level 1

:: International trade ::

The law or principle of _____ holds that under free trade, an agent will produce more of and consume less of a good for which they have a _____ . _____ is the economic reality describing the work gains from trade for individuals, firms, or nations, which arise from differences in their factor endowments or technological progress. In an economic model, agents have a _____ over others in producing a particular good if they can produce that good at a lower relative opportunity cost or autarky price, i.e. at a lower relative marginal cost prior to trade. One shouldn't compare the monetary costs of production or even the resource costs of production. Instead, one must compare the opportunity costs of producing goods across countries.

Exam Probability: **Low**

31. *Answer choices:*

(see index for correct answer)

- a. Special drawing rights
- b. Harberger-Laursen-Metzler effect
- c. Comparative advantage
- d. Asian Clearing Union

Guidance: level 1

:: Debt ::

_____ is when something, usually money, is owed by one party, the borrower or _____ or, to a second party, the lender or creditor. _____ is a deferred payment, or series of payments, that is owed in the future, which is what differentiates it from an immediate purchase. The _____ may be owed by sovereign state or country, local government, company, or an individual. Commercial _____ is generally subject to contractual terms regarding the amount and timing of repayments of principal and interest. Loans, bonds, notes, and mortgages are all types of _____ . The term can also be used metaphorically to cover moral obligations and other interactions not based on economic value. For example, in Western cultures, a person who has been helped by a second person is sometimes said to owe a " _____ of gratitude" to the second person.

Exam Probability: **Low**

32. *Answer choices:*

(see index for correct answer)

- a. Household debt
- b. Arrears
- c. Consumer debt
- d. Debt

Guidance: level 1

:: Electronic feedback ::

_____ occurs when outputs of a system are routed back as inputs as part of a chain of cause-and-effect that forms a circuit or loop. The system can then be said to feed back into itself. The notion of cause-and-effect has to be handled carefully when applied to _____ systems.

Exam Probability: **High**

33. *Answer choices:*

(see index for correct answer)

- a. Positive feedback
- b. feedback loop

Guidance: level 1

:: Cash flow ::

_____ s are narrowly interconnected with the concepts of value, interest rate and liquidity. A _____ that shall happen on a future day tN can be transformed into a _____ of the same value in t0.

Exam Probability: **Low**

34. *Answer choices:*

(see index for correct answer)

- a. Operating cash flow

- b. Cash flow
- c. Cash flow hedge
- d. Cash carrier

Guidance: level 1

:: Poker strategy ::

_____ is any measure taken to guard a thing against damage caused by outside forces. _____ can be provided to physical objects, including organisms, to systems, and to intangible things like civil and political rights. Although the mechanisms for providing _____ vary widely, the basic meaning of the term remains the same. This is illustrated by an explanation found in a manual on electrical wiring.

Exam Probability: **Low**

35. *Answer choices:*
(see index for correct answer)

- a. Position
- b. Fundamental theorem of poker
- c. M-ratio
- d. Protection

Guidance: level 1

:: Environmental economics ::

_____ is the process of people maintaining change in a balanced environment, in which the exploitation of resources, the direction of investments, the orientation of technological development and institutional change are all in harmony and enhance both current and future potential to meet human needs and aspirations. For many in the field, _____ is defined through the following interconnected domains or pillars: environment, economic and social, which according to Fritjof Capra is based on the principles of Systems Thinking. Sub-domains of sustainable development have been considered also: cultural, technological and political. While sustainable development may be the organizing principle for _____ for some, for others, the two terms are paradoxical . Sustainable development is the development that meets the needs of the present without compromising the ability of future generations to meet their own needs. Brundtland Report for the World Commission on Environment and Development introduced the term of sustainable development.

Exam Probability: **Medium**

36. *Answer choices:*
(see index for correct answer)

- a. Global Development and Environment Institute
- b. Bequest value
- c. Calvert Social Index
- d. Sustainability

Guidance: level 1

:: ::

In regulatory jurisdictions that provide for it , _____ is a group of laws and organizations designed to ensure the rights of consumers as well as fair trade, competition and accurate information in the marketplace. The laws are designed to prevent the businesses that engage in fraud or specified unfair practices from gaining an advantage over competitors. They may also provides additional protection for those most vulnerable in society. _____ laws are a form of government regulation that aim to protect the rights of consumers. For example, a government may require businesses to disclose detailed information about products—particularly in areas where safety or public health is an issue, such as food.

Exam Probability: **Medium**

37. *Answer choices:*

(see index for correct answer)

- a. surface-level diversity
- b. similarity-attraction theory
- c. interpersonal communication
- d. Character

Guidance: level 1

:: Analysis ::

_____ is the process of breaking a complex topic or substance into smaller parts in order to gain a better understanding of it. The technique has been applied in the study of mathematics and logic since before Aristotle , though _____ as a formal concept is a relatively recent development.

38. *Answer choices:*

(see index for correct answer)

- a. Narrative logic
- b. Gompertz constant
- c. Analysis
- d. Situational analysis

Guidance: level 1

:: Semiconductor companies ::

_____ Corporation is a Japanese multinational conglomerate corporation headquartered in Konan, Minato, Tokyo. Its diversified business includes consumer and professional electronics, gaming, entertainment and financial services. The company owns the largest music entertainment business in the world, the largest video game console business and one of the largest video game publishing businesses, and is one of the leading manufacturers of electronic products for the consumer and professional markets, and a leading player in the film and television entertainment industry. _____ was ranked 97th on the 2018 Fortune Global 500 list.

Exam Probability: **High**

39. *Answer choices:*

(see index for correct answer)

- a. Vishay Intertechnology
- b. SVTC Technologies
- c. Fujitsu
- d. Reading Works

Guidance: level 1

:: Infographics ::

A _____ is a symbolic representation of information according to visualization technique. _____ s have been used since ancient times, but became more prevalent during the Enlightenment. Sometimes, the technique uses a three-dimensional visualization which is then projected onto a two-dimensional surface. The word graph is sometimes used as a synonym for _____ .

Exam Probability: **High**

40. *Answer choices:*

(see index for correct answer)

- a. Treemapping
- b. FusionCharts
- c. Blueprint
- d. Isotype

Guidance: level 1

:: Mathematical finance ::

In economics and finance, _____ , also known as present discounted value, is the value of an expected income stream determined as of the date of valuation. The _____ is always less than or equal to the future value because money has interest-earning potential, a characteristic referred to as the time value of money, except during times of negative interest rates, when the _____ will be more than the future value. Time value can be described with the simplified phrase, "A dollar today is worth more than a dollar tomorrow". Here, `worth more` means that its value is greater. A dollar today is worth more than a dollar tomorrow because the dollar can be invested and earn a day's worth of interest, making the total accumulate to a value more than a dollar by tomorrow. Interest can be compared to rent. Just as rent is paid to a landlord by a tenant without the ownership of the asset being transferred, interest is paid to a lender by a borrower who gains access to the money for a time before paying it back. By letting the borrower have access to the money, the lender has sacrificed the exchange value of this money, and is compensated for it in the form of interest. The initial amount of the borrowed funds is less than the total amount of money paid to the lender.

Exam Probability: **Low**

41. *Answer choices:*

(see index for correct answer)

- a. Consumer math
- b. Econophysics
- c. Present value
- d. Risk-neutral measure

Guidance: level 1

:: Consumer theory ::

_____ is the quantity of a good that consumers are willing and able to purchase at various prices during a given period of time.

Exam Probability: **High**

42. *Answer choices:*

(see index for correct answer)

- a. Preference
- b. Demand
- c. Engel curve
- d. Expenditure function

Guidance: level 1

:: Asset ::

In financial accounting, an _____ is any resource owned by the business. Anything tangible or intangible that can be owned or controlled to produce value and that is held by a company to produce positive economic value is an _____ . Simply stated, _____ s represent value of ownership that can be converted into cash . The balance sheet of a firm records the monetary value of the _____ s owned by that firm. It covers money and other valuables belonging to an individual or to a business.

43. *Answer choices:*

(see index for correct answer)

- a. Fixed asset
- b. Asset

Guidance: level 1

:: Basic financial concepts ::

_____ is a sustained increase in the general price level of goods and services in an economy over a period of time. When the general price level rises, each unit of currency buys fewer goods and services; consequently, _____ reflects a reduction in the purchasing power per unit of money a loss of real value in the medium of exchange and unit of account within the economy. The measure of _____ is the _____ rate, the annualized percentage change in a general price index, usually the consumer price index, over time. The opposite of _____ is deflation.

Exam Probability: **Low**

44. *Answer choices:*

(see index for correct answer)

- a. Inflation
- b. Base effect

- c. Financial transaction
- d. Present value of costs

Guidance: level 1

:: Business law ::

_____ is where a person's financial liability is limited to a fixed sum, most commonly the value of a person's investment in a company or partnership. If a company with _____ is sued, then the claimants are suing the company, not its owners or investors. A shareholder in a limited company is not personally liable for any of the debts of the company, other than for the amount already invested in the company and for any unpaid amount on the shares in the company, if any. The same is true for the members of a _____ partnership and the limited partners in a limited partnership. By contrast, sole proprietors and partners in general partnerships are each liable for all the debts of the business .

Exam Probability: **Low**

45. *Answer choices:*

(see index for correct answer)

- a. Apparent authority
- b. Tacit relocation
- c. Limited liability limited partnership
- d. Limited liability

Guidance: level 1

:: Information technology ::

_____ is the use of computers to store, retrieve, transmit, and manipulate data, or information, often in the context of a business or other enterprise. IT is considered to be a subset of information and communications technology . An _____ system is generally an information system, a communications system or, more specifically speaking, a computer system – including all hardware, software and peripheral equipment – operated by a limited group of users.

Exam Probability: **High**

46. *Answer choices:*

(see index for correct answer)

- a. Attra
- b. Information technology
- c. Iomart Group plc
- d. Mobile file management

Guidance: level 1

:: Corporate crime ::

_____ LLP, based in Chicago, was an American holding company. Formerly one of the "Big Five" accounting firms , the firm had provided auditing, tax, and consulting services to large corporations. By 2001, it had become one of the world's largest multinational companies.

Exam Probability: **High**

47. *Answer choices:*

(see index for correct answer)

- a. NatWest Three
- b. Holdings of American International Group
- c. Equity Funding
- d. Titan Corporation

Guidance: level 1

:: Competition regulators ::

The _____ is an independent agency of the United States government, established in 1914 by the _____ Act. Its principal mission is the promotion of consumer protection and the elimination and prevention of anticompetitive business practices, such as coercive monopoly. It is headquartered in the _____ Building in Washington, D.C.

Exam Probability: **Medium**

48. *Answer choices:*

(see index for correct answer)

- a. Competition Authority
- b. Federal Trade Commission
- c. Competition Bureau
- d. Competition Appeal Tribunal

Guidance: level 1

:: Survey methodology ::

An _____ is a conversation where questions are asked and answers are given. In common parlance, the word "_____" refers to a one-on-one conversation between an _____ er and an _____ ee. The _____ er asks questions to which the _____ ee responds, usually so information may be transferred from _____ ee to _____ er . Sometimes, information can be transferred in both directions. It is a communication, unlike a speech, which produces a one-way flow of information.

Exam Probability: **Low**

49. *Answer choices:*

(see index for correct answer)

- a. Interview
- b. Sampling
- c. Group concept mapping

- d. World Association for Public Opinion Research

Guidance: level 1

:: Financial markets ::

A _____ is a financial market in which long-term debt or equity-backed securities are bought and sold. _____ s channel the wealth of savers to those who can put it to long-term productive use, such as companies or governments making long-term investments. Financial regulators like the Bank of England and the U.S. Securities and Exchange Commission oversee _____ s to protect investors against fraud, among other duties.

Exam Probability: **Medium**

50. *Answer choices:*

(see index for correct answer)

- a. Fundamentally based indexes
- b. Market maker
- c. Systematic trading
- d. Capital market

Guidance: level 1

:: Data collection ::

A _____ is an utterance which typically functions as a request for information. _____ s can thus be understood as a kind of illocutionary act in the field of pragmatics or as special kinds of propositions in frameworks of formal semantics such as alternative semantics or inquisitive semantics. The information requested is expected to be provided in the form of an answer.

_____ s are often conflated with interrogatives, which are the grammatical forms typically used to achieve them. Rhetorical _____ s, for example, are interrogative in form but may not be considered true _____ s as they are not expected to be answered. Conversely, non-interrogative grammatical structures may be considered _____ s as in the case of the imperative sentence "tell me your name".

Exam Probability: **Medium**

51. *Answer choices:*

(see index for correct answer)

- a. BanxQuote
- b. Human-based computation game
- c. Question
- d. SensoMotoric Instruments

Guidance: level 1

:: Project management ::

_____ is the right to exercise power, which can be formalized by a state and exercised by way of judges, appointed executives of government, or the ecclesiastical or priestly appointed representatives of a God or other deities.

Exam Probability: **Low**

52. *Answer choices:*

- a. Authority
- b. Hart Mason Index
- c. Project
- d. PRINCE2

Guidance: level 1

:: Health promotion ::

_____ , as defined by the World _____ Organization , is "a state of complete physical, mental and social well-being and not merely the absence of disease or infirmity." This definition has been subject to controversy, as it may have limited value for implementation. _____ may be defined as the ability to adapt and manage physical, mental and social challenges throughout life.

Exam Probability: **High**

53. *Answer choices:*

(see index for correct answer)

- a. High-deductible health plan
- b. Lifestyle management programme
- c. Health promotion
- d. Health

Guidance: level 1

:: Decision theory ::

A _____ is a deliberate system of principles to guide decisions and achieve rational outcomes. A _____ is a statement of intent, and is implemented as a procedure or protocol. Policies are generally adopted by a governance body within an organization. Policies can assist in both subjective and objective decision making. Policies to assist in subjective decision making usually assist senior management with decisions that must be based on the relative merits of a number of factors, and as a result are often hard to test objectively, e.g. work-life balance _____ . In contrast policies to assist in objective decision making are usually operational in nature and can be objectively tested, e.g. password _____ .

Exam Probability: **Low**

54. *Answer choices:*

(see index for correct answer)

- a. Fuzzy-trace theory

- b. Decision-theoretic rough sets
- c. ERulemaking
- d. Policy

Guidance: level 1

:: Actuarial science ::

_____ is the possibility of losing something of value. Values can be gained or lost when taking _____ resulting from a given action or inaction, foreseen or unforeseen . _____ can also be defined as the intentional interaction with uncertainty. Uncertainty is a potential, unpredictable, and uncontrollable outcome; _____ is a consequence of action taken in spite of uncertainty.

Exam Probability: **Medium**

55. *Answer choices:*

(see index for correct answer)

- a. Panjer recursion
- b. Risk
- c. Reliability theory
- d. Area compatibility factor

Guidance: level 1

:: Land value taxation ::

_____ , sometimes referred to as dry _____ , is the solid surface of Earth that is not permanently covered by water. The vast majority of human activity throughout history has occurred in _____ areas that support agriculture, habitat, and various natural resources. Some life forms have developed from predecessor species that lived in bodies of water.

Exam Probability: **High**

56. *Answer choices:*

(see index for correct answer)

- a. Physiocracy
- b. Georgism
- c. Land
- d. Harry Gunnison Brown

Guidance: level 1

:: Mereology ::

_____ , in the abstract, is what belongs to or with something, whether as an attribute or as a component of said thing. In the context of this article, it is one or more components , whether physical or incorporeal, of a person's estate; or so belonging to, as in being owned by, a person or jointly a group of people or a legal entity like a corporation or even a society. Depending on the nature of the _____ , an owner of _____ has the right to consume, alter, share, redefine, rent, mortgage, pawn, sell, exchange, transfer, give away or destroy it, or to exclude others from doing these things, as well as to perhaps abandon it; whereas regardless of the nature of the _____ , the owner thereof has the right to properly use it , or at the very least exclusively keep it.

Exam Probability: **High**

57. *Answer choices:*

(see index for correct answer)

- a. Non-wellfounded mereology
- b. Meronomy
- c. Mereological essentialism
- d. Property

Guidance: level 1

:: Management ::

In organizational studies, _____ is the efficient and effective development of an organization's resources when they are needed. Such resources may include financial resources, inventory, human skills, production resources, or information technology and natural resources.

Exam Probability: **Medium**

58. *Answer choices:*

(see index for correct answer)

- a. middle manager
- b. Resource management
- c. Public sector consulting
- d. Focused improvement

Guidance: level 1

:: Human resource management ::

_____ encompasses values and behaviors that contribute to the unique social and psychological environment of a business. The _____ influences the way people interact, the context within which knowledge is created, the resistance they will have towards certain changes, and ultimately the way they share knowledge. _____ represents the collective values, beliefs and principles of organizational members and is a product of factors such as history, product, market, technology, strategy, type of employees, management style, and national culture; culture includes the organization's vision, values, norms, systems, symbols, language, assumptions, environment, location, beliefs and habits.

59. *Answer choices:*

(see index for correct answer)

- a. Human resources
- b. Employee retention
- c. Organization chart
- d. Organizational culture

Guidance: level 1

Management

Management is the administration of an organization, whether it is a business, a not-for-profit organization, or government body. Management includes the activities of setting the strategy of an organization and coordinating the efforts of its employees (or of volunteers) to accomplish its objectives through the application of available resources, such as financial, natural, technological, and human resources.

:: Generally Accepted Accounting Principles ::

In accounting, _____ is the income that a business have from its normal business activities, usually from the sale of goods and services to customers. _____ is also referred to as sales or turnover. Some companies receive _____ from interest, royalties, or other fees. _____ may refer to business income in general, or it may refer to the amount, in a monetary unit, earned during a period of time, as in "Last year, Company X had _____ of $42 million". Profits or net income generally imply total _____ minus total expenses in a given period. In accounting, in the balance statement it is a subsection of the Equity section and _____ increases equity, it is often referred to as the "top line" due to its position on the income statement at the very top. This is to be contrasted with the "bottom line" which denotes net income .

Exam Probability: **High**

1. *Answer choices:*

(see index for correct answer)

- a. Revenue
- b. Operating statement
- c. Cost principle
- d. Gross sales

Guidance: level 1

:: Human resource management ::

_____ encompasses values and behaviors that contribute to the unique social and psychological environment of a business. The _____ influences the way people interact, the context within which knowledge is created, the resistance they will have towards certain changes, and ultimately the way they share knowledge. _____ represents the collective values, beliefs and principles of organizational members and is a product of factors such as history, product, market, technology, strategy, type of employees, management style, and national culture; culture includes the organization's vision, values, norms, systems, symbols, language, assumptions, environment, location, beliefs and habits.

Exam Probability: **High**

2. *Answer choices:*

(see index for correct answer)

- a. Co-determination
- b. Applicant tracking system
- c. Bonus payment
- d. Organizational culture

Guidance: level 1

:: Management ::

_____ is a process by which entities review the quality of all factors involved in production. ISO 9000 defines _____ as "A part of quality management focused on fulfilling quality requirements".

3. *Answer choices:*

(see index for correct answer)

- a. Quality control
- b. Court of Assistants
- c. Productive efficiency
- d. Profitable growth

Guidance: level 1

:: Export and import control ::

" _____ " means the Government Service which is responsible for the administration of _____ law and the collection of duties and taxes and which also has the responsibility for the application of other laws and regulations relating to the importation, exportation, movement or storage of goods.

Exam Probability: **Medium**

4. *Answer choices:*

(see index for correct answer)

- a. GOST R Conformity Declaration
- b. Customs

- c. Export of cryptography
- d. CoCom

Guidance: level 1

:: Employment discrimination ::

A _____ is a metaphor used to represent an invisible barrier that keeps a given demographic from rising beyond a certain level in a hierarchy.

Exam Probability: **High**

5. *Answer choices:*
(see index for correct answer)

- a. New South Wales selection bias
- b. Employment discrimination law in the European Union
- c. MacBride Principles
- d. LGBT employment discrimination in the United States

Guidance: level 1

:: Management accounting ::

In economics, _____ s, indirect costs or overheads are business expenses that are not dependent on the level of goods or services produced by the business. They tend to be time-related, such as interest or rents being paid per month, and are often referred to as overhead costs. This is in contrast to variable costs, which are volume-related and unknown at the beginning of the accounting year. For a simple example, such as a bakery, the monthly rent for the baking facilities, and the monthly payments for the security system and basic phone line are _____ s, as they do not change according to how much bread the bakery produces and sells. On the other hand, the wage costs of the bakery are variable, as the bakery will have to hire more workers if the production of bread increases. Economists reckon _____ as a entry barrier for new entrepreneurs.

Exam Probability: **High**

6. *Answer choices:*

(see index for correct answer)

- a. Customer profitability
- b. Semi-variable cost
- c. Cost accounting
- d. Certified Management Accountant

Guidance: level 1

:: Organizational theory ::

A _____ is an organizational theory that claims that there is no best way to organize a corporation, to lead a company, or to make decisions. Instead, the optimal course of action is contingent upon the internal and external situation. A contingent leader effectively applies their own style of leadership to the right situation.

Exam Probability: **High**

7. *Answer choices:*

(see index for correct answer)

- a. Formal consensus
- b. Organigraph
- c. Imprinting
- d. Organization development

Guidance: level 1

:: Teams ::

A _____ usually refers to a group of individuals who work together from different geographic locations and rely on communication technology such as email, FAX, and video or voice conferencing services in order to collaborate. The term can also refer to groups or teams that work together asynchronously or across organizational levels. Powell, Piccoli and Ives define _____ s as "groups of geographically, organizationally and/or time dispersed workers brought together by information and telecommunication technologies to accomplish one or more organizational tasks." According to Ale Ebrahim et. al. , _____ s can also be defined as "small temporary groups of geographically, organizationally and/or time dispersed knowledge workers who coordinate their work predominantly with electronic information and communication technologies in order to accomplish one or more organization tasks."

Exam Probability: **Low**

8. *Answer choices:*

(see index for correct answer)

- a. Virtual team
- b. team composition

Guidance: level 1

:: ::

_____ involves decision making. It can include judging the merits of multiple options and selecting one or more of them. One can make a _____ between imagined options or between real options followed by the corresponding action. For example, a traveler might choose a route for a journey based on the preference of arriving at a given destination as soon as possible. The preferred route can then follow from information such as the length of each of the possible routes, traffic conditions, etc. The arrival at a _____ can include more complex motivators such as cognition, instinct, and feeling.

Exam Probability: **Medium**

9. *Answer choices:*

(see index for correct answer)

- a. personal values
- b. similarity-attraction theory
- c. hierarchical
- d. Choice

Guidance: level 1

:: ::

_____ is the practice of protecting the natural environment by individuals, organizations and governments. Its objectives are to conserve natural resources and the existing natural environment and, where possible, to repair damage and reverse trends.

10. *Answer choices:*

(see index for correct answer)

- a. functional perspective
- b. deep-level diversity
- c. Environmental protection
- d. similarity-attraction theory

Guidance: level 1

:: Analysis ::

_____ is the process of breaking a complex topic or substance into smaller parts in order to gain a better understanding of it. The technique has been applied in the study of mathematics and logic since before Aristotle , though _____ as a formal concept is a relatively recent development.

Exam Probability: **Low**

11. *Answer choices:*

(see index for correct answer)

- a. Engineering analysis
- b. Configurational analysis
- c. Divergent question

- d. Analysis

Guidance: level 1

:: Supply chain management ::

_____ is the process of finding and agreeing to terms, and acquiring goods, services, or works from an external source, often via a tendering or competitive bidding process. _____ is used to ensure the buyer receives goods, services, or works at the best possible price when aspects such as quality, quantity, time, and location are compared. Corporations and public bodies often define processes intended to promote fair and open competition for their business while minimizing risks such as exposure to fraud and collusion.

Exam Probability: **Medium**

12. *Answer choices:*

(see index for correct answer)

- a. Dealer Business System
- b. Security risk
- c. Reverse auction
- d. Reverse logistics

Guidance: level 1

:: Market research ::

_____ is an organized effort to gather information about target markets or customers. It is a very important component of business strategy. The term is commonly interchanged with marketing research; however, expert practitioners may wish to draw a distinction, in that marketing research is concerned specifically about marketing processes, while _____ is concerned specifically with markets.

Exam Probability: **High**

13. *Answer choices:*

(see index for correct answer)

- a. Market research
- b. Email marketing
- c. BrandZ
- d. LRMR

Guidance: level 1

:: ::

A _____ is a professional who provides expert advice in a particular area such as security , management, education, accountancy, law, human resources, marketing , finance, engineering, science or any of many other specialized fields.

Exam Probability: **Low**

14. *Answer choices:*

(see index for correct answer)

- a. Consultant
- b. levels of analysis
- c. Sarbanes-Oxley act of 2002
- d. hierarchical perspective

Guidance: level 1

:: Organizational theory ::

_____ is the process of groups of organisms working or acting together for common, mutual, or some underlying benefit, as opposed to working in competition for selfish benefit. Many animal and plant species cooperate both with other members of their own species and with members of other species .

Exam Probability: **Medium**

15. *Answer choices:*

(see index for correct answer)

- a. Requisite organization
- b. Cooperation
- c. Organizational effectiveness
- d. resource dependence

:: ::

A _____ is a leader's method of providing direction, implementing plans, and motivating people. Various authors have proposed identifying many different _____ s as exhibited by leaders in the political, business or other fields. Studies on _____ are conducted in the military field, expressing an approach that stresses a holistic view of leadership, including how a leader's physical presence determines how others perceive that leader. The factors of physical presence in this context include military bearing, physical fitness, confidence, and resilience. The leader's intellectual capacity helps to conceptualize solutions and to acquire knowledge to do the job. A leader's conceptual abilities apply agility, judgment, innovation, interpersonal tact, and domain knowledge. Domain knowledge encompasses tactical and technical knowledge as well as cultural and geopolitical awareness. Daniel Goleman in his article "Leadership that Gets Results" talks about six styles of leadership.

Exam Probability: **High**

16. *Answer choices:*

(see index for correct answer)

- a. cultural
- b. levels of analysis
- c. interpersonal communication
- d. corporate values

:: Critical thinking ::

In psychology, _____ is regarded as the cognitive process resulting in the selection of a belief or a course of action among several alternative possibilities. Every _____ process produces a final choice, which may or may not prompt action.

Exam Probability: **Medium**

17. *Answer choices:*

(see index for correct answer)

- a. Scholarly method
- b. Scientific temper
- c. Decision-making
- d. Explanatory power

Guidance: level 1

:: ::

Business is the activity of making one's living or making money by producing or buying and selling products . Simply put, it is "any activity or enterprise entered into for profit. It does not mean it is a company, a corporation, partnership, or have any such formal organization, but it can range from a street peddler to General Motors."

18. *Answer choices:*

(see index for correct answer)

- a. Firm
- b. open system
- c. co-culture
- d. empathy

Guidance: level 1

:: ::

An _____ is a contingent motivator. Traditional _____ s are extrinsic motivators which reward actions to yield a desired outcome. The effectiveness of traditional _____ s has changed as the needs of Western society have evolved. While the traditional _____ model is effective when there is a defined procedure and goal for a task, Western society started to require a higher volume of critical thinkers, so the traditional model became less effective. Institutions are now following a trend in implementing strategies that rely on intrinsic motivations rather than the extrinsic motivations that the traditional _____ s foster.

Exam Probability: **High**

19. *Answer choices:*

(see index for correct answer)

- a. Incentive
- b. hierarchical perspective
- c. cultural
- d. open system

Guidance: level 1

:: Poker strategy ::

_____ is any measure taken to guard a thing against damage caused by outside forces. _____ can be provided to physical objects, including organisms, to systems, and to intangible things like civil and political rights. Although the mechanisms for providing _____ vary widely, the basic meaning of the term remains the same. This is illustrated by an explanation found in a manual on electrical wiring.

Exam Probability: **High**

20. *Answer choices:*

(see index for correct answer)

- a. Protection
- b. M-ratio
- c. Slow play
- d. Q-ratio

Guidance: level 1

:: Management ::

_____ is the identification, evaluation, and prioritization of risks followed by coordinated and economical application of resources to minimize, monitor, and control the probability or impact of unfortunate events or to maximize the realization of opportunities.

Exam Probability: **High**

21. *Answer choices:*

(see index for correct answer)

- a. Mushroom management
- b. Meeting system
- c. Earned schedule
- d. Product differentiation

Guidance: level 1

:: ::

The _____ is a political and economic union of 28 member states that are located primarily in Europe. It has an area of 4,475,757 km2 and an estimated population of about 513 million. The EU has developed an internal single market through a standardised system of laws that apply in all member states in those matters, and only those matters, where members have agreed to act as one. EU policies aim to ensure the free movement of people, goods, services and capital within the internal market, enact legislation in justice and home affairs and maintain common policies on trade, agriculture, fisheries and regional development. For travel within the Schengen Area, passport controls have been abolished. A monetary union was established in 1999 and came into full force in 2002 and is composed of 19 EU member states which use the euro currency.

Exam Probability: **Medium**

22. *Answer choices:*

(see index for correct answer)

- a. Sarbanes-Oxley act of 2002
- b. functional perspective
- c. European Union
- d. co-culture

Guidance: level 1

:: Management ::

A _____ is an idea of the future or desired result that a person or a group of people envisions, plans and commits to achieve. People endeavor to reach _____ s within a finite time by setting deadlines.

Exam Probability: **Low**

23. *Answer choices:*

(see index for correct answer)

- a. Bed management
- b. Goal
- c. Production flow analysis
- d. Industrial forensics

Guidance: level 1

:: ::

_____ or accountancy is the measurement, processing, and communication of financial information about economic entities such as businesses and corporations. The modern field was established by the Italian mathematician Luca Pacioli in 1494. _____ , which has been called the "language of business", measures the results of an organization's economic activities and conveys this information to a variety of users, including investors, creditors, management, and regulators. Practitioners of _____ are known as accountants. The terms " _____ " and "financial reporting" are often used as synonyms.

24. *Answer choices:*

(see index for correct answer)

- a. surface-level diversity
- b. Accounting
- c. functional perspective
- d. corporate values

Guidance: level 1

:: Training ::

_____ is teaching, or developing in oneself or others, any skills and knowledge that relate to specific useful competencies. _____ has specific goals of improving one's capability, capacity, productivity and performance. It forms the core of apprenticeships and provides the backbone of content at institutes of technology . In addition to the basic _____ required for a trade, occupation or profession, observers of the labor-market recognize as of 2008 the need to continue _____ beyond initial qualifications: to maintain, upgrade and update skills throughout working life. People within many professions and occupations may refer to this sort of _____ as professional development.

Exam Probability: **Medium**

25. *Answer choices:*

(see index for correct answer)

- a. Training
- b. Voluntary Protection Program
- c. Leonardo da Vinci programme
- d. Hot potato

Guidance: level 1

:: ::

In sales, commerce and economics, a _____ is the recipient of a good, service, product or an idea - obtained from a seller, vendor, or supplier via a financial transaction or exchange for money or some other valuable consideration.

Exam Probability: **High**

26. *Answer choices:*

(see index for correct answer)

- a. Customer
- b. empathy
- c. cultural
- d. deep-level diversity

Guidance: level 1

:: Strategic management ::

_____ is a strategic planning technique used to help a person or organization identify strengths, weaknesses, opportunities, and threats related to business competition or project planning. It is intended to specify the objectives of the business venture or project and identify the internal and external factors that are favorable and unfavorable to achieving those objectives. Users of a _____ often ask and answer questions to generate meaningful information for each category to make the tool useful and identify their competitive advantage. SWOT has been described as the tried-and-true tool of strategic analysis.

Exam Probability: **Low**

27. *Answer choices:*

(see index for correct answer)

- a. Rule of three
- b. International business strategy
- c. Earlyvangelist
- d. SWOT analysis

Guidance: level 1

:: Management ::

The _____ is a strategy performance management tool – a semi-standard structured report, that can be used by managers to keep track of the execution of activities by the staff within their control and to monitor the consequences arising from these actions.

Exam Probability: **Medium**

28. *Answer choices:*

(see index for correct answer)

- a. Duality
- b. SimulTrain
- c. Social risk management
- d. Director

Guidance: level 1

:: Industrial agreements ::

_____ is a process of negotiation between employers and a group of employees aimed at agreements to regulate working salaries, working conditions, benefits, and other aspects of workers' compensation and rights for workers. The interests of the employees are commonly presented by representatives of a trade union to which the employees belong. The collective agreements reached by these negotiations usually set out wage scales, working hours, training, health and safety, overtime, grievance mechanisms, and rights to participate in workplace or company affairs.

29. *Answer choices:*

(see index for correct answer)

- a. Compulsory arbitration
- b. Collective bargaining
- c. Bargaining unit
- d. Court of Arbitration

Guidance: level 1

:: Management ::

A _____ is when two or more people come together to discuss one or more topics, often in a formal or business setting, but _____ s also occur in a variety of other environments. Many various types of _____ s exist.

Exam Probability: **Medium**

30. *Answer choices:*

(see index for correct answer)

- a. Omnex
- b. Value migration
- c. Risk management
- d. Meeting

:: Statistical terminology ::

_____ es can be learned implicitly within cultural contexts. People may develop _____ es toward or against an individual, an ethnic group, a sexual or gender identity, a nation, a religion, a social class, a political party, theoretical paradigms and ideologies within academic domains, or a species. _____ ed means one-sided, lacking a neutral viewpoint, or not having an open mind. _____ can come in many forms and is related to prejudice and intuition.

Exam Probability: **High**

31. *Answer choices:*

(see index for correct answer)

- a. Iterated conditional modes
- b. Inherent zero
- c. Statistical epidemiology
- d. Covariate

:: Mereology ::

_____ , in the abstract, is what belongs to or with something, whether as an attribute or as a component of said thing. In the context of this article, it is one or more components , whether physical or incorporeal, of a person's estate; or so belonging to, as in being owned by, a person or jointly a group of people or a legal entity like a corporation or even a society. Depending on the nature of the _____ , an owner of _____ has the right to consume, alter, share, redefine, rent, mortgage, pawn, sell, exchange, transfer, give away or destroy it, or to exclude others from doing these things, as well as to perhaps abandon it; whereas regardless of the nature of the _____ , the owner thereof has the right to properly use it , or at the very least exclusively keep it.

Exam Probability: **Medium**

32. *Answer choices:*

(see index for correct answer)

- a. Mereology
- b. Mereotopology
- c. Mereological nihilism
- d. Property

Guidance: level 1

:: Discrimination ::

In social psychology, a _____ is an over-generalized belief about a particular category of people. _____ s are generalized because one assumes that the _____ is true for each individual person in the category. While such generalizations may be useful when making quick decisions, they may be erroneous when applied to particular individuals. _____ s encourage prejudice and may arise for a number of reasons.

Exam Probability: **Medium**

33. *Answer choices:*

(see index for correct answer)

- a. Stereotype
- b. Economic discrimination
- c. Anti-Americanism

Guidance: level 1

:: ::

A _____ or GM is an executive who has overall responsibility for managing both the revenue and cost elements of a company's income statement, known as profit & loss responsibility. A _____ usually oversees most or all of the firm's marketing and sales functions as well as the day-to-day operations of the business. Frequently, the _____ is responsible for effective planning, delegating, coordinating, staffing, organizing, and decision making to attain desirable profit making results for an organization .

34. *Answer choices:*

(see index for correct answer)

- a. surface-level diversity
- b. similarity-attraction theory
- c. General manager
- d. information systems assessment

Guidance: level 1

:: Production and manufacturing ::

Automatic _____ in continuous production processes is a combination of control engineering and chemical engineering disciplines that uses industrial control systems to achieve a production level of consistency, economy and safety which could not be achieved purely by human manual control. It is implemented widely in industries such as oil refining, pulp and paper manufacturing, chemical processing and power generating plants.

Exam Probability: **Medium**

35. *Answer choices:*

(see index for correct answer)

- a. Foundation Fieldbus H1
- b. Process control

- c. First pass yield
- d. Craft production

Guidance: level 1

:: Materials ::

A _____ , also known as a feedstock, unprocessed material, or primary commodity, is a basic material that is used to produce goods, finished products, energy, or intermediate materials which are feedstock for future finished products. As feedstock, the term connotes these materials are bottleneck assets and are highly important with regard to producing other products. An example of this is crude oil, which is a _____ and a feedstock used in the production of industrial chemicals, fuels, plastics, and pharmaceutical goods; lumber is a _____ used to produce a variety of products including all types of furniture. The term " _____ " denotes materials in minimally processed or unprocessed in states; e.g., raw latex, crude oil, cotton, coal, raw biomass, iron ore, air, logs, or water i.e. "...any product of agriculture, forestry, fishing and any other mineral that is in its natural form or which has undergone the transformation required to prepare it for internationally marketing in substantial volumes."

Exam Probability: **Medium**

36. *Answer choices:*
(see index for correct answer)

- a. Cellulose fiber
- b. Layered double hydroxides
- c. Raw material

- d. Rubblization

Guidance: level 1

:: Project management ::

A _____ is a team whose members usually belong to different groups, functions and are assigned to activities for the same project. A team can be divided into sub-teams according to need. Usually _____ s are only used for a defined period of time. They are disbanded after the project is deemed complete. Due to the nature of the specific formation and disbandment, _____ s are usually in organizations.

Exam Probability: **Low**

37. *Answer choices:*

(see index for correct answer)

- a. American Society of Professional Estimators
- b. The International Association of Project and Program Management
- c. Metra potential method
- d. Project team

Guidance: level 1

:: Decision theory ::

A _____ is a deliberate system of principles to guide decisions and achieve rational outcomes. A _____ is a statement of intent, and is implemented as a procedure or protocol. Policies are generally adopted by a governance body within an organization. Policies can assist in both subjective and objective decision making. Policies to assist in subjective decision making usually assist senior management with decisions that must be based on the relative merits of a number of factors, and as a result are often hard to test objectively, e.g. work-life balance _____. In contrast policies to assist in objective decision making are usually operational in nature and can be objectively tested, e.g. password _____.

Exam Probability: **Medium**

38. *Answer choices:*

(see index for correct answer)

- a. TOPSIS
- b. Lock-in
- c. Policy
- d. Health management system

Guidance: level 1

:: ::

The _____ is an agreement signed by Canada, Mexico, and the United States, creating a trilateral trade bloc in North America. The agreement came into force on January 1, 1994, and superseded the 1988 Canada–United States Free Trade Agreement between the United States and Canada. The NAFTA trade bloc is one of the largest trade blocs in the world by gross domestic product.

Exam Probability: **Low**

39. *Answer choices:*

(see index for correct answer)

- a. process perspective
- b. North American Free Trade Agreement
- c. Character
- d. functional perspective

Guidance: level 1

:: Statistical terminology ::

_____ is the ability to avoid wasting materials, energy, efforts, money, and time in doing something or in producing a desired result. In a more general sense, it is the ability to do things well, successfully, and without waste. In more mathematical or scientific terms, it is a measure of the extent to which input is well used for an intended task or function . It often specifically comprises the capability of a specific application of effort to produce a specific outcome with a minimum amount or quantity of waste, expense, or unnecessary effort. _____ refers to very different inputs and outputs in different fields and industries.

40. *Answer choices:*

(see index for correct answer)

- a. Conditional expectation
- b. Efficiency
- c. Innovations vector
- d. Standardised mortality rate

Guidance: level 1

:: Meetings ::

A _____ is a body of one or more persons that is subordinate to a deliberative assembly. Usually, the assembly sends matters into a _____ as a way to explore them more fully than would be possible if the assembly itself were considering them. _____ s may have different functions and their type of work differ depending on the type of the organization and its needs.

41. *Answer choices:*

(see index for correct answer)

- a. Over the Air
- b. Parley

- c. Committee
- d. AEI World Forum

Guidance: level 1

:: Statistical terminology ::

_____ is the magnitude or dimensions of a thing. _____ can be measured as length, width, height, diameter, perimeter, area, volume, or mass.

Exam Probability: **Medium**

42. *Answer choices:*

(see index for correct answer)

- a. Neutral vector
- b. Drift rate
- c. Size
- d. Skewness risk

Guidance: level 1

:: Employee relations ::

_____ ownership, or employee share ownership, is an ownership interest in a company held by the company's workforce. The ownership interest may be facilitated by the company as part of employees' remuneration or incentive compensation for work performed, or the company itself may be employee owned.

Exam Probability: **Medium**

43. *Answer choices:*

(see index for correct answer)

- a. Industry Federation of the State of Rio de Janeiro
- b. Fringe benefit
- c. Employee handbook
- d. Employee stock

Guidance: level 1

:: ::

_____ is the administration of an organization, whether it is a business, a not-for-profit organization, or government body. _____ includes the activities of setting the strategy of an organization and coordinating the efforts of its employees to accomplish its objectives through the application of available resources, such as financial, natural, technological, and human resources. The term " _____ " may also refer to those people who manage an organization.

Exam Probability: **High**

44. *Answer choices:*

(see index for correct answer)

- a. hierarchical
- b. hierarchical perspective
- c. functional perspective
- d. levels of analysis

Guidance: level 1

:: Management ::

_____ is a method of quality control which employs statistical methods to monitor and control a process. This helps to ensure that the process operates efficiently, producing more specification-conforming products with less waste . SPC can be applied to any process where the "conforming product" output can be measured. Key tools used in SPC include run charts, control charts, a focus on continuous improvement, and the design of experiments. An example of a process where SPC is applied is manufacturing lines.

Exam Probability: **Medium**

45. *Answer choices:*

(see index for correct answer)

- a. Facilitator
- b. Central administration
- c. Just in time

- d. Automated decision support

Guidance: level 1

:: Personality tests ::

The Myers–Briggs Type Indicator is an introspective self-report questionnaire with the purpose of indicating differing psychological preferences in how people perceive the world around them and make decisions. . Though the test superficially resembles some psychological theories it is commonly classified as pseudoscience, especially as pertains to its supposed predictive abilities.

Exam Probability: **Medium**

46. *Answer choices:*

(see index for correct answer)

- a. Myers-Briggs Type Indicator
- b. Johari window
- c. personality quiz
- d. Keirsey Temperament Sorter

Guidance: level 1

:: Human resource management ::

_____ , also known as management by results , was first popularized by Peter Drucker in his 1954 book The Practice of Management. _____ is the process of defining specific objectives within an organization that management can convey to organization members, then deciding on how to achieve each objective in sequence. This process allows managers to take work that needs to be done one step at a time to allow for a calm, yet productive work environment. This process also helps organization members to see their accomplishments as they achieve each objective, which reinforces a positive work environment and a sense of achievement. An important part of MBO is the measurement and comparison of an employee`s actual performance with the standards set. Ideally, when employees themselves have been involved with the goal-setting and choosing the course of action to be followed by them, they are more likely to fulfill their responsibilities. According to George S. Odiorne, the system of _____ can be described as a process whereby the superior and subordinate jointly identify common goals, define each individual`s major areas of responsibility in terms of the results expected of him or her, and use these measures as guides for operating the unit and assessing the contribution of each of its members.

Exam Probability: **High**

47. *Answer choices:*

(see index for correct answer)

- a. Open plan
- b. Technical performance measure
- c. Public service motivation
- d. T-shaped skills

Guidance: level 1

_____ is both a research area and a practical skill encompassing the ability of an individual or organization to "lead" or guide other individuals, teams, or entire organizations. Specialist literature debates various viewpoints, contrasting Eastern and Western approaches to _____ , and also United States versus European approaches. U.S. academic environments define _____ as "a process of social influence in which a person can enlist the aid and support of others in the accomplishment of a common task".

Exam Probability: **Medium**

48. *Answer choices:*

(see index for correct answer)

- a. Leadership
- b. personal values
- c. functional perspective
- d. deep-level diversity

Guidance: level 1

:: Human resource management ::

_____ involves improving the effectiveness of organizations and the individuals and teams within them. Training may be viewed as related to immediate changes in organizational effectiveness via organized instruction, while development is related to the progress of longer-term organizational and employee goals. While _____ technically have differing definitions, the two are oftentimes used interchangeably and/or together. _____ has historically been a topic within applied psychology but has within the last two decades become closely associated with human resources management, talent management, human resources development, instructional design, human factors, and knowledge management.

Exam Probability: **Low**

49. *Answer choices:*

(see index for correct answer)

- a. Open-book management
- b. Applicant tracking system
- c. Workforce modeling
- d. Training and development

Guidance: level 1

:: Costs ::

In economics, _____ is the total economic cost of production and is made up of variable cost, which varies according to the quantity of a good produced and includes inputs such as labour and raw materials, plus fixed cost, which is independent of the quantity of a good produced and includes inputs that cannot be varied in the short term: fixed costs such as buildings and machinery, including sunk costs if any. Since cost is measured per unit of time, it is a flow variable.

Exam Probability: **High**

50. *Answer choices:*

(see index for correct answer)

- a. Direct materials cost
- b. Incremental cost-effectiveness ratio
- c. Road Logistics Costing in South Africa
- d. Total cost

Guidance: level 1

:: Summary statistics ::

_____ is the number of occurrences of a repeating event per unit of time. It is also referred to as temporal _____ , which emphasizes the contrast to spatial _____ and angular _____ . The period is the duration of time of one cycle in a repeating event, so the period is the reciprocal of the _____ . For example: if a newborn baby's heart beats at a _____ of 120 times a minute, its period—the time interval between beats—is half a second . _____ is an important parameter used in science and engineering to specify the rate of oscillatory and vibratory phenomena, such as mechanical vibrations, audio signals , radio waves, and light.

Exam Probability: **Medium**

51. *Answer choices:*

(see index for correct answer)

- a. Quantile
- b. Five-number summary
- c. Mean percentage error
- d. Quartile

Guidance: level 1

:: Project management ::

A _____ is a type of bar chart that illustrates a project schedule, named after its inventor, Henry Gantt , who designed such a chart around the years 1910–1915. Modern _____ s also show the dependency relationships between activities and current schedule status.

52. *Answer choices:*

(see index for correct answer)

- a. Gantt chart
- b. Participatory impact pathways analysis
- c. Authority
- d. Code name

Guidance: level 1

:: Time management ::

_____ is the process of planning and exercising conscious control of time spent on specific activities, especially to increase effectiveness, efficiency, and productivity. It involves a juggling act of various demands upon a person relating to work, social life, family, hobbies, personal interests and commitments with the finiteness of time. Using time effectively gives the person "choice" on spending/managing activities at their own time and expediency.

Exam Probability: **Low**

53. *Answer choices:*

(see index for correct answer)

- a. Maestro concept

- b. Time Trek
- c. Time management
- d. Time perception

Guidance: level 1

:: Hospitality management ::

A _____ is an establishment that provides paid lodging on a short-term basis. Facilities provided may range from a modest-quality mattress in a small room to large suites with bigger, higher-quality beds, a dresser, a refrigerator and other kitchen facilities, upholstered chairs, a flat screen television, and en-suite bathrooms. Small, lower-priced _____ s may offer only the most basic guest services and facilities. Larger, higher-priced _____ s may provide additional guest facilities such as a swimming pool, business centre , childcare, conference and event facilities, tennis or basketball courts, gymnasium, restaurants, day spa, and social function services. _____ rooms are usually numbered to allow guests to identify their room. Some boutique, high-end _____ s have custom decorated rooms. Some _____ s offer meals as part of a room and board arrangement. In the United Kingdom, a _____ is required by law to serve food and drinks to all guests within certain stated hours. In Japan, capsule _____ s provide a tiny room suitable only for sleeping and shared bathroom facilities.

Exam Probability: **Medium**

54. *Answer choices:*

(see index for correct answer)

- a. RateGain

- b. Restaurant management
- c. IHM Pusa
- d. Hotel

Guidance: level 1

:: Management occupations ::

_____ is the process of designing, launching and running a new business, which is often initially a small business. The people who create these businesses are called entrepreneurs.

Exam Probability: **High**

55. *Answer choices:*

(see index for correct answer)

- a. entrepreneurial
- b. Pit manager
- c. Entrepreneurship
- d. Chief design officer

Guidance: level 1

:: Project management ::

_____ and Theory Y are theories of human work motivation and management. They were created by Douglas McGregor while he was working at the MIT Sloan School of Management in the 1950s, and developed further in the 1960s. McGregor's work was rooted in motivation theory alongside the works of Abraham Maslow, who created the hierarchy of needs. The two theories proposed by McGregor describe contrasting models of workforce motivation applied by managers in human resource management, organizational behavior, organizational communication and organizational development. _____ explains the importance of heightened supervision, external rewards, and penalties, while Theory Y highlights the motivating role of job satisfaction and encourages workers to approach tasks without direct supervision. Management use of _____ and Theory Y can affect employee motivation and productivity in different ways, and managers may choose to implement strategies from both theories into their practices.

Exam Probability: **Medium**

56. *Answer choices:*

(see index for correct answer)

- a. Project engineering
- b. Theory X
- c. Resource leveling
- d. NEC Engineering and Construction Contract

Guidance: level 1

:: Management ::

A _____ is a formal written document containing business goals, the methods on how these goals can be attained, and the time frame within which these goals need to be achieved. It also describes the nature of the business, background information on the organization, the organization's financial projections, and the strategies it intends to implement to achieve the stated targets. In its entirety, this document serves as a road map that provides direction to the business.

Exam Probability: **Medium**

57. *Answer choices:*

(see index for correct answer)

- a. Process capability
- b. Provectus IT Inc
- c. Business plan
- d. Best current practice

Guidance: level 1

:: ::

_____ is a means of protection from financial loss. It is a form of risk management, primarily used to hedge against the risk of a contingent or uncertain loss

Exam Probability: **Medium**

58. *Answer choices:*

(see index for correct answer)

- a. levels of analysis
- b. Insurance
- c. Sarbanes-Oxley act of 2002
- d. personal values

Guidance: level 1

:: Business law ::

A _____ is a group of people who jointly supervise the activities of an organization, which can be either a for-profit business, nonprofit organization, or a government agency. Such a board's powers, duties, and responsibilities are determined by government regulations and the organization's own constitution and bylaws. These authorities may specify the number of members of the board, how they are to be chosen, and how often they are to meet.

Exam Probability: **Medium**

59. *Answer choices:*

(see index for correct answer)

- a. Statutory liability
- b. Jurisdictional strike
- c. Economic torts

- d. Independent contractor

Guidance: level 1

Business law

Corporate law (also known as business law) is the body of law governing the rights, relations, and conduct of persons, companies, organizations and businesses. It refers to the legal practice relating to, or the theory of corporations. Corporate law often describes the law relating to matters which derive directly from the life-cycle of a corporation. It thus encompasses the formation, funding, governance, and death of a corporation.

:: Employment discrimination ::

_____ is a form of discrimination based on race, gender, religion, national origin, physical or mental disability, age, sexual orientation, and gender identity by employers. Earnings differentials or occupational differentiation—where differences in pay come from differences in qualifications or responsibilities—should not be confused with _____. Discrimination can be intended and involve disparate treatment of a group or be unintended, yet create disparate impact for a group.

Exam Probability: **Medium**

1. *Answer choices:*

(see index for correct answer)

- a. Employment discrimination law in the European Union
- b. Employment discrimination
- c. Glass ceiling
- d. Marriage bars

Guidance: level 1

:: ::

An _____ is a written sworn statement of fact voluntarily made by an affiant or deponent under an oath or affirmation administered by a person authorized to do so by law. Such statement is witnessed as to the authenticity of the affiant's signature by a taker of oaths, such as a notary public or commissioner of oaths. An _____ is a type of verified statement or showing, or in other words, it contains a verification, meaning it is under oath or penalty of perjury, and this serves as evidence to its veracity and is required for court proceedings.

Exam Probability: **High**

2. *Answer choices:*

(see index for correct answer)

- a. process perspective
- b. surface-level diversity

- c. corporate values
- d. levels of analysis

Guidance: level 1

:: Stock market ::

_____ is freedom from, or resilience against, potential harm caused by others. Beneficiaries of _____ may be of persons and social groups, objects and institutions, ecosystems or any other entity or phenomenon vulnerable to unwanted change by its environment.

Exam Probability: **Low**

3. *Answer choices:*

(see index for correct answer)

- a. Security
- b. Stop price
- c. Wash sale
- d. Mark Twain effect

Guidance: level 1

:: Sexual harassment in the United States ::

In law, a _____ , reasonable man, or the man on the Clapham omnibus is a hypothetical person of legal fiction crafted by the courts and communicated through case law and jury instructions.

Exam Probability: **Low**

4. *Answer choices:*

(see index for correct answer)

- a. Sandy Gallin
- b. Puerto Rican Day Parade attacks
- c. Fitzgerald v. Barnstable School Committee
- d. Alexander v. Yale

Guidance: level 1

:: ::

The _____ is an intergovernmental organization that is concerned with the regulation of international trade between nations. The WTO officially commenced on 1 January 1995 under the Marrakesh Agreement, signed by 124 nations on 15 April 1994, replacing the General Agreement on Tariffs and Trade , which commenced in 1948. It is the largest international economic organization in the world.

Exam Probability: **High**

5. *Answer choices:*

(see index for correct answer)

- a. surface-level diversity
- b. deep-level diversity
- c. empathy
- d. World Trade Organization

Guidance: level 1

:: Contract law ::

In the law of contracts, the _____ , also referred to as an unequivocal and absolute acceptance requirement, states that an offer must be accepted exactly with no modifications. The offeror is the master of one's own offer. An attempt to accept the offer on different terms instead creates a counter-offer, and this constitutes a rejection of the original offer.

Exam Probability: **Low**

6. *Answer choices:*

(see index for correct answer)

- a. French contract law
- b. Peppercorn
- c. Community Benefits Agreement
- d. Interconnect agreement

:: ::

Punishment is the imposition of an undesirable or unpleasant outcome upon a group or individual, meted out by an authority—in contexts ranging from child discipline to criminal law—as a response and deterrent to a particular action or behaviour that is deemed undesirable or unacceptable. The reasoning may be to condition a child to avoid self-endangerment, to impose social conformity , to defend norms, to protect against future harms , and to maintain the law—and respect for rule of law—under which the social group is governed. Punishment may be self-inflicted as with self-flagellation and mortification of the flesh in the religious setting, but is most often a form of social coercion.

Exam Probability: **Medium**

7. *Answer choices:*

(see index for correct answer)

- a. open system
- b. personal values
- c. Punitive
- d. corporate values

:: Legal terms ::

A _____ is any "lesser" criminal act in some common law legal systems. _____ s are generally punished less severely than felonies, but theoretically more so than administrative infractions and regulatory offences. Many _____ s are punished with monetary fines.

Exam Probability: **High**

8. *Answer choices:*

(see index for correct answer)

- a. Ambiguity
- b. Government interest
- c. Punitive damages
- d. Misdemeanor

Guidance: level 1

:: ::

_____ is the consumption and saving opportunity gained by an entity within a specified timeframe, which is generally expressed in monetary terms. For households and individuals, " _____ is the sum of all the wages, salaries, profits, interest payments, rents, and other forms of earnings received in a given period of time."

Exam Probability: **Low**

9. *Answer choices:*

(see index for correct answer)

- a. open system
- b. hierarchical
- c. Income
- d. corporate values

Guidance: level 1

:: Legal doctrines and principles ::

In law, a _____ is an event sufficiently related to an injury that the courts deem the event to be the cause of that injury. There are two types of causation in the law: cause-in-fact, and proximate cause. Cause-in-fact is determined by the "but for" test: But for the action, the result would not have happened. The action is a necessary condition, but may not be a sufficient condition, for the resulting injury. A few circumstances exist where the but for test is ineffective . Since but-for causation is very easy to show , a second test is used to determine if an action is close enough to a harm in a "chain of events" to be legally valid. This test is called _____ .

_____ is a key principle of Insurance and is concerned with how the loss or damage actually occurred. There are several competing theories of _____ . For an act to be deemed to cause a harm, both tests must be met; _____ is a legal limitation on cause-in-fact.

Exam Probability: **Medium**

10. *Answer choices:*

(see index for correct answer)

- a. Unilateral mistake
- b. unconscionable contract
- c. Proximate cause
- d. Eminent domain

Guidance: level 1

:: Real property law ::

A _____ is the grant of authority or rights, stating that the granter formally recognizes the prerogative of the recipient to exercise the rights specified. It is implicit that the granter retains superiority , and that the recipient admits a limited status within the relationship, and it is within that sense that _____ s were historically granted, and that sense is retained in modern usage of the term.

Exam Probability: **High**

11. *Answer choices:*

(see index for correct answer)

- a. Charter
- b. Lateral and subjacent support
- c. NES Financial
- d. Attornment

Guidance: level 1

:: Promotion and marketing communications ::

In everyday language, _____ refers to exaggerated or false praise. In law, _____ is a promotional statement or claim that expresses subjective rather than objective views, which no "reasonable person" would take literally. _____ serves to "puff up" an exaggerated image of what is being described and is especially featured in testimonials.

Exam Probability: **Low**

12. *Answer choices:*

(see index for correct answer)

- a. Helicopter banner
- b. 8coupons
- c. National Consumer Panel
- d. Custom media

Guidance: level 1

:: ::

Credit is the trust which allows one party to provide money or resources to another party wherein the second party does not reimburse the first party immediately , but promises either to repay or return those resources at a later date. In other words, credit is a method of making reciprocity formal, legally enforceable, and extensible to a large group of unrelated people.

Exam Probability: **Medium**

13. *Answer choices:*

(see index for correct answer)

- a. process perspective
- b. Character
- c. Consumer credit
- d. open system

Guidance: level 1

:: Business law ::

In the United States, the United Kingdom, Australia, Canada and South Africa, _____ relates to the doctrines of the law of agency. It is relevant particularly in corporate law and constitutional law. _____ refers to a situation where a reasonable third party would understand that an agent had authority to act. This means a principal is bound by the agent's actions, even if the agent had no actual authority, whether express or implied. It raises an estoppel because the third party is given an assurance, which he relies on and would be inequitable for the principal to deny the authority given. _____ can legally be found, even if actual authority has not been given.

Exam Probability: **High**

14. *Answer choices:*

(see index for correct answer)

- a. Starting a Business Index
- b. Apparent authority
- c. Holder
- d. Statutory liability

Guidance: level 1

:: Fraud ::

In law, _____ is intentional deception to secure unfair or unlawful gain, or to deprive a victim of a legal right. _____ can violate civil law , a criminal law , or it may cause no loss of money, property or legal right but still be an element of another civil or criminal wrong. The purpose of _____ may be monetary gain or other benefits, for example by obtaining a passport, travel document, or driver`s license, or mortgage _____ , where the perpetrator may attempt to qualify for a mortgage by way of false statements.

Exam Probability: **Low**

15. *Answer choices:*

(see index for correct answer)

- a. Card not present transaction
- b. Unconscious fraud
- c. Fraud
- d. Missing trader fraud

:: ::

A _____ is a person who trades in commodities produced by other people. Historically, a _____ is anyone who is involved in business or trade. _____ s have operated for as long as industry, commerce, and trade have existed. During the 16th-century, in Europe, two different terms for _____ s emerged: One term, meerseniers, described local traders such as bakers, grocers, etc.; while a new term, koopman (Dutch: koopman, described _____ s who operated on a global stage, importing and exporting goods over vast distances, and offering added-value services such as credit and finance.

Exam Probability: **Low**

16. *Answer choices:*

(see index for correct answer)

- a. surface-level diversity
- b. Merchant
- c. open system
- d. Character

:: Business law ::

_____ is where a person's financial liability is limited to a fixed sum, most commonly the value of a person's investment in a company or partnership. If a company with _____ is sued, then the claimants are suing the company, not its owners or investors. A shareholder in a limited company is not personally liable for any of the debts of the company, other than for the amount already invested in the company and for any unpaid amount on the shares in the company, if any. The same is true for the members of a _____ partnership and the limited partners in a limited partnership. By contrast, sole proprietors and partners in general partnerships are each liable for all the debts of the business .

Exam Probability: **High**

17. *Answer choices:*

(see index for correct answer)

- a. Business license
- b. Ordinary course of business
- c. Wrongful trading
- d. Novation

Guidance: level 1

:: ::

Employment is a relationship between two parties, usually based on a contract where work is paid for, where one party, which may be a corporation, for profit, not-for-profit organization, co-operative or other entity is the employer and the other is the employee. Employees work in return for payment, which may be in the form of an hourly wage, by piecework or an annual salary, depending on the type of work an employee does or which sector she or he is working in. Employees in some fields or sectors may receive gratuities, bonus payment or stock options. In some types of employment, employees may receive benefits in addition to payment. Benefits can include health insurance, housing, disability insurance or use of a gym. Employment is typically governed by employment laws, regulations or legal contracts.

Exam Probability: **Medium**

18. *Answer choices:*

(see index for correct answer)

- a. process perspective
- b. hierarchical perspective
- c. Personnel
- d. functional perspective

Guidance: level 1

:: ::

The _____ is the central philosophical concept in the deontological moral philosophy of Immanuel Kant. Introduced in Kant's 1785 Groundwork of the Metaphysics of Morals, it may be defined as a way of evaluating motivations for action.

Exam Probability: **Medium**

19. *Answer choices:*

(see index for correct answer)

- a. co-culture
- b. levels of analysis
- c. similarity-attraction theory
- d. Categorical imperative

Guidance: level 1

:: Contract law ::

_____ is a doctrine in contract law that describes terms that are so extremely unjust, or overwhelmingly one-sided in favor of the party who has the superior bargaining power, that they are contrary to good conscience. Typically, an unconscionable contract is held to be unenforceable because no reasonable or informed person would otherwise agree to it. The perpetrator of the conduct is not allowed to benefit, because the consideration offered is lacking, or is so obviously inadequate, that to enforce the contract would be unfair to the party seeking to escape the contract.

20. *Answer choices:*

(see index for correct answer)

- a. Pre-existing duty rule
- b. Garnishment
- c. Condition subsequent
- d. Implied warranty

Guidance: level 1

:: Progressive Era in the United States ::

The Clayton Antitrust Act of 1914 , was a part of United States antitrust law with the goal of adding further substance to the U.S. antitrust law regime; the _____ sought to prevent anticompetitive practices in their incipiency. That regime started with the Sherman Antitrust Act of 1890, the first Federal law outlawing practices considered harmful to consumers . The _____ specified particular prohibited conduct, the three-level enforcement scheme, the exemptions, and the remedial measures.

Exam Probability: **Low**

21. *Answer choices:*

(see index for correct answer)

- a. Mann Act

- b. Clayton Antitrust Act
- c. pragmatism

Guidance: level 1

:: Forgery ::

_____ is a white-collar crime that generally refers to the false making or material alteration of a legal instrument with the specific intent to defraud anyone . Tampering with a certain legal instrument may be forbidden by law in some jurisdictions but such an offense is not related to _____ unless the tampered legal instrument was actually used in the course of the crime to defraud another person or entity. Copies, studio replicas, and reproductions are not considered forgeries, though they may later become forgeries through knowing and willful misrepresentations.

Exam Probability: **Medium**

22. *Answer choices:*

(see index for correct answer)

- a. Forgery Act 1861
- b. Copy-evident document
- c. Void pantograph
- d. Signature forgery

Guidance: level 1

:: Real property law ::

_____ , sometimes colloquially described as 'squatter's rights', is a legal principle under which a person who does not have legal title to a piece of property—usually land —acquires legal ownership based on continuous possession or occupation of the land without the permission of its legal owner.

Exam Probability: **Low**

23. *Answer choices:*

(see index for correct answer)

- a. Deed
- b. Project 70 Land Acquisition and Borrowing Act
- c. Adverse possession
- d. Emphyteusis

Guidance: level 1

:: Debt ::

_____ is the trust which allows one party to provide money or resources to another party wherein the second party does not reimburse the first party immediately , but promises either to repay or return those resources at a later date. In other words, _____ is a method of making reciprocity formal, legally enforceable, and extensible to a large group of unrelated people.

24. *Answer choices:*

(see index for correct answer)

- a. Bad debt
- b. Teacher Loan Forgiveness
- c. Credit cycle
- d. Least developed country

Guidance: level 1

:: ::

A _____ is a formal written enactment of a legislative authority that governs the legal entities of a city, state, or country by way of consent. Typically, _____ s command or prohibit something, or declare policy. _____ s are rules made by legislative bodies; they are distinguished from case law or precedent, which is decided by courts, and regulations issued by government agencies.

Exam Probability: **Low**

25. *Answer choices:*

(see index for correct answer)

- a. open system
- b. functional perspective

- c. Statute
- d. co-culture

Guidance: level 1

:: Monopoly (economics) ::

A _____ is a form of intellectual property that gives its owner the legal right to exclude others from making, using, selling, and importing an invention for a limited period of years, in exchange for publishing an enabling public disclosure of the invention. In most countries _____ rights fall under civil law and the _____ holder needs to sue someone infringing the _____ in order to enforce his or her rights. In some industries _____ s are an essential form of competitive advantage; in others they are irrelevant.

Exam Probability: **Low**

26. *Answer choices:*
(see index for correct answer)

- a. Privatization
- b. De facto monopoly
- c. Patent
- d. Public utility

Guidance: level 1

:: Contract law ::

A _____ cannot be enforced by law. _____s are different from voidable contracts, which are contracts that may be nullified. However, when a contract is being written and signed, there is no automatic mechanism available in every situation that can be utilized to detect the validity or enforceability of that contract. Practically, a contract can be declared to be void by a court of law. So the main question is that under what conditions can a contract be deemed as void

Exam Probability: **Medium**

27. *Answer choices:*

(see index for correct answer)

- a. Impracticability
- b. Talent holding deal
- c. Unjust enrichment
- d. Cost-plus-incentive fee

Guidance: level 1

:: Legal terms ::

An _____ is a legal and equitable remedy in the form of a special court order that compels a party to do or refrain from specific acts. "When a court employs the extraordinary remedy of _____ , it directs the conduct of a party, and does so with the backing of its full coercive powers." A party that fails to comply with an _____ faces criminal or civil penalties, including possible monetary sanctions and even imprisonment. They can also be charged with contempt of court. Counter _____ s are _____ s that stop or reverse the enforcement of another _____ .

Exam Probability: **Low**

28. *Answer choices:*

(see index for correct answer)

- a. Adjustment
- b. Further and better particulars
- c. Bifurcation
- d. Injunction

Guidance: level 1

:: ::

_____ , or auditory perception, is the ability to perceive sounds by detecting vibrations, changes in the pressure of the surrounding medium through time, through an organ such as the ear. The academic field concerned with _____ is auditory science.

29. *Answer choices:*

(see index for correct answer)

- a. open system
- b. deep-level diversity
- c. cultural
- d. hierarchical

Guidance: level 1

:: Legal doctrines and principles ::

_____ is a doctrine that a party is responsible for acts of their agents. For example, in the United States, there are circumstances when an employer is liable for acts of employees performed within the course of their employment. This rule is also called the master-servant rule, recognized in both common law and civil law jurisdictions.

Exam Probability: **Low**

30. *Answer choices:*

(see index for correct answer)

- a. Caveat emptor
- b. Act of state

- c. Assumption of risk
- d. Mutual mistake

Guidance: level 1

:: ::

A _____ is a person who holds a legal or ethical relationship of trust with one or more other parties . Typically, a _____ prudently takes care of money or other assets for another person. One party, for example, a corporate trust company or the trust department of a bank, acts in a _____ capacity to another party, who, for example, has entrusted funds to the _____ for safekeeping or investment. Likewise, financial advisers, financial planners, and; asset managers, including managers of pension plans, endowments, and other tax-exempt assets, are considered fiduciaries under applicable statutes and laws. In a _____ relationship, one person, in a position of vulnerability, justifiably vests confidence, good faith, reliance, and trust in another whose aid, advice, or protection is sought in some matter. In such a relation good conscience requires the _____ to act at all times for the sole benefit and interest of the one who trusts.

Exam Probability: **Medium**

31. *Answer choices:*

(see index for correct answer)

- a. hierarchical perspective
- b. corporate values
- c. similarity-attraction theory
- d. Fiduciary

:: Business law ::

An _____ is a clause in a contract that requires the parties to resolve their disputes through an arbitration process. Although such a clause may or may not specify that arbitration occur within a specific jurisdiction, it always binds the parties to a type of resolution outside the courts, and is therefore considered a kind of forum selection clause.

Exam Probability: **Low**

32. *Answer choices:*

(see index for correct answer)

- a. Apparent authority
- b. Arbitration clause
- c. Voidable floating charge
- d. Lien

:: Trade secrets ::

The _____ of 1996 was a 6 title Act of Congress dealing with a wide range of issues, including not only industrial espionage , but the insanity defense, matters regarding the Boys & Girls Clubs of America, requirements for presentence investigation reports, and the United States Sentencing Commission reports regarding encryption or scrambling technology, and other technical and minor amendments.

Exam Probability: **High**

33. *Answer choices:*

(see index for correct answer)

- a. WD-40
- b. Economic Espionage Act
- c. DVD Copy Control Association, Inc. v. Bunner
- d. Illegal number

Guidance: level 1

:: Abuse of the legal system ::

_____ occurs when a person is restricted in their personal movement within any area without justification or consent. Actual physical restraint is not necessary for _____ to occur. A _____ claim may be made based upon private acts, or upon wrongful governmental detention. For detention by the police, proof of _____ provides a basis to obtain a writ of habeas corpus.

34. *Answer choices:*

(see index for correct answer)

- a. Forum shopping
- b. False imprisonment
- c. Obstruction of Justice

Guidance: level 1

:: ::

_____ is a process under which executive or legislative actions are subject to review by the judiciary. A court with authority for _____ may invalidate laws, acts and governmental actions that are incompatible with a higher authority: an executive decision may be invalidated for being unlawful or a statute may be invalidated for violating the terms of a constitution.

_____ is one of the checks and balances in the separation of powers: the power of the judiciary to supervise the legislative and executive branches when the latter exceed their authority. The doctrine varies between jurisdictions, so the procedure and scope of _____ may differ between and within countries.

35. *Answer choices:*

(see index for correct answer)

- a. surface-level diversity
- b. imperative
- c. similarity-attraction theory
- d. hierarchical

Guidance: level 1

:: Business law ::

An _____ is a natural person, business, or corporation that provides goods or services to another entity under terms specified in a contract or within a verbal agreement. Unlike an employee, an _____ does not work regularly for an employer but works as and when required, during which time they may be subject to law of agency. _____ s are usually paid on a freelance basis. Contractors often work through a limited company or franchise, which they themselves own, or may work through an umbrella company.

Exam Probability: **Low**

36. *Answer choices:*

(see index for correct answer)

- a. Independent contractor
- b. Closed shop
- c. Complex structured finance transactions
- d. Commercial law

Guidance: level 1

In law, an _____ is the process in which cases are reviewed, where parties request a formal change to an official decision. _____ s function both as a process for error correction as well as a process of clarifying and interpreting law. Although appellate courts have existed for thousands of years, common law countries did not incorporate an affirmative right to _____ into their jurisprudence until the 19th century.

Exam Probability: **High**

37. *Answer choices:*

(see index for correct answer)

- a. process perspective
- b. corporate values
- c. co-culture
- d. Sarbanes-Oxley act of 2002

Guidance: level 1

:: Marketing ::

_____ or stock is the goods and materials that a business holds for the ultimate goal of resale .

Exam Probability: **High**

38. *Answer choices:*

(see index for correct answer)

- a. Negotiation
- b. Content marketing
- c. Generic brand
- d. Inventory

Guidance: level 1

:: ::

_____ is the collection of mechanisms, processes and relations by which corporations are controlled and operated. Governance structures and principles identify the distribution of rights and responsibilities among different participants in the corporation and include the rules and procedures for making decisions in corporate affairs. _____ is necessary because of the possibility of conflicts of interests between stakeholders, primarily between shareholders and upper management or among shareholders.

Exam Probability: **Medium**

39. *Answer choices:*

(see index for correct answer)

- a. empathy

- b. Corporate governance
- c. interpersonal communication
- d. corporate values

Guidance: level 1

:: ::

A _____ loan or, simply, _____ is used either by purchasers of real property to raise funds to buy real estate, or alternatively by existing property owners to raise funds for any purpose, while putting a lien on the property being _____ d. The loan is "secured" on the borrower's property through a process known as _____ origination. This means that a legal mechanism is put into place which allows the lender to take possession and sell the secured property to pay off the loan in the event the borrower defaults on the loan or otherwise fails to abide by its terms. The word _____ is derived from a Law French term used in Britain in the Middle Ages meaning "death pledge" and refers to the pledge ending when either the obligation is fulfilled or the property is taken through foreclosure. A _____ can also be described as "a borrower giving consideration in the form of a collateral for a benefit ".

Exam Probability: High

40. *Answer choices:*

(see index for correct answer)

- a. personal values
- b. surface-level diversity
- c. Mortgage

- d. information systems assessment

Guidance: level 1

:: Majority–minority relations ::

_____ , also known as reservation in India and Nepal, positive discrimination / action in the United Kingdom, and employment equity in Canada and South Africa, is the policy of promoting the education and employment of members of groups that are known to have previously suffered from discrimination. Historically and internationally, support for _____ has sought to achieve goals such as bridging inequalities in employment and pay, increasing access to education, promoting diversity, and redressing apparent past wrongs, harms, or hindrances.

Exam Probability: **Low**

41. *Answer choices:*
(see index for correct answer)

- a. positive discrimination
- b. cultural dissonance
- c. Affirmative action

Guidance: level 1

:: Business law ::

A _____ is a contractual arrangement calling for the lessee to pay the lessor for use of an asset. Property, buildings and vehicles are common assets that are _____ d. Industrial or business equipment is also _____ d.

Exam Probability: **High**

42. *Answer choices:*

(see index for correct answer)

- a. Lease
- b. Forged endorsement
- c. Refusal to deal
- d. United Kingdom commercial law

Guidance: level 1

:: Chemical industry ::

The _____ for the Protection of Literary and Artistic Works, usually known as the _____ , is an international agreement governing copyright, which was first accepted in Berne, Switzerland, in 1886.

Exam Probability: **Medium**

43. *Answer choices:*

(see index for correct answer)

- a. Chemical leasing
- b. Berne Convention
- c. ConverDyn
- d. High production volume chemicals

Guidance: level 1

:: ::

Advertising is a marketing communication that employs an openly sponsored, non-personal message to promote or sell a product, service or idea. Sponsors of advertising are typically businesses wishing to promote their products or services. Advertising is differentiated from public relations in that an advertiser pays for and has control over the message. It differs from personal selling in that the message is non-personal, i.e., not directed to a particular individual. Advertising is communicated through various mass media, including traditional media such as newspapers, magazines, television, radio, outdoor advertising or direct mail; and new media such as search results, blogs, social media, websites or text messages. The actual presentation of the message in a medium is referred to as an _____ , or "ad" or advert for short.

Exam Probability: **Low**

44. *Answer choices:*

(see index for correct answer)

- a. Sarbanes-Oxley act of 2002
- b. Character
- c. functional perspective

- d. corporate values

Guidance: level 1

:: Business law ::

A _____ is a form of security interest granted over an item of property to secure the payment of a debt or performance of some other obligation. The owner of the property, who grants the _____ , is referred to as the _____ ee and the person who has the benefit of the _____ is referred to as the _____ or or _____ holder.

Exam Probability: **High**

45. *Answer choices:*

(see index for correct answer)

- a. Trusted Computing
- b. Lien
- c. Refusal to deal
- d. Hundi

Guidance: level 1

:: ::

A _____ is the party who initiates a lawsuit before a court. By doing so, the _____ seeks a legal remedy; if this search is successful, the court will issue judgment in favor of the _____ and make the appropriate court order . " _____ " is the term used in civil cases in most English-speaking jurisdictions, the notable exception being England and Wales, where a _____ has, since the introduction of the Civil Procedure Rules in 1999, been known as a "claimant", but that term also has other meanings. In criminal cases, the prosecutor brings the case against the defendant, but the key complaining party is often called the "complainant".

Exam Probability: **Low**

46. *Answer choices:*

(see index for correct answer)

- a. Plaintiff
- b. hierarchical
- c. Character
- d. Sarbanes-Oxley act of 2002

Guidance: level 1

:: Statutory law ::

_____ or statute law is written law set down by a body of legislature or by a singular legislator . This is as opposed to oral or customary law; or regulatory law promulgated by the executive or common law of the judiciary. Statutes may originate with national, state legislatures or local municipalities.

47. *Answer choices:*

(see index for correct answer)

- a. incorporation by reference
- b. statute law
- c. Statute of repose
- d. Statutory Law

Guidance: level 1

:: Patent law ::

A _____ is generally any statement intended to specify or delimit the scope of rights and obligations that may be exercised and enforced by parties in a legally recognized relationship. In contrast to other terms for legally operative language, the term _____ usually implies situations that involve some level of uncertainty, waiver, or risk.

Exam Probability: **Low**

48. *Answer choices:*

(see index for correct answer)

- a. Disclaimer
- b. Compulsory license

- c. Patentleft
- d. Patent prosecution

Guidance: level 1

:: Project management ::

A _____ is a source or supply from which a benefit is produced and it has some utility. _____ s can broadly be classified upon their availability—they are classified into renewable and non-renewable _____ s.Examples of non renewable _____ s are coal ,crude oil natural gas nuclear energy etc. Examples of renewable _____ s are air,water,wind,solar energy etc. They can also be classified as actual and potential on the basis of level of development and use, on the basis of origin they can be classified as biotic and abiotic, and on the basis of their distribution, as ubiquitous and localized . An item becomes a _____ with time and developing technology. Typically, _____ s are materials, energy, services, staff, knowledge, or other assets that are transformed to produce benefit and in the process may be consumed or made unavailable. Benefits of _____ utilization may include increased wealth, proper functioning of a system, or enhanced well-being. From a human perspective a natural _____ is anything obtained from the environment to satisfy human needs and wants. From a broader biological or ecological perspective a _____ satisfies the needs of a living organism .

Exam Probability: **Medium**

49. *Answer choices:*

(see index for correct answer)

- a. Resource
- b. Master of Science in Project Management

- c. Project planning
- d. Grandfather principle

Guidance: level 1

:: Business law ::

A _____ , also known as the sole trader, individual entrepreneurship or proprietorship, is a type of enterprise that is owned and run by one person and in which there is no legal distinction between the owner and the business entity. A sole trader does not necessarily work `alone'—it is possible for the sole trader to employ other people.

Exam Probability: **Low**

50. *Answer choices:*

(see index for correct answer)

- a. Sole proprietorship
- b. Equity of redemption
- c. United Kingdom commercial law
- d. Participation

Guidance: level 1

:: Business law ::

A _____ is a business entity created by two or more parties, generally characterized by shared ownership, shared returns and risks, and shared governance. Companies typically pursue _____ s for one of four reasons: to access a new market, particularly emerging markets; to gain scale efficiencies by combining assets and operations; to share risk for major investments or projects; or to access skills and capabilities.

Exam Probability: **Medium**

51. *Answer choices:*

(see index for correct answer)

- a. Valuation using the Market Penetration Model
- b. Lien
- c. Joint venture
- d. Relational contract

Guidance: level 1

:: ::

_____ is a marketing communication that employs an openly sponsored, non-personal message to promote or sell a product, service or idea. Sponsors of _____ are typically businesses wishing to promote their products or services. _____ is differentiated from public relations in that an advertiser pays for and has control over the message. It differs from personal selling in that the message is non-personal, i.e., not directed to a particular individual. _____ is communicated through various mass media, including traditional media such as newspapers, magazines, television, radio, outdoor _____ or direct mail; and new media such as search results, blogs, social media, websites or text messages. The actual presentation of the message in a medium is referred to as an advertisement, or "ad" or advert for short.

Exam Probability: **High**

52. *Answer choices:*

(see index for correct answer)

- a. hierarchical perspective
- b. Advertising
- c. open system
- d. corporate values

Guidance: level 1

:: ::

_____ is a type of government support for the citizens of that society. _____ may be provided to people of any income level, as with social security , but it is usually intended to ensure that the poor can meet their basic human needs such as food and shelter. _____ attempts to provide poor people with a minimal level of well-being, usually either a free- or a subsidized-supply of certain goods and social services, such as healthcare, education, and vocational training.

Exam Probability: **High**

53. *Answer choices:*

(see index for correct answer)

- a. hierarchical perspective
- b. similarity-attraction theory
- c. surface-level diversity
- d. functional perspective

Guidance: level 1

:: Sureties ::

In finance, a _____ , _____ bond or guaranty involves a promise by one party to assume responsibility for the debt obligation of a borrower if that borrower defaults. The person or company providing the promise is also known as a " _____ " or as a "guarantor".

Exam Probability: **High**

54. *Answer choices:*

(see index for correct answer)

- a. Supersedeas bond
- b. Aval
- c. Payment bond
- d. Little Miller Act

Guidance: level 1

:: Generally Accepted Accounting Principles ::

Expenditure is an outflow of money to another person or group to pay for an item or service, or for a category of costs. For a tenant, rent is an _____ . For students or parents, tuition is an _____ . Buying food, clothing, furniture or an automobile is often referred to as an _____ . An _____ is a cost that is "paid" or "remitted", usually in exchange for something of value. Something that seems to cost a great deal is "expensive". Something that seems to cost little is "inexpensive". " _____ s of the table" are _____ s of dining, refreshments, a feast, etc.

Exam Probability: **High**

55. *Answer choices:*

(see index for correct answer)

- a. Earnings before interest and taxes
- b. Gross profit

- c. Reserve
- d. Cost principle

Guidance: level 1

:: Legal doctrines and principles ::

In some common law jurisdictions, _____ is a defense to a tort claim based on negligence. If it is available, the defense completely bars plaintiffs from any recovery if they contribute to their own injury through their own negligence.

Exam Probability: **Medium**

56. *Answer choices:*
(see index for correct answer)

- a. Act of state doctrine
- b. Assumption of risk
- c. Contributory negligence
- d. Acquiescence

Guidance: level 1

:: ::

_____ is a means of protection from financial loss. It is a form of risk management, primarily used to hedge against the risk of a contingent or uncertain loss

57. *Answer choices:*

(see index for correct answer)

- a. functional perspective
- b. Sarbanes-Oxley act of 2002
- c. Insurance
- d. deep-level diversity

Guidance: level 1

:: Investment ::

In finance, the benefit from an _____ is called a return. The return may consist of a gain realised from the sale of property or an _____, unrealised capital appreciation , or _____ income such as dividends, interest, rental income etc., or a combination of capital gain and income. The return may also include currency gains or losses due to changes in foreign currency exchange rates.

58. *Answer choices:*

(see index for correct answer)

- a. Investing online
- b. CAN SLIM
- c. CPP Investment Board
- d. Land banking

Guidance: level 1

:: Real property law ::

A _____ is any legal instrument in writing which passes, affirms or confirms an interest, right, or property and that is signed, attested, delivered, and in some jurisdictions, sealed. It is commonly associated with transferring title to property. The _____ has a greater presumption of validity and is less rebuttable than an instrument signed by the party to the _____ . A _____ can be unilateral or bilateral. _____ s include conveyances, commissions, licenses, patents, diplomas, and conditionally powers of attorney if executed as _____ s. The _____ is the modern descendant of the medieval charter, and delivery is thought to symbolically replace the ancient ceremony of livery of seisin.

Exam Probability: **High**

59. *Answer choices:*

(see index for correct answer)

- a. Disseisor

- b. Deed
- c. NES Financial
- d. Thomond deeds

Guidance: level 1

Finance

Finance is a field that is concerned with the allocation (investment) of assets and liabilities over space and time, often under conditions of risk or uncertainty. Finance can also be defined as the science of money management. Participants in the market aim to price assets based on their risk level, fundamental value, and their expected rate of return. Finance can be split into three sub-categories: public finance, corporate finance and personal finance.

:: Financial accounting ::

In accounting, _____ is the value of an asset according to its balance sheet account balance. For assets, the value is based on the original cost of the asset less any depreciation, amortization or impairment costs made against the asset. Traditionally, a company's _____ is its total assets minus intangible assets and liabilities. However, in practice, depending on the source of the calculation, _____ may variably include goodwill, intangible assets, or both. The value inherent in its workforce, part of the intellectual capital of a company, is always ignored. When intangible assets and goodwill are explicitly excluded, the metric is often specified to be "tangible _____".

Exam Probability: **Medium**

1. *Answer choices:*

(see index for correct answer)

- a. Book value
- b. Asset swap
- c. Equity method
- d. Valuation

Guidance: level 1

:: Budgets ::

A _____ is a financial plan for a defined period, often one year. It may also include planned sales volumes and revenues, resource quantities, costs and expenses, assets, liabilities and cash flows. Companies, governments, families and other organizations use it to express strategic plans of activities or events in measurable terms.

Exam Probability: **High**

2. *Answer choices:*

(see index for correct answer)

- a. Budget
- b. Zero budget
- c. Zero deficit budget
- d. Participatory budgeting

Guidance: level 1

:: Mathematical finance ::

In economics and finance, _____ , also known as present discounted value, is the value of an expected income stream determined as of the date of valuation. The _____ is always less than or equal to the future value because money has interest-earning potential, a characteristic referred to as the time value of money, except during times of negative interest rates, when the _____ will be more than the future value. Time value can be described with the simplified phrase, "A dollar today is worth more than a dollar tomorrow". Here, `worth more` means that its value is greater. A dollar today is worth more than a dollar tomorrow because the dollar can be invested and earn a day's worth of interest, making the total accumulate to a value more than a dollar by tomorrow. Interest can be compared to rent. Just as rent is paid to a landlord by a tenant without the ownership of the asset being transferred, interest is paid to a lender by a borrower who gains access to the money for a time before paying it back. By letting the borrower have access to the money, the lender has sacrificed the exchange value of this money, and is compensated for it in the form of interest. The initial amount of the borrowed funds is less than the total amount of money paid to the lender.

Exam Probability: **High**

3. *Answer choices:*

(see index for correct answer)

- a. Binomial options pricing model
- b. No-arbitrage bounds
- c. Present value
- d. Adjusted present value

Guidance: level 1

:: ::

_____ s and acquisitions are transactions in which the ownership of companies, other business organizations, or their operating units are transferred or consolidated with other entities. As an aspect of strategic management, M&A can allow enterprises to grow or downsize, and change the nature of their business or competitive position.

Exam Probability: **High**

4. *Answer choices:*

(see index for correct answer)

- a. Merger
- b. deep-level diversity
- c. functional perspective
- d. open system

Guidance: level 1

:: Banking ::

_____ refers to a broad area of finance involving the collection, handling, and usage of cash. It involves assessing market liquidity, cash flow, and investments.

Exam Probability: **Low**

5. *Answer choices:*

(see index for correct answer)

- a. Highly confident letter
- b. Banking software
- c. Variance risk premium
- d. Numbered bank account

Guidance: level 1

:: Market research ::

_____ , an acronym for Information through Disguised Experimentation is an annual market research fair conducted by the students of IIM-Lucknow. Students create games and use various other simulated environments to capture consumers' subconscious thoughts. This innovative method of market research removes the sensitization effect that might bias peoples answers to questions. This ensures that the most truthful answers are captured to research questions. The games are designed in such a way that the observers can elicit all the required information just by observing and noting down the behaviour and the responses of the participants.

Exam Probability: **Medium**

6. *Answer choices:*

(see index for correct answer)

- a. INDEX
- b. Cambashi
- c. Multistage sampling

- d. Product Intelligence

Guidance: level 1

:: Financial markets ::

The _____ , also called the aftermarket and follow on public offering is the financial market in which previously issued financial instruments such as stock, bonds, options, and futures are bought and sold. Another frequent usage of " _____ " is to refer to loans which are sold by a mortgage bank to investors such as Fannie Mae and Freddie Mac.

Exam Probability: **Low**

7. *Answer choices:*

(see index for correct answer)

- a. GEOS
- b. Shelf registration
- c. Precautionary demand
- d. Secondary market

Guidance: level 1

:: Accounting terminology ::

A _____ contains all the accounts for recording transactions relating to a company's assets, liabilities, owners' equity, revenue, and expenses. In modern accounting software or ERP, the _____ works as a central repository for accounting data transferred from all subledgers or modules like accounts payable, accounts receivable, cash management, fixed assets, purchasing and projects. The _____ is the backbone of any accounting system which holds financial and non-financial data for an organization. The collection of all accounts is known as the _____ . Each account is known as a ledger account. In a manual or non-computerized system this may be a large book. The statement of financial position and the statement of income and comprehensive income are both derived from the _____ . Each account in the _____ consists of one or more pages. The _____ is where posting to the accounts occurs. Posting is the process of recording amounts as credits , and amounts as debits , in the pages of the _____ . Additional columns to the right hold a running activity total .

Exam Probability: **High**

8. *Answer choices:*

(see index for correct answer)

- a. Total absorption costing
- b. Cash flow management
- c. Impairment cost
- d. General ledger

Guidance: level 1

:: Inventory ::

_____ is a system of inventory in which updates are made on a periodic basis. This differs from perpetual inventory systems, where updates are made as seen fit.

Exam Probability: **High**

9. *Answer choices:*

(see index for correct answer)

- a. just-in-time manufacturing
- b. Lower of cost or market
- c. Inventory bounce
- d. Perpetual inventory

Guidance: level 1

:: ::

A _____ , in the word's original meaning, is a sheet of paper on which one performs work. They come in many forms, most commonly associated with children's school work assignments, tax forms, and accounting or other business environments. Software is increasingly taking over the paper-based _____ .

Exam Probability: **Medium**

10. *Answer choices:*

(see index for correct answer)

- a. hierarchical perspective
- b. co-culture
- c. process perspective
- d. Character

:: Generally Accepted Accounting Principles ::

_____ , also referred to as the bottom line, net income, or net earnings is a measure of the profitability of a venture after accounting for all costs and taxes. It is the actual profit, and includes the operating expenses that are excluded from gross profit.

Exam Probability: **High**

11. *Answer choices:*

(see index for correct answer)

- a. Petty cash
- b. Engagement letter
- c. Operating statement
- d. Net profit

:: Cash flow ::

In corporate finance, _____ or _____ to firm is a way of looking at a business's cash flow to see what is available for distribution among all the securities holders of a corporate entity. This may be useful to parties such as equity holders, debt holders, preferred stock holders, and convertible security holders when they want to see how much cash can be extracted from a company without causing issues to its operations.

Exam Probability: **Low**

12. *Answer choices:*

(see index for correct answer)

- a. Valuation using discounted cash flows
- b. Cash flow loan
- c. First Chicago Method
- d. Cash flow hedge

Guidance: level 1

:: ::

In business, economics or investment, market _____ is a market's feature whereby an individual or firm can quickly purchase or sell an asset without causing a drastic change in the asset's price. _____ is about how big the trade-off is between the speed of the sale and the price it can be sold for. In a liquid market, the trade-off is mild: selling quickly will not reduce the price much. In a relatively illiquid market, selling it quickly will require cutting its price by some amount.

Exam Probability: **Medium**

13. *Answer choices:*

(see index for correct answer)

- a. Liquidity
- b. deep-level diversity
- c. empathy
- d. open system

Guidance: level 1

:: ::

The _____ is a private, non-profit organization standard-setting body whose primary purpose is to establish and improve Generally Accepted Accounting Principles within the United States in the public's interest. The Securities and Exchange Commission designated the FASB as the organization responsible for setting accounting standards for public companies in the US. The FASB replaced the American Institute of Certified Public Accountants' Accounting Principles Board on July 1, 1973.

14. *Answer choices:*

(see index for correct answer)

- a. deep-level diversity
- b. interpersonal communication
- c. hierarchical
- d. corporate values

Guidance: level 1

:: Basel II ::

A _____ is the risk of default on a debt that may arise from a borrower failing to make required payments. In the first resort, the risk is that of the lender and includes lost principal and interest, disruption to cash flows, and increased collection costs. The loss may be complete or partial. In an efficient market, higher levels of _____ will be associated with higher borrowing costs. Because of this, measures of borrowing costs such as yield spreads can be used to infer _____ levels based on assessments by market participants.

Exam Probability: **Medium**

15. *Answer choices:*

(see index for correct answer)

- a. Credit risk
- b. Legal risk
- c. Advanced measurement approach
- d. Standardized approach

Guidance: level 1

:: Government bonds ::

A _____ or sovereign bond is a bond issued by a national government, generally with a promise to pay periodic interest payments called coupon payments and to repay the face value on the maturity date. The aim of a _____ is to support government spending. _____ s are usually denominated in the country's own currency, in which case the government cannot be forced to default, although it may choose to do so. If a government is close to default on its debt the media often refer to this as a sovereign debt crisis.

Exam Probability: **Medium**

16. *Answer choices:*

(see index for correct answer)

- a. Government bond
- b. Direct operations
- c. GDP-linked bond
- d. South Carolina v. Baker

:: Inventory ::

Costs are associated with particular goods using one of the several formulas, including specific identification, first-in first-out , or average cost. Costs include all costs of purchase, costs of conversion and other costs that are incurred in bringing the inventories to their present location and condition. Costs of goods made by the businesses include material, labor, and allocated overhead. The costs of those goods which are not yet sold are deferred as costs of inventory until the inventory is sold or written down in value.

Exam Probability: **Low**

17. *Answer choices:*

(see index for correct answer)

- a. Average cost method
- b. Phantom inventory
- c. Stock demands
- d. New old stock

:: Investment ::

The _____ is a measure of an investment's rate of return. The term internal refers to the fact that the calculation excludes external factors, such as the risk-free rate, inflation, the cost of capital, or various financial risks.

18. *Answer choices:*

(see index for correct answer)

- a. Foreign portfolio investment
- b. Active management
- c. rebalancing
- d. Internal rate of return

Guidance: level 1

:: ::

From an accounting perspective, _____ is crucial because _____ and _____ taxes considerably affect the net income of most companies and because they are subject to laws and regulations .

19. *Answer choices:*

(see index for correct answer)

- a. co-culture
- b. empathy
- c. cultural
- d. Sarbanes-Oxley act of 2002

Guidance: level 1

:: Generally Accepted Accounting Principles ::

In business and accounting, _____ is an entity's income minus cost of goods sold, expenses and taxes for an accounting period. It is computed as the residual of all revenues and gains over all expenses and losses for the period, and has also been defined as the net increase in shareholders' equity that results from a company's operations. In the context of the presentation of financial statements, the IFRS Foundation defines _____ as synonymous with profit and loss. The difference between revenue and the cost of making a product or providing a service, before deducting overheads, payroll, taxation, and interest payments. This is different from operating income .

Exam Probability: **Low**

20. *Answer choices:*

(see index for correct answer)

- a. Net realizable value
- b. Access to finance
- c. Net profit
- d. Net income

:: Pension funds ::

_____ s typically have large amounts of money to invest and are the major investors in listed and private companies. They are especially important to the stock market where large institutional investors dominate. The largest 300 _____ s collectively hold about $6 trillion in assets. In January 2008, The Economist reported that Morgan Stanley estimates that _____ s worldwide hold over US$20 trillion in assets, the largest for any category of investor ahead of mutual funds, insurance companies, currency reserves, sovereign wealth funds, hedge funds, or private equity.

Exam Probability: **Low**

21. *Answer choices:*

(see index for correct answer)

- a. Pension led funding
- b. Texas Municipal Retirement System
- c. Pension buyout

:: Interest rates ::

An _____ is the amount of interest due per period, as a proportion of the amount lent, deposited or borrowed . The total interest on an amount lent or borrowed depends on the principal sum, the _____ , the compounding frequency, and the length of time over which it is lent, deposited or borrowed.

Exam Probability: **Low**

22. *Answer choices:*

(see index for correct answer)

- a. Interest rate
- b. Official bank rate
- c. Forward interest rate
- d. Forex swap

Guidance: level 1

:: Financial economics ::

_____ , Inc. is an independent investment research and financial publishing firm based in New York City, New York, United States, founded in 1931 by Arnold Bernhard. _____ is best known for publishing The _____ Investment Survey, a stock analysis newsletter that is among the most highly regarded and widely used independent investment research resources in global investment and trading markets, tracking approximately 1,700 publicly traded stocks in over 99 industries.

Exam Probability: **Low**

23. *Answer choices:*

(see index for correct answer)

- a. Value Line
- b. Indexation
- c. Customer value
- d. Triangular arbitrage

Guidance: level 1

:: Financial ratios ::

The _____ shows the percentage of how profitable a company's assets are in generating revenue.

Exam Probability: **Low**

24. *Answer choices:*

(see index for correct answer)

- a. stock turnover
- b. Return on assets
- c. price-to-cash flow ratio
- d. Short interest ratio

Guidance: level 1

:: Money ::

Cash and _____ s are the most liquid current assets found on a business's balance sheet. _____ s are short-term commitments "with temporarily idle cash and easily convertible into a known cash amount". An investment normally counts to be a _____ when it has a short maturity period of 90 days or less, and can be included in the cash and _____ s balance from the date of acquisition when it carries an insignificant risk of changes in the asset value; with more than 90 days maturity, the asset is not considered as cash and _____ s. Equity investments mostly are excluded from _____ s, unless they are essentially _____ s, for instance, if the preferred shares acquired within a short maturity period and with specified recovery date.

Exam Probability: **Medium**

25. *Answer choices:*

(see index for correct answer)

- a. Cash equivalent
- b. Money creation
- c. World Money Fair
- d. Purse bid

Guidance: level 1

:: Occupations ::

An _____ is a practitioner of accounting or accountancy, which is the measurement, disclosure or provision of assurance about financial information that helps managers, investors, tax authorities and others make decisions about allocating resource.

Exam Probability: **High**

26. *Answer choices:*

(see index for correct answer)

- a. Monumental masonry
- b. Accountant
- c. Designated Pilot Examiner
- d. Amateur professionalism

Guidance: level 1

:: Bonds (finance) ::

An _____ is a legal contract that reflects or covers a debt or purchase obligation. It specifically refers to two types of practices: in historical usage, an _____ d servant status, and in modern usage, it is an instrument used for commercial debt or real estate transaction.

Exam Probability: **High**

27. *Answer choices:*

(see index for correct answer)

- a. Synthetic bond
- b. Indenture
- c. Eurobond
- d. Bond market index

Guidance: level 1

:: Notes (finance) ::

A _____ , sometimes referred to as a note payable, is a legal instrument , in which one party promises in writing to pay a determinate sum of money to the other , either at a fixed or determinable future time or on demand of the payee, under specific terms.

Exam Probability: **Low**

28. *Answer choices:*
(see index for correct answer)

- a. Promissory note
- b. note payable
- c. A notes
- d. Demand Note

Guidance: level 1

:: ::

Business is the activity of making one`s living or making money by producing or buying and selling products . Simply put, it is "any activity or enterprise entered into for profit. It does not mean it is a company, a corporation, partnership, or have any such formal organization, but it can range from a street peddler to General Motors."

Exam Probability: **Medium**

29. *Answer choices:*

(see index for correct answer)

- a. Firm
- b. cultural
- c. process perspective
- d. empathy

Guidance: level 1

:: Financial ratios ::

The _____ is a financial ratio indicating the relative proportion of shareholders` equity and debt used to finance a company`s assets. Closely related to leveraging, the ratio is also known as risk, gearing or leverage. The two components are often taken from the firm`s balance sheet or statement of financial position , but the ratio may also be calculated using market values for both, if the company`s debt and equity are publicly traded, or using a combination of book value for debt and market value for equity financially.

Exam Probability: **Low**

30. *Answer choices:*

(see index for correct answer)

- a. Beta
- b. Operating margin
- c. Market-to-book
- d. interest margin

Guidance: level 1

:: Auditing ::

_____ , as defined by accounting and auditing, is a process for assuring of an organization`s objectives in operational effectiveness and efficiency, reliable financial reporting, and compliance with laws, regulations and policies. A broad concept, _____ involves everything that controls risks to an organization.

31. *Answer choices:*

(see index for correct answer)

- a. Auditing Standards Board
- b. Management audit
- c. Internal control
- d. Audit working papers

Guidance: level 1

:: Basel II ::

All businesses take risks based on two factors: the probability an adverse circumstance will come about and the cost of such adverse circumstance.Risk management is the study of how to control risks and balance the possibility of gains.

Exam Probability: **Low**

32. *Answer choices:*

(see index for correct answer)

- a. Foundation IRB
- b. Standardized approach
- c. Market risk

- d. Operational risk

Guidance: level 1

:: Debt ::

_____ , in finance and economics, is payment from a borrower or deposit-taking financial institution to a lender or depositor of an amount above repayment of the principal sum , at a particular rate. It is distinct from a fee which the borrower may pay the lender or some third party. It is also distinct from dividend which is paid by a company to its shareholders from its profit or reserve, but not at a particular rate decided beforehand, rather on a pro rata basis as a share in the reward gained by risk taking entrepreneurs when the revenue earned exceeds the total costs.

Exam Probability: **High**

33. *Answer choices:*

(see index for correct answer)

- a. Debt club
- b. External debt
- c. Interest
- d. Troubled Debt Restructuring

Guidance: level 1

:: Financial ratios ::

The _____ is a liquidity ratio that measures whether a firm has enough resources to meet its short-term obligations. It compares a firm's current assets to its current liabilities, and is expressed as follows.

Exam Probability: **Low**

34. *Answer choices:*

(see index for correct answer)

- a. Operating ratio
- b. Debt-to-income ratio
- c. Net interest income
- d. Loan-to-value ratio

Guidance: level 1

:: Corporate finance ::

_____ in corporate finance is the way a corporation finances its assets through some combination of equity, debt, or hybrid securities.

Exam Probability: **Medium**

35. *Answer choices:*

(see index for correct answer)

- a. Accord and satisfaction
- b. Cashier balancing
- c. Capital structure
- d. Capitalization table

Guidance: level 1

:: ::

A _____ is the process of presenting a topic to an audience. It is typically a demonstration, introduction, lecture, or speech meant to inform, persuade, inspire, motivate, or to build good will or to present a new idea or product. The term can also be used for a formal or ritualized introduction or offering, as with the _____ of a debutante. _____ s in certain formats are also known as keynote address.

Exam Probability: **High**

36. *Answer choices:*
(see index for correct answer)

- a. corporate values
- b. information systems assessment
- c. surface-level diversity
- d. Presentation

:: Derivatives (finance) ::

A _____ or _____ row is a line of closely spaced shrubs and sometimes trees, planted and trained to form a barrier or to mark the boundary of an area, such as between neighbouring properties. _____ s used to separate a road from adjoining fields or one field from another, and of sufficient age to incorporate larger trees, are known as _____ rows. Often they serve as windbreaks to improve conditions for the adjacent crops, as in bocage country. When clipped and maintained, _____ s are also a simple form of topiary.

Exam Probability: **Low**

37. *Answer choices:*

(see index for correct answer)

- a. Ratio spread
- b. Hedge
- c. Forward start option
- d. fundamental value

:: Accounting terminology ::

_____ is a legally enforceable claim for payment held by a business for goods supplied and/or services rendered that customers/clients have ordered but not paid for. These are generally in the form of invoices raised by a business and delivered to the customer for payment within an agreed time frame.
_____ is shown in a balance sheet as an asset. It is one of a series of accounting transactions dealing with the billing of a customer for goods and services that the customer has ordered. These may be distinguished from notes receivable, which are debts created through formal legal instruments called promissory notes.

Exam Probability: **Low**

38. *Answer choices:*

(see index for correct answer)

- a. Double-entry accounting
- b. Absorption costing
- c. Fund accounting
- d. Accounts receivable

Guidance: level 1

:: ::

An _____ is the production of goods or related services within an economy. The major source of revenue of a group or company is the indicator of its relevant _____ . When a large group has multiple sources of revenue generation, it is considered to be working in different industries.

Manufacturing _____ became a key sector of production and labour in European and North American countries during the Industrial Revolution, upsetting previous mercantile and feudal economies. This came through many successive rapid advances in technology, such as the production of steel and coal.

Exam Probability: **High**

39. *Answer choices:*

(see index for correct answer)

- a. corporate values
- b. surface-level diversity
- c. Industry
- d. functional perspective

Guidance: level 1

:: Generally Accepted Accounting Principles ::

Financial statements prepared and presented by a company typically follow an external standard that specifically guides their preparation. These standards vary across the globe and are typically overseen by some combination of the private accounting profession in that specific nation and the various government regulators. Variations across countries may be considerable, making cross-country evaluation of financial data challenging.

Exam Probability: **High**

40. *Answer choices:*

(see index for correct answer)

- a. Gross income
- b. Generally accepted accounting principles
- c. Operating income before depreciation and amortization
- d. Long-term liabilities

Guidance: level 1

:: Financial accounting ::

_____ in accounting is the process of treating investments in associate companies. Equity accounting is usually applied where an investor entity holds 20–50% of the voting stock of the associate company. The investor records such investments as an asset on its balance sheet. The investor's proportional share of the associate company's net income increases the investment , and proportional payments of dividends decrease it. In the investor's income statement, the proportional share of the investor's net income or net loss is reported as a single-line item.

41. *Answer choices:*

(see index for correct answer)

- a. Accounting identity
- b. Deferred Acquisition Costs
- c. SEC filing
- d. Mark-to-market accounting

Guidance: level 1

:: ::

_____ or accountancy is the measurement, processing, and communication of financial information about economic entities such as businesses and corporations. The modern field was established by the Italian mathematician Luca Pacioli in 1494. _____ , which has been called the "language of business", measures the results of an organization's economic activities and conveys this information to a variety of users, including investors, creditors, management, and regulators. Practitioners of _____ are known as accountants. The terms " _____ " and "financial reporting" are often used as synonyms.

42. *Answer choices:*

(see index for correct answer)

- a. hierarchical perspective
- b. personal values
- c. empathy
- d. similarity-attraction theory

Guidance: level 1

:: Shareholders ::

A _____ is a payment made by a corporation to its shareholders, usually as a distribution of profits. When a corporation earns a profit or surplus, the corporation is able to re-invest the profit in the business and pay a proportion of the profit as a _____ to shareholders. Distribution to shareholders may be in cash or, if the corporation has a _____ reinvestment plan, the amount can be paid by the issue of further shares or share repurchase. When _____ s are paid, shareholders typically must pay income taxes, and the corporation does not receive a corporate income tax deduction for the _____ payments.

Exam Probability: **Low**

43. *Answer choices:*

(see index for correct answer)

- a. Friedman doctrine
- b. Activist shareholder
- c. Proxy statement
- d. Dividend

:: Generally Accepted Accounting Principles ::

_____ is the accounting classification of an account. It is part of double-entry book-keeping technique.

Exam Probability: **Low**

44. *Answer choices:*

(see index for correct answer)

- a. Management accounting principles
- b. Profit
- c. Depreciation
- d. Generally accepted accounting principles

:: Generally Accepted Accounting Principles ::

Expenditure is an outflow of money to another person or group to pay for an item or service, or for a category of costs. For a tenant, rent is an _____ . For students or parents, tuition is an _____ . Buying food, clothing, furniture or an automobile is often referred to as an _____ . An _____ is a cost that is "paid" or "remitted", usually in exchange for something of value. Something that seems to cost a great deal is "expensive". Something that seems to cost little is "inexpensive". " _____ s of the table" are _____ s of dining, refreshments, a feast, etc.

Exam Probability: **High**

45. *Answer choices:*

(see index for correct answer)

- a. Expense
- b. Revenue recognition
- c. Gross income
- d. Fixed investment

Guidance: level 1

:: ::

_____ is the collection of techniques, skills, methods, and processes used in the production of goods or services or in the accomplishment of objectives, such as scientific investigation. _____ can be the knowledge of techniques, processes, and the like, or it can be embedded in machines to allow for operation without detailed knowledge of their workings. Systems applying _____ by taking an input, changing it according to the system`s use, and then producing an outcome are referred to as _____ systems or technological systems.

Exam Probability: **Medium**

46. *Answer choices:*
(see index for correct answer)

- a. cultural
- b. similarity-attraction theory
- c. corporate values
- d. Technology

Guidance: level 1

:: Economics terminology ::

A corporation`s share capital or _____ is the portion of a corporation`s equity that has been obtained by the issue of shares in the corporation to a shareholder, usually for cash. "Share capital" may also denote the number and types of shares that compose a corporation`s share structure.

47. *Answer choices:*

(see index for correct answer)

- a. Capital stock
- b. External costs
- c. economic profit
- d. Capital cost

Guidance: level 1

:: Business economics ::

In finance, _____ is the risk of losses caused by interest rate changes. The prices of most financial instruments, such as stocks and bonds move inversely with interest rates, so investors are subject to capital loss when rates rise.

Exam Probability: **High**

48. *Answer choices:*

(see index for correct answer)

- a. Inorganic growth
- b. Risk financing
- c. Rate risk

- d. Trade name

Guidance: level 1

:: Fixed income market ::

In finance, the _____ is a curve showing several yields or interest rates across different contract lengths for a similar debt contract. The curve shows the relation between the interest rate and the time to maturity, known as the "term", of the debt for a given borrower in a given currency. For example, the U.S. dollar interest rates paid on U.S. Treasury securities for various maturities are closely watched by many traders, and are commonly plotted on a graph such as the one on the right which is informally called "the _____". More formal mathematical descriptions of this relation are often called the term structure of interest rates.

Exam Probability: **Low**

49. *Answer choices:*
(see index for correct answer)

- a. Fixed-income attribution
- b. Bond market
- c. Bond Exchange of South Africa
- d. Inter-dealer broker

Guidance: level 1

_____ is the production of products for use or sale using labour and machines, tools, chemical and biological processing, or formulation. The term may refer to a range of human activity, from handicraft to high tech, but is most commonly applied to industrial design, in which raw materials are transformed into finished goods on a large scale. Such finished goods may be sold to other manufacturers for the production of other, more complex products, such as aircraft, household appliances, furniture, sports equipment or automobiles, or sold to wholesalers, who in turn sell them to retailers, who then sell them to end users and consumers.

Exam Probability: **Low**

50. *Answer choices:*

(see index for correct answer)

- a. empathy
- b. Character
- c. cultural
- d. Manufacturing

Guidance: level 1

A _____ is an organization, usually a group of people or a company, authorized to act as a single entity and recognized as such in law. Early incorporated entities were established by charter . Most jurisdictions now allow the creation of new _____ s through registration.

Exam Probability: **High**

51. *Answer choices:*

(see index for correct answer)

- a. hierarchical
- b. corporate values
- c. deep-level diversity
- d. Corporation

Guidance: level 1

:: Basic financial concepts ::

_____ is a sustained increase in the general price level of goods and services in an economy over a period of time.When the general price level rises, each unit of currency buys fewer goods and services; consequently, _____ reflects a reduction in the purchasing power per unit of money a loss of real value in the medium of exchange and unit of account within the economy. The measure of _____ is the _____ rate, the annualized percentage change in a general price index, usually the consumer price index, over time. The opposite of _____ is deflation.

52. *Answer choices:*

(see index for correct answer)

- a. Forward guidance
- b. Inflation
- c. Short interest
- d. Deflation

Guidance: level 1

:: ::

The U.S. _____ is an independent agency of the United States federal government. The SEC holds primary responsibility for enforcing the federal securities laws, proposing securities rules, and regulating the securities industry, the nation's stock and options exchanges, and other activities and organizations, including the electronic securities markets in the United States.

53. *Answer choices:*

(see index for correct answer)

- a. levels of analysis
- b. information systems assessment

- c. empathy
- d. Character

Guidance: level 1

:: ::

_____ focuses on ratios, equities and debts. It is useful for portfolio management,distribution of dividend,capital raising,hedging and looking after fluctuations in foreign currency and product cycles.Financial managers are the people who will do research and based on the research, decide what sort of capital to obtain in order to fund the company`s assets as well as maximizing the value of the firm for all the stakeholders. It also refers to the efficient and effective management of money in such a manner as to accomplish the objectives of the organization. It is the specialized function directly associated with the top management. The significance of this function is not seen in the `Line` but also in the capacity of the `Staff` in overall of a company. It has been defined differently by different experts in the field.

Exam Probability: **High**

54. *Answer choices:*

(see index for correct answer)

- a. corporate values
- b. functional perspective
- c. deep-level diversity
- d. Financial management

:: Stock market ::

A _____ or stock divide increases the number of shares in a company. The price is adjusted such that the before and after market capitalization of the company remains the same and dilution does not occur. Options and warrants are included.

Exam Probability: **High**

55. *Answer choices:*

(see index for correct answer)

- a. Direct finance
- b. Indian Depository Receipt
- c. Stock split
- d. Concentrated stock

:: ::

_____ is the consumption and saving opportunity gained by an entity within a specified timeframe, which is generally expressed in monetary terms. For households and individuals, " _____ is the sum of all the wages, salaries, profits, interest payments, rents, and other forms of earnings received in a given period of time."

Exam Probability: **High**

56. *Answer choices:*

(see index for correct answer)

- a. Income
- b. empathy
- c. Sarbanes-Oxley act of 2002
- d. functional perspective

Guidance: level 1

:: Financial risk ::

The _____ on a financial investment is the expected value of its return . It is a measure of the center of the distribution of the random variable that is the return.

Exam Probability: **High**

57. *Answer choices:*

(see index for correct answer)

- a. Capital Requirements Directive
- b. Financial risk management
- c. Fuel price risk management
- d. Bielard, Biehl and Kaiser five-way model

Guidance: level 1

:: Financial markets ::

For an individual, a _____ is the minimum amount of money by which the expected return on a risky asset must exceed the known return on a risk-free asset in order to induce an individual to hold the risky asset rather than the risk-free asset. It is positive if the person is risk averse. Thus it is the minimum willingness to accept compensation for the risk.

Exam Probability: **Medium**

58. *Answer choices:*

(see index for correct answer)

- a. Block trade
- b. Swap spread
- c. Capital market
- d. Risk premium

:: Legal terms ::

_____ s may be governments, corporations or investment trusts.
_____ s are legally responsible for the obligations of the issue and for reporting financial conditions, material developments and any other operational activities as required by the regulations of their jurisdictions.

Exam Probability: **Medium**

59. *Answer choices:*

(see index for correct answer)

- a. Issuer
- b. Arbitrariness
- c. Legal benefit
- d. In-chambers opinion

Human resource management

Human resource (HR) management is the strategic approach to the effective management of organization workers so that they help the business gain a competitive advantage. It is designed to maximize employee performance in service of an employer's strategic objectives. HR is primarily concerned with the management of people within organizations, focusing on policies and on systems. HR departments are responsible for overseeing employee-benefits design, employee recruitment, training and development, performance appraisal, and rewarding (e.g., managing pay and benefit systems). HR also concerns itself with organizational change and industrial relations, that is, the balancing of organizational practices with requirements arising from collective bargaining and from governmental laws.

:: Occupations ::

An _____ is a person who has a position of authority in a hierarchical organization. The term derives from the late Latin from officiarius, meaning "official".

Exam Probability: **High**

1. *Answer choices:*

(see index for correct answer)

- a. Paraprofessional
- b. Officer
- c. Grubber
- d. Footage broker

Guidance: level 1

:: ::

_____ is a common standard in United States labor law arbitration that is used in labor union contracts in the United States as a form of job security.

Exam Probability: **Low**

2. *Answer choices:*

(see index for correct answer)

- a. cultural
- b. Just cause
- c. information systems assessment
- d. co-culture

Guidance: level 1

:: United States employment discrimination case law ::

_____ , 490 U.S. 228 , was an important decision by the United States Supreme Court on the issues of prescriptive sex discrimination and employer liability for sex discrimination. The employee, Ann Hopkins, sued her former employer, the accounting firm Price Waterhouse. She argued that the firm denied her partnership because she didn't fit the partners' idea of what a female employee should look like and act like. The employer failed to prove that it would have denied her partnership anyway, and the Court held that constituted sex discrimination under Title VII of the Civil Rights Act of 1964. The significance of the Supreme Court's ruling was twofold. First, it established that gender stereotyping is actionable as sex discrimination. Second, it established the mixed-motive framework that enables employees to prove discrimination when other, lawful reasons for the adverse employment action exist alongside discriminatory motivations or reasons.

Exam Probability: **High**

3. *Answer choices:*

(see index for correct answer)

- a. Kloeckner v. Solis
- b. New York City Transit Authority v. Beazer

- c. Shyamala Rajender v. University of Minnesota
- d. Price Waterhouse v. Hopkins

Guidance: level 1

:: Employment compensation ::

_____ refers to various incentive plans introduced by businesses that provide direct or indirect payments to employees that depend on company's profitability in addition to employees' regular salary and bonuses. In publicly traded companies these plans typically amount to allocation of shares to employees. One of the earliest pioneers of _____ was Englishman Theodore Cooke Taylor, who is known to have introduced the practice in his woollen mills during the late 1800s .

Exam Probability: **Medium**

4. *Answer choices:*

(see index for correct answer)

- a. The Theory of Wages
- b. Pay scale
- c. Australian Fair Pay Commission
- d. Profit sharing

Guidance: level 1

:: Psychometrics ::

_____ is a dynamic, structured, interactive process where a neutral third party assists disputing parties in resolving conflict through the use of specialized communication and negotiation techniques. All participants in _____ are encouraged to actively participate in the process. _____ is a "party-centered" process in that it is focused primarily upon the needs, rights, and interests of the parties. The mediator uses a wide variety of techniques to guide the process in a constructive direction and to help the parties find their optimal solution. A mediator is facilitative in that she/he manages the interaction between parties and facilitates open communication. _____ is also evaluative in that the mediator analyzes issues and relevant norms , while refraining from providing prescriptive advice to the parties .

Exam Probability: **High**

5. *Answer choices:*

(see index for correct answer)

- a. Classical test theory
- b. Mediation
- c. Reaction time
- d. Assessment Systems Corporation

Guidance: level 1

:: Parental leave ::

_____ is a type of employment discrimination that occurs when expectant women are fired, not hired, or otherwise discriminated against due to their pregnancy or intention to become pregnant. Common forms of _____ include not being hired due to visible pregnancy or likelihood of becoming pregnant, being fired after informing an employer of one's pregnancy, being fired after maternity leave, and receiving a pay dock due to pregnancy. Convention on the Elimination of All Forms of Discrimination against Women prohibits dismissal on the grounds of maternity or pregnancy and ensures right to maternity leave or comparable social benefits. The Maternity Protection Convention C 183 proclaims adequate protection for pregnancy as well. Though women have some protection in the United States because of the _____ Act of 1978, it has not completely curbed the incidence of _____. The Equal Rights Amendment could ensure more robust sex equality ensuring that women and men could both work and have children at the same time.

Exam Probability: **High**

6. *Answer choices:*

(see index for correct answer)

- a. Sara Hlupekile Longwe
- b. Parental leave economics
- c. Pregnancy discrimination
- d. Motherhood penalty

Guidance: level 1

:: Management ::

The term _____ refers to measures designed to increase the degree of autonomy and self-determination in people and in communities in order to enable them to represent their interests in a responsible and self-determined way, acting on their own authority. It is the process of becoming stronger and more confident, especially in controlling one`s life and claiming one`s rights.

_____ as action refers both to the process of self- _____ and to professional support of people, which enables them to overcome their sense of powerlessness and lack of influence, and to recognize and use their resources. To do work with power.

Exam Probability: **Medium**

7. *Answer choices:*

(see index for correct answer)

- a. Top development
- b. Coworking
- c. Scrum
- d. U-procedure and Theory U

Guidance: level 1

:: Human resource management ::

Frederick Herzberg, an American psychologist, originally developed the concept of ` _____ ` in 1968, in an article that he published on pioneering studies at A T&T. The concept stemmed from Herzberg's motivator-hygiene theory, which is based on the premise that job attitude is a construct of two independent factors, namely job satisfaction and job dissatisfaction. Job satisfaction encompasses intrinsic factors that arise from the work itself, including achievement and advancement; whilst job dissatisfaction stems from factors external to the actual work, including company policy and the quality of supervision.

Exam Probability: **Medium**

8. *Answer choices:*

(see index for correct answer)

- a. Individual development plan
- b. Human resources
- c. Job enrichment
- d. Behavioral Competencies

Guidance: level 1

:: ::

A _____ service is an online platform which people use to build social networks or social relationship with other people who share similar personal or career interests, activities, backgrounds or real-life connections.

9. *Answer choices:*

(see index for correct answer)

- a. surface-level diversity
- b. deep-level diversity
- c. information systems assessment
- d. Social networking

Guidance: level 1

:: Employment compensation ::

_____ is time off from work that workers can use to stay home to address their health and safety needs without losing pay. Paid _____ is a statutory requirement in many nations. Most European, many Latin American, a few African and a few Asian countries have legal requirements for paid _____ .

10. *Answer choices:*

(see index for correct answer)

- a. salary sacrifice
- b. Gender pay gap

- c. Pension insurance contract
- d. Employees%27 Compensation Appeals Board

Guidance: level 1

:: Television terminology ::

Distance education or long-_____ is the education of students who may not always be physically present at a school. Traditionally, this usually involved correspondence courses wherein the student corresponded with the school via post. Today it involves online education. Courses that are conducted are either hybrid, blended or 100% _____ . Massive open online courses , offering large-scale interactive participation and open access through the World Wide Web or other network technologies, are recent developments in distance education. A number of other terms are used roughly synonymously with distance education.

Exam Probability: **High**

11. *Answer choices:*
(see index for correct answer)

- a. Distance learning
- b. nonprofit
- c. not-for-profit
- d. multiplexing

Guidance: level 1

A _____ is a systematic way of determining the value/worth of a job in relation to other jobs in an organization. It tries to make a systematic comparison between jobs to assess their relative worth for the purpose of establishing a rational pay structure. _____ needs to be differentiated from job analysis. Job analysis is a systematic way of gathering information about a job. Every _____ method requires at least some basic job analysis in order to provide factual information about the jobs concerned. Thus, _____ begins with job analysis and ends at that point where the worth of a job is ascertained for achieving pay equity between jobs and different roles.

Exam Probability: **Medium**

12. *Answer choices:*

(see index for correct answer)

- a. information systems assessment
- b. personal values
- c. empathy
- d. co-culture

Guidance: level 1

:: Power (social and political) ::

_____ is a form of reverence gained by a leader who has strong interpersonal relationship skills. _____ , as an aspect of personal power, becomes particularly important as organizational leadership becomes increasingly about collaboration and influence, rather than command and control.

Exam Probability: **High**

13. *Answer choices:*

(see index for correct answer)

- a. need for power
- b. Hard power
- c. Referent power

Guidance: level 1

:: Management ::

In organizational studies, _____ is the efficient and effective development of an organization's resources when they are needed. Such resources may include financial resources, inventory, human skills, production resources, or information technology and natural resources.

Exam Probability: **Medium**

14. *Answer choices:*

(see index for correct answer)

- a. Managerial economics
- b. Control limits
- c. Reval
- d. Resource management

Guidance: level 1

:: ::

_____ is a form of government characterized by strong central power and limited political freedoms. Individual freedoms are subordinate to the state and there is no constitutional accountability and rule of law under an authoritarian regime. Authoritarian regimes can be autocratic with power concentrated in one person or it can be more spread out between multiple officials and government institutions. Juan Linz's influential 1964 description of _____ characterized authoritarian political systems by four qualities.

Exam Probability: **Low**

15. *Answer choices:*

(see index for correct answer)

- a. cultural
- b. information systems assessment
- c. Authoritarianism
- d. co-culture

:: Survey methodology ::

An _____ is a conversation where questions are asked and answers are given. In common parlance, the word "_____" refers to a one-on-one conversation between an _____ er and an _____ ee. The _____ er asks questions to which the _____ ee responds, usually so information may be transferred from _____ ee to _____ er . Sometimes, information can be transferred in both directions. It is a communication, unlike a speech, which produces a one-way flow of information.

Exam Probability: **Medium**

16. *Answer choices:*

(see index for correct answer)

- a. Administrative error
- b. Public opinion
- c. Self-report study
- d. Interview

:: Educational assessment and evaluation ::

An _____ is a component of a competence to do a certain kind of work at a certain level. Outstanding _____ can be considered "talent". An _____ may be physical or mental. _____ is inborn potential to do certain kinds of work whether developed or undeveloped. Ability is developed knowledge, understanding, learned or acquired abilities or attitude. The innate nature of _____ is in contrast to skills and achievement, which represent knowledge or ability that is gained through learning.

Exam Probability: **High**

17. *Answer choices:*

(see index for correct answer)

- a. Illinois School Report Card
- b. Aptitude
- c. Heidi Hayes Jacobs
- d. Grading

Guidance: level 1

:: Employment discrimination ::

A _____ is a metaphor used to represent an invisible barrier that keeps a given demographic from rising beyond a certain level in a hierarchy.

Exam Probability: **Low**

18. *Answer choices:*

(see index for correct answer)

- a. Marriage bars
- b. LGBT employment discrimination in the United States
- c. Glass ceiling
- d. New South Wales selection bias

Guidance: level 1

:: Management ::

_____ is a set of activities that ensure goals are met in an effective and efficient manner. _____ can focus on the performance of an organization, a department, an employee, or the processes in place to manage particular tasks. _____ standards are generally organized and disseminated by senior leadership at an organization, and by task owners.

Exam Probability: **Medium**

19. *Answer choices:*

(see index for correct answer)

- a. Continuous monitoring
- b. Concept of the Corporation
- c. Performance management
- d. Supply management

:: Trade unions ::

A _____ , in North America, or union branch , in the United Kingdom and other countries, is a local branch of a usually national trade union. The terms used for sub-branches of _____ s vary from country to country and include "shop committee", "shop floor committee", "board of control", "chapel", and others.

Exam Probability: **Low**

20. *Answer choices:*

(see index for correct answer)

- a. Vigilance committee
- b. Local union
- c. General union
- d. National trade union center

Guidance: level 1

:: Meetings ::

A _____ is a formal meeting of the representatives of different countries, constituent states, organizations, trade unions, political parties or other groups. The term, originally denoting a parley during battle in the Late Middle Ages, is derived from the Latin _____ us.

Exam Probability: **High**

21. *Answer choices:*

(see index for correct answer)

- a. Brown bag seminar
- b. Awayday
- c. European Architecture Students Assembly
- d. Popular assembly

Guidance: level 1

:: ::

_____ is a form of development in which a person called a coach supports a learner or client in achieving a specific personal or professional goal by providing training and guidance. The learner is sometimes called a coachee. Occasionally, _____ may mean an informal relationship between two people, of whom one has more experience and expertise than the other and offers advice and guidance as the latter learns; but _____ differs from mentoring in focusing on specific tasks or objectives, as opposed to more general goals or overall development.

Exam Probability: **High**

22. *Answer choices:*

(see index for correct answer)

- a. Coaching
- b. corporate values
- c. process perspective
- d. Sarbanes-Oxley act of 2002

Guidance: level 1

:: Management ::

A _____ describes the rationale of how an organization creates, delivers, and captures value, in economic, social, cultural or other contexts. The process of _____ construction and modification is also called _____ innovation and forms a part of business strategy.

Exam Probability: **High**

23. *Answer choices:*

(see index for correct answer)

- a. Executive compensation
- b. Third-generation balanced scorecard
- c. Business model

- d. Duality

Guidance: level 1

:: Employment compensation ::

The formula commonly used by compensation professionals to assess the competitiveness of an employee's pay level involves calculating a "" _____ "". _____ is the short form for Comparative ratio.

Exam Probability: **Medium**

24. *Answer choices:*

(see index for correct answer)

- a. Wage regulation
- b. Wage payment systems
- c. Compa-ratio
- d. Employees%27 Compensation Appeals Board

Guidance: level 1

:: Unemployment ::

The _____ is the negative relationship between the levels of unemployment and wages that arises when these variables are expressed in local terms. According to David Blanchflower and Andrew Oswald , the _____ summarizes the fact that "A worker who is employed in an area of high unemployment earns less than an identical individual who works in a region with low joblessness."

Exam Probability: **High**

25. *Answer choices:*

(see index for correct answer)

- a. Wage curve
- b. Male unemployment
- c. Misery index
- d. Growth recession

Guidance: level 1

:: Employment compensation ::

A _____ is an agreement between a company and an employee specifying that the employee will receive certain significant benefits if employment is terminated. Most definitions specify the employment termination is as a result of a merger or takeover, also known as "Change-in-control benefits", but more recently the term has been used to describe perceived excessive CEO severance packages unrelated to change in ownership . The benefits may include severance pay, cash bonuses, stock options, or other benefits.

26. *Answer choices:*

(see index for correct answer)

- a. Compa-ratio
- b. Long service leave
- c. Streamlining Claims Processing for Federal Contractor Employees Act
- d. Cafeteria plan

Guidance: level 1

:: Financial terminology ::

_____ is the cost of maintaining a certain standard of living. Changes in the _____ over time are often operationalized in a cost-of-living index. _____ calculations are also used to compare the cost of maintaining a certain standard of living in different geographic areas. Differences in _____ between locations can also be measured in terms of purchasing power parity rates.

Exam Probability: **Low**

27. *Answer choices:*

(see index for correct answer)

- a. Sovereign credit risk

- b. RNPV
- c. Skin in the game
- d. Global tactical asset allocation

Guidance: level 1

:: Recruitment ::

Recruitment refers to the overall process of attracting, shortlisting, selecting and appointing suitable candidates for jobs within an organization. Recruitment can also refer to processes involved in choosing individuals for unpaid roles. Managers, human resource generalists and recruitment specialists may be tasked with carrying out recruitment, but in some cases public-sector employment agencies, commercial recruitment agencies, or specialist search consultancies are used to undertake parts of the process. Internet-based technologies which support all aspects of recruitment have become widespread.

Exam Probability: **Medium**

28. *Answer choices:*
(see index for correct answer)

- a. Work-at-home scheme
- b. Avature
- c. Disclosure Scotland
- d. Employee referral

Guidance: level 1

:: Organizational behavior ::

Greenberg introduced the concept of _____ with regard to how an employee judges the behaviour of the organization and the employee's resulting attitude and behaviour. .

Exam Probability: **Medium**

29. *Answer choices:*

(see index for correct answer)

- a. Conformity
- b. Organizational storytelling
- c. Organizational justice
- d. Burnout

Guidance: level 1

:: Human resource management ::

_____ is a core function of human resource management and it is related to the specification of contents, methods and relationship of jobs in order to satisfy technological and organizational requirements as well as the social and personal requirements of the job holder or the employee. Its principles are geared towards how the nature of a person's job affects their attitudes and behavior at work, particularly relating to characteristics such as skill variety and autonomy. The aim of a _____ is to improve job satisfaction, to improve through-put, to improve quality and to reduce employee problems .

Exam Probability: **Medium**

30. *Answer choices:*

(see index for correct answer)

- a. Administrative services organization
- b. Employeeship
- c. Adaptive performance
- d. Vendor management system

Guidance: level 1

:: Psychometrics ::

In statistics and research, _____ is typically a measure based on the correlations between different items on the same test . It measures whether several items that propose to measure the same general construct produce similar scores. For example, if a respondent expressed agreement with the statements "I like to ride bicycles" and "I've enjoyed riding bicycles in the past", and disagreement with the statement "I hate bicycles", this would be indicative of good _____ of the test.

Exam Probability: **Low**

31. *Answer choices:*

(see index for correct answer)

- a. Reliability
- b. Assessment day
- c. Internal consistency
- d. Jensen box

Guidance: level 1

:: Survey methodology ::

A _____ is the procedure of systematically acquiring and recording information about the members of a given population. The term is used mostly in connection with national population and housing _____ es; other common _____ es include agriculture, business, and traffic _____ es. The United Nations defines the essential features of population and housing _____ es as "individual enumeration, universality within a defined territory, simultaneity and defined periodicity", and recommends that population _____ es be taken at least every 10 years. United Nations recommendations also cover _____ topics to be collected, official definitions, classifications and other useful information to co-ordinate international practice.

Exam Probability: **High**

32. *Answer choices:*

(see index for correct answer)

- a. Swiss Centre of Expertise in the Social Sciences
- b. Political forecasting
- c. Scale analysis
- d. Public opinion

Guidance: level 1

:: ::

A _____ seeks to further a particular profession, the interests of individuals engaged in that profession and the public interest. In the United States, such an association is typically a nonprofit organization for tax purposes.

Exam Probability: **Low**

33. *Answer choices:*

(see index for correct answer)

- a. interpersonal communication
- b. hierarchical perspective
- c. empathy
- d. process perspective

Guidance: level 1

:: ::

In educational development, _____ provides a person, often a student, focus for selecting a career or subject to undertake in the future. Often educational institutions provide career counsellors to assist students with their educational development.

Exam Probability: **Low**

34. *Answer choices:*

(see index for correct answer)

- a. hierarchical perspective
- b. Career development
- c. similarity-attraction theory
- d. imperative

Guidance: level 1

:: Occupations ::

_____ means a restricted practice or a restriction on the use of an occupational title, requiring a license. A license created under a "practice act" requires a license before performing a certain activity, such as driving a car on public roads. A license created under a "title act" restricts the use of a given occupational title to licensees, but anyone can perform the activity itself under a less restricted title. For example, in Oregon, anyone can practice counseling, but only licensees can call themselves "Licensed Professional Counselors." Thus depending on the type of law,practicing without a license may carry civil or criminal penalties or may be perfectly legal. For some occupations and professions, licensing is often granted through a professional body or a licensing board composed of practitioners who oversee the applications for licenses. This often involves accredited training and examinations, but varies a great deal for different activities and in different countries.

Exam Probability: **Low**

35. *Answer choices:*

(see index for correct answer)

- a. Signwriter
- b. Licensure
- c. International Standard Classification of Occupations
- d. Sarpanch

Guidance: level 1

:: Trade unions in the United States ::

The _____ is an American labor union representing over 670,000 employees of the federal government, about 5,000 employees of the District of Columbia, and a few hundred private sector employees, mostly in and around federal facilities. AFGE is the largest union for civilian, non-postal federal employees and the largest union for District of Columbia employees who report directly to the mayor . It is affiliated with the AFL-CIO.

Exam Probability: **Medium**

36. *Answer choices:*

(see index for correct answer)

- a. American Federation of State, County and Municipal Employees
- b. Pride at Work
- c. American Federation of Government Employees
- d. Professional Flight Attendants Association

Guidance: level 1

:: Systems thinking ::

Systems theory is the interdisciplinary study of systems. A system is a cohesive conglomeration of interrelated and interdependent parts that is either natural or man-made. Every system is delineated by its spatial and temporal boundaries, surrounded and influenced by its environment, described by its structure and purpose or nature and expressed in its functioning. In terms of its effects, a system can be more than the sum of its parts if it expresses synergy or emergent behavior. Changing one part of the system usually affects other parts and the whole system, with predictable patterns of behavior. For systems that are self-learning and self-adapting, the positive growth and adaptation depend upon how well the system is adjusted with its environment. Some systems function mainly to support other systems by aiding in the maintenance of the other system to prevent failure. The goal of systems theory is systematically discovering a system's dynamics, constraints, conditions and elucidating principles that can be discerned and applied to systems at every level of nesting, and in every field for achieving optimized equifinality.

Exam Probability: **Medium**

37. *Answer choices:*
(see index for correct answer)

- a. World Future Society
- b. Club of Rome
- c. Interdependence
- d. Involution

Guidance: level 1

:: Meetings ::

A _____ is a body of one or more persons that is subordinate to a deliberative assembly. Usually, the assembly sends matters into a _____ as a way to explore them more fully than would be possible if the assembly itself were considering them. _____ s may have different functions and their type of work differ depending on the type of the organization and its needs.

Exam Probability: **High**

38. *Answer choices:*

(see index for correct answer)

- a. Official function
- b. Mighty Men Conference
- c. Evoma
- d. Committee

Guidance: level 1

:: Production and manufacturing ::

_____ is a theory of management that analyzes and synthesizes workflows. Its main objective is improving economic efficiency, especially labor productivity. It was one of the earliest attempts to apply science to the engineering of processes and to management. _____ is sometimes known as Taylorism after its founder, Frederick Winslow Taylor.

39. *Answer choices:*

(see index for correct answer)

- a. Pegging report
- b. Dynamic Manufacturing Network
- c. Traditional engineering
- d. Scientific management

Guidance: level 1

:: ::

_____ is the means to see, hear, or become aware of something or someone through our fundamental senses. The term _____ derives from the Latin word perceptio, and is the organization, identification, and interpretation of sensory information in order to represent and understand the presented information, or the environment.

Exam Probability: **High**

40. *Answer choices:*

(see index for correct answer)

- a. similarity-attraction theory
- b. cultural

- c. deep-level diversity
- d. Perception

Guidance: level 1

:: ::

Refresher/_____ is the process of learning a new or the same old skill or trade for the same group of personnel. Refresher/_____ is required to be provided on regular basis to avoid personnel obsolescence due to technological changes & the individuals memory capacity. This short term instruction course shall serve to re-acquaint personnel with skills previously learnt or to bring one`s knowledge or skills up-to-date so that skills stay sharp. This kind of training could be provided annually or more frequently as maybe required, based on the importance of consistency of the task of which the skill is involved. Examples of refreshers are cGMP, GDP, HSE trainings.

_____ shall also be conducted for an employee, when the employee is rated as 'not qualified' for a skill or knowledge, as determined based on the assessment of answers in the training questionnaire of the employee.

Exam Probability: **Medium**

41. *Answer choices:*

(see index for correct answer)

- a. interpersonal communication
- b. personal values
- c. Retraining
- d. cultural

:: Business law ::

In professional sports, a _____ is a player who is eligible to freely sign with any club or franchise; i.e., not under contract to any specific team. The term is also used in reference to a player who is under contract at present but who is allowed to solicit offers from other teams. In some circumstances, the _____ 's options are limited by league rules.

Exam Probability: **Low**

42. *Answer choices:*

(see index for correct answer)

- a. Enhanced use lease
- b. Certificate of incorporation
- c. Free agent
- d. Lien

:: Management education ::

_____ refers to simulation games that are used as an educational tool for teaching business. _____ s may be carried out for various business training such as: general management, finance, organizational behaviour, human resources, etc. Often, the term "business simulation" is used with the same meaning.

Exam Probability: **Low**

43. *Answer choices:*

(see index for correct answer)

- a. Master of Management
- b. Fachwirt
- c. Business game
- d. Training simulation

Guidance: level 1

:: Business models ::

A _____ is a diagram that is used to document the primary strategic goals being pursued by an organization or management team. It is an element of the documentation associated with the Balanced Scorecard, and in particular is characteristic of the second generation of Balanced Scorecard designs that first appeared during the mid-1990s. The first diagrams of this type appeared in the early 1990s, and the idea of using this type of diagram to help document Balanced Scorecard was discussed in a paper by Drs. Robert S. Kaplan and David P. Norton in 1996.

44. *Answer choices:*

(see index for correct answer)

- a. Professional open source
- b. Strategy map
- c. Paid To Click
- d. Cooperative

Guidance: level 1

:: Employment compensation ::

The _____ has been successfully used by a variety of public and private companies for many decades. These plans combine leadership, total workforce education, and widespread employee participation with a reward system linked to organization performance. The _____ is a gainsharing program in which employees share in pre-established cost savings, based upon employee effort. Formal employee participation is necessary with the _____ , as well as periodic progress reporting and an incentive formula.

Exam Probability: **Low**

45. *Answer choices:*

(see index for correct answer)

- a. Golden handcuffs

- b. Severance package
- c. Pension insurance contract
- d. New York Disability Benefits Law

Guidance: level 1

:: Business ::

_____ is a trade policy that does not restrict imports or exports; it can also be understood as the free market idea applied to international trade. In government, _____ is predominantly advocated by political parties that hold liberal economic positions while economically left-wing and nationalist political parties generally support protectionism, the opposite of _____.

Exam Probability: **Low**

46. *Answer choices:*
(see index for correct answer)

- a. CyberAlert, Inc.
- b. American Environmental Assessment and Solutions Inc.
- c. E-lancing
- d. Viability study

Guidance: level 1

:: Production and manufacturing ::

_____ is a set of techniques and tools for process improvement. Though as a shortened form it may be found written as 6S, it should not be confused with the methodology known as 6S .

Exam Probability: **High**

47. *Answer choices:*

(see index for correct answer)

- a. Shifting bottleneck heuristic
- b. Six Sigma
- c. Expediting
- d. Woodworking machine

Guidance: level 1

:: ::

_____ is the withdrawal from one`s position or occupation or from one`s active working life. A person may also semi-retire by reducing work hours.

Exam Probability: **Medium**

48. *Answer choices:*

(see index for correct answer)

- a. Retirement
- b. personal values
- c. levels of analysis
- d. empathy

Guidance: level 1

:: Employment compensation ::

A _____ , also known as a flexible spending arrangement, is one of a number of tax-advantaged financial accounts, resulting in payroll tax savings. Before the Patient Protection and Affordable Care Act, one significant disadvantage to using an FSA was that funds not used by the end of the plan year were forfeited to the employer, known as the "use it or lose it" rule. Under the terms of the Affordable Care Act, a plan may permit an employee to carry over up to $500 into the following year without losing the funds.

Exam Probability: **Medium**

49. *Answer choices:*
(see index for correct answer)

- a. The Theory of Wages
- b. Employee stock ownership plan
- c. Wage regulation
- d. Flexible spending account

:: Hazard analysis ::

A _____ is an agent which has the potential to cause harm to a vulnerable target. The terms " _____ " and "risk" are often used interchangeably. However, in terms of risk assessment, they are two very distinct terms. A _____ is any agent that can cause harm or damage to humans, property, or the environment. Risk is defined as the probability that exposure to a _____ will lead to a negative consequence, or more simply, a _____ poses no risk if there is no exposure to that _____ .

Exam Probability: **Medium**

50. *Answer choices:*

(see index for correct answer)

- a. Hazard identification
- b. Risk assessment
- c. Swiss cheese model
- d. Hazardous Materials Identification System

:: Workplace ::

_____ or occupational violence refers to violence, usually in the form of physical abuse or threat, that creates a risk to the health and safety of an employee or multiple employees. The National Institute for Occupational Safety and Health defines worker on worker, personal relationship, customer/client, and criminal intent all as categories of violence in the workplace. These four categories are further broken down into three levels: Level one displays early warning signs of violence, Level two is slightly more violent, and level three is significantly violent. Many workplaces have initiated programs and protocols to protect their workers as the Occupational Health Act of 1970 states that employers must provide an environment in which employees are free of harm or harmful conditions.

Exam Probability: **Low**

51. *Answer choices:*

(see index for correct answer)

- a. Queen bee syndrome
- b. Workplace democracy
- c. Workplace wellness
- d. Discrimination based on hair texture

Guidance: level 1

:: Human resource management ::

_____ is a process for identifying and developing new leaders who can replace old leaders when they leave, retire or die. _____ increases the availability of experienced and capable employees that are prepared to assume these roles as they become available. Taken narrowly, "replacement planning" for key roles is the heart of _____ .

Exam Probability: **High**

52. *Answer choices:*

(see index for correct answer)

- a. Employee retention
- b. Multiculturalism
- c. Job enlargement
- d. Restructuring

Guidance: level 1

:: Occupational safety and health law ::

The _____ of 1970 is a US labor law governing the federal law of occupational health and safety in the private sector and federal government in the United States. It was enacted by Congress in 1970 and was signed by President Richard Nixon on December 29, 1970. Its main goal is to ensure that employers provide employees with an environment free from recognized hazards, such as exposure to toxic chemicals, excessive noise levels, mechanical dangers, heat or cold stress, or unsanitary conditions. The Act created the Occupational Safety and Health Administration and the National Institute for Occupational Safety and Health .

53. *Answer choices:*

(see index for correct answer)

- a. Employment Standards Act of British Columbia
- b. Labor Standards Act
- c. Factories Act 1961
- d. Factory and Workshop Act 1895

Guidance: level 1

:: Workplace ::

A _____ , also referred to as a performance review, performance evaluation, development discussion, or employee appraisal is a method by which the job performance of an employee is documented and evaluated. _____ s are a part of career development and consist of regular reviews of employee performance within organizations.

Exam Probability: **Medium**

54. *Answer choices:*

(see index for correct answer)

- a. Performance appraisal
- b. Hostile environment sexual harassment

- c. Workplace incivility
- d. Workplace relationships

Guidance: level 1

:: Workplace ::

A _____ is a process through which feedback from an employee's subordinates, colleagues, and supervisor, as well as a self-evaluation by the employee themselves is gathered. Such feedback can also include, when relevant, feedback from external sources who interact with the employee, such as customers and suppliers or other interested stakeholders. _____ is so named because it solicits feedback regarding an employee's behavior from a variety of points of view . It therefore may be contrasted with "downward feedback" , or "upward feedback" delivered to supervisory or management employees by subordinates only.

Exam Probability: **Medium**

55. *Answer choices:*
(see index for correct answer)

- a. Performance appraisal
- b. Toxic workplace
- c. Workplace deviance
- d. 360-degree feedback

Guidance: level 1

:: Self ::

_____ is a conscious or subconscious process in which people attempt to influence the perceptions of other people about a person, object or event. They do so by regulating and controlling information in social interaction. It was first conceptualized by Erving Goffman in 1959 in The Presentation of Self in Everyday Life, and then was expanded upon in 1967. An example of _____ theory in play is in sports such as soccer. At an important game, a player would want to showcase themselves in the best light possible, because there are college recruiters watching. This person would have the flashiest pair of cleats and try and perform their best to show off their skills. Their main goal may be to impress the college recruiters in a way that maximizes their chances of being chosen for a college team rather than winning the game.

Exam Probability: **Low**

56. *Answer choices:*

(see index for correct answer)

- a. ecological self
- b. Impression management
- c. Egocentrism
- d. Narcissism

Guidance: level 1

:: Labour relations ::

_____ is a field of study that can have different meanings depending on the context in which it is used. In an international context, it is a subfield of labor history that studies the human relations with regard to work – in its broadest sense – and how this connects to questions of social inequality. It explicitly encompasses unregulated, historical, and non-Western forms of labor. Here, _____ define "for or with whom one works and under what rules. These rules determine the type of work, type and amount of remuneration, working hours, degrees of physical and psychological strain, as well as the degree of freedom and autonomy associated with the work."

Exam Probability: **Low**

57. *Answer choices:*

(see index for correct answer)

- a. Labor relations
- b. Big labor
- c. Whipsaw strike
- d. Featherbedding

Guidance: level 1

:: ::

The _____ or labour force is the labour pool in employment. It is generally used to describe those working for a single company or industry, but can also apply to a geographic region like a city, state, or country. Within a company, its value can be labelled as its "_____ in Place". The _____ of a country includes both the employed and the unemployed. The labour force participation rate, LFPR , is the ratio between the labour force and the overall size of their cohort . The term generally excludes the employers or management, and can imply those involved in manual labour. It may also mean all those who are available for work.

Exam Probability: **Medium**

58. *Answer choices:*

(see index for correct answer)

- a. personal values
- b. Workforce
- c. process perspective
- d. empathy

Guidance: level 1

:: Workplace ::

_____ is asystematic determination of a subject's merit, worth and significance, using criteria governed by a set of standards. It can assist an organization, program, design, project or any other intervention or initiative to assess any aim, realisable concept/proposal, or any alternative, to help in decision-making; or to ascertain the degree of achievement or value in regard to the aim and objectives and results of any such action that has been completed. The primary purpose of _____ , in addition to gaining insight into prior or existing initiatives, is to enable reflection and assist in the identification of future change.

Exam Probability: **Medium**

59. *Answer choices:*
(see index for correct answer)

- a. Discrimination based on hair texture
- b. Evaluation
- c. Workplace revenge
- d. Emotions in the workplace

Guidance: level 1

Information systems

Information systems (IS) are formal, sociotechnical, organizational systems designed to collect, process, store, and distribute information. In a sociotechnical perspective Information Systems are composed by four components: technology, process, people and organizational structure.

:: E-commerce ::

Electronic governance or e-governance is the application of information and communication technology for delivering government services, exchange of information, communication transactions, integration of various stand-alone systems and services between _____ , government-to-business , government-to-government , government-to-employees as well as back-office processes and interactions within the entire government framework. Through e-governance, government services are made available to citizens in a convenient, efficient, and transparent manner. The three main target groups that can be distinguished in governance concepts are government, citizens, andbusinesses/interest groups. In e-governance, there are no distinct boundaries.

Exam Probability: **Low**

1. *Answer choices:*

(see index for correct answer)

- a. SupaDupa
- b. Online wallet
- c. Social commerce
- d. Government-to-citizen

Guidance: level 1

:: ::

A _____ is a discussion or informational website published on the World Wide Web consisting of discrete, often informal diary-style text entries . Posts are typically displayed in reverse chronological order, so that the most recent post appears first, at the top of the web page. Until 2009, _____ s were usually the work of a single individual, occasionally of a small group, and often covered a single subject or topic. In the 2010s, "multi-author _____ s" emerged, featuring the writing of multiple authors and sometimes professionally edited. MABs from newspapers, other media outlets, universities, think tanks, advocacy groups, and similar institutions account for an increasing quantity of _____ traffic. The rise of Twitter and other "micro _____ ging" systems helps integrate MABs and single-author _____ s into the news media. _____ can also be used as a verb, meaning to maintain or add content to a _____ .

Exam Probability: **High**

2. *Answer choices:*

(see index for correct answer)

- a. Sarbanes-Oxley act of 2002
- b. hierarchical
- c. open system
- d. hierarchical perspective

Guidance: level 1

:: Management ::

In organizational studies, _____ is the efficient and effective development of an organization's resources when they are needed. Such resources may include financial resources, inventory, human skills, production resources, or information technology and natural resources.

Exam Probability: **Low**

3. *Answer choices:*

(see index for correct answer)

- a. Resource management
- b. Purchasing management
- c. Value migration
- d. Organizational space

Guidance: level 1

:: Tag editors ::

_____ is a media player, media library, Internet radio broadcaster, and mobile device management application developed by Apple Inc. It was announced on January 9, 2001. It is used to play, download, and organize digital multimedia files, including music and video, on personal computers running the macOS and Windows operating systems. Content must be purchased through the _____ Store, whereas _____ is the software letting users manage their purchases.

Exam Probability: **Medium**

4. *Answer choices:*

(see index for correct answer)

- a. MediaMonkey
- b. ExifTool
- c. ITunes
- d. Windows Media Player

Guidance: level 1

:: Virtual reality ::

An _____ , a concept in Hinduism that means "descent", refers to the material appearance or incarnation of a deity on earth. The relative verb to "alight, to make one's appearance" is sometimes used to refer to any guru or revered human being.

Exam Probability: **Low**

5. *Answer choices:*

(see index for correct answer)

- a. Avatar
- b. Blue Brain Project
- c. Unigine
- d. Surround sound

:: Information technology management ::

The term _____ is used to refer to periods when a system is unavailable. _____ or outage duration refers to a period of time that a system fails to provide or perform its primary function. Reliability, availability, recovery, and unavailability are related concepts. The unavailability is the proportion of a time-span that a system is unavailable or offline. This is usually a result of the system failing to function because of an unplanned event, or because of routine maintenance .

Exam Probability: **Medium**

6. *Answer choices:*

(see index for correct answer)

- a. Automic
- b. Downtime
- c. High Availability Application Architecture
- d. Campustours

:: User interfaces ::

The _____ , in the industrial design field of human–computer interaction, is the space where interactions between humans and machines occur. The goal of this interaction is to allow effective operation and control of the machine from the human end, whilst the machine simultaneously feeds back information that aids the operators' decision-making process. Examples of this broad concept of _____ s include the interactive aspects of computer operating systems, hand tools, heavy machinery operator controls, and process controls. The design considerations applicable when creating _____ s are related to or involve such disciplines as ergonomics and psychology.

Exam Probability: **Medium**

7. *Answer choices:*

(see index for correct answer)

- a. MachPanel
- b. Baifox
- c. User interface
- d. Direct mode

Guidance: level 1

:: Payment systems ::

An _____ is an electronic telecommunications device that enables customers of financial institutions to perform financial transactions, such as cash withdrawals, deposits, transfer funds, or obtaining account information, at any time and without the need for direct interaction with bank staff.

8. *Answer choices:*

(see index for correct answer)

- a. 3V
- b. Wire transfer
- c. Automated teller machine
- d. CNG Processing

Guidance: level 1

:: Information technology ::

_____ is the reorientation of product and service designs to focus on the end user as an individual consumer, in contrast with an earlier era of only organization-oriented offerings . Technologies whose first commercialization was at the inter-organization level thus have potential for later _____ .
The emergence of the individual consumer as the primary driver of product and service design is most commonly associated with the IT industry, as large business and government organizations dominated the early decades of computer usage and development. Thus the microcomputer revolution, in which electronic computing moved from exclusively enterprise and government use to include personal computing, is a cardinal example of _____ . But many technology-based products, such as calculators and mobile phones, have also had their origins in business markets, and only over time did they become dominated by high-volume consumer usage, as these products commoditized and prices fell. An example of enterprise software that became consumer software is optical character recognition software, which originated with banks and postal systems but eventually became personal productivity software.

9. *Answer choices:*

(see index for correct answer)

- a. Information Technology Generalist
- b. Information and communications technology
- c. Omniview technology
- d. E-Governance

Guidance: level 1

:: Information technology management ::

_____ is a collective term for all approaches to prepare , support and help individuals, teams, and organizations in making organizational change. The most common change drivers include: technological evolution, process reviews, crisis, and consumer habit changes; pressure from new business entrants, acquisitions, mergers, and organizational restructuring. It includes methods that redirect or redefine the use of resources, business process, budget allocations, or other modes of operation that significantly change a company or organization. Organizational _____ considers the full organization and what needs to change, while _____ may be used solely to refer to how people and teams are affected by such organizational transition. It deals with many different disciplines, from behavioral and social sciences to information technology and business solutions.

10. *Answer choices:*

(see index for correct answer)

- a. Change management
- b. Pathology Messaging Implementation Project
- c. Information Technology Infrastructure Library
- d. Mobile business development

Guidance: level 1

:: Network architecture ::

An _____ is a controlled private network that allows access to partners, vendors and suppliers or an authorized set of customers – normally to a subset of the information accessible from an organization's intranet. An _____ is similar to a DMZ in that it provides access to needed services for authorized parties, without granting access to an organization's entire network. An _____ is a private network organization.

Exam Probability: **Medium**

11. *Answer choices:*

(see index for correct answer)

- a. Extranet
- b. client-server

Guidance: level 1

:: Information systems ::

_____ , Chief Digital Information Officer or Information Technology Director, is a job title commonly given to the most senior executive in an enterprise who works for the traditional information technology and computer systems that support enterprise goals.

Exam Probability: **Medium**

12. *Answer choices:*

(see index for correct answer)

- a. Chief information officer
- b. Knowledge management
- c. Ucode system
- d. Digital marketing system

Guidance: level 1

:: Procurement practices ::

_____ or commercially available off-the-shelf products are packaged solutions which are then adapted to satisfy the needs of the purchasing organization, rather than the commissioning of custom-made, or bespoke, solutions. A related term, Mil-COTS, refers to COTS products for use by the U.S. military.

13. *Answer choices:*

(see index for correct answer)

- a. Commercial off-the-shelf
- b. Construction by configuration

Guidance: level 1

:: Business ::

_____ is a sourcing model in which individuals or organizations obtain goods and services, including ideas and finances, from a large, relatively open and often rapidly-evolving group of internet users; it divides work between participants to achieve a cumulative result. The word _____ itself is a portmanteau of crowd and outsourcing, and was coined in 2005. As a mode of sourcing, _____ existed prior to the digital age .

14. *Answer choices:*

(see index for correct answer)

- a. Crowdsourcing
- b. Local multiplier effect
- c. Westnile Distilling Company Limited
- d. Values scales

:: Data management ::

An _____ is a term used in data warehousing to refer to a system that is used to process the day-to-day transactions of an organization. These systems are designed in a manner that processing of day-to-day transactions is performed efficiently and the integrity of the transactional data is preserved.

Exam Probability: **Low**

15. *Answer choices:*

(see index for correct answer)

- a. Inverted index
- b. Retention period
- c. Copyright
- d. Semantic warehousing

:: ::

_____ is a free email service developed by Google. Users can access _____ on the web and using third-party programs that synchronize email content through POP or IMAP protocols. _____ started as a limited beta release on April 1, 2004 and ended its testing phase on July 7, 2009.

Exam Probability: **Low**

16. *Answer choices:*

(see index for correct answer)

- a. functional perspective
- b. personal values
- c. Gmail
- d. empathy

Guidance: level 1

:: Information and communication technologies for development ::

_____ is a non-profit initiative established with the goal of transforming education for children around the world; this goal was to be achieved by creating and distributing educational devices for the developing world, and by creating software and content for those devices.

Exam Probability: **Medium**

17. *Answer choices:*

(see index for correct answer)

- a. One Laptop per Child
- b. Lemote
- c. Development informatics
- d. Community informatics

Guidance: level 1

:: Business planning ::

_____ is an organization's process of defining its strategy, or direction, and making decisions on allocating its resources to pursue this strategy. It may also extend to control mechanisms for guiding the implementation of the strategy. _____ became prominent in corporations during the 1960s and remains an important aspect of strategic management. It is executed by strategic planners or strategists, who involve many parties and research sources in their analysis of the organization and its relationship to the environment in which it competes.

Exam Probability: **Low**

18. *Answer choices:*
(see index for correct answer)

- a. Stakeholder management
- b. Exit planning
- c. Business war games

- d. Strategic planning

Guidance: level 1

:: Data management ::

Given organizations' increasing dependency on information technology to run their operations, Business continuity planning covers the entire organization, and Disaster recovery focuses on IT.

Exam Probability: **Medium**

19. *Answer choices:*

(see index for correct answer)

- a. Disaster recovery plan
- b. Automated tiered storage
- c. Tuple
- d. Data custodian

Guidance: level 1

:: ::

A _____ is a knowledge base website on which users collaboratively modify content and structure directly from the web browser. In a typical _____, text is written using a simplified markup language and often edited with the help of a rich-text editor.

20. *Answer choices:*

(see index for correct answer)

- a. levels of analysis
- b. functional perspective
- c. Wiki
- d. deep-level diversity

Guidance: level 1

:: Google services ::

_____ is a time-management and scheduling calendar service developed by Google. It became available in beta release April 13, 2006, and in general release in July 2009, on the web and as mobile apps for the Android and iOS platforms.

21. *Answer choices:*

(see index for correct answer)

- a. Google WiFi
- b. Google Business Solutions
- c. Google Maps
- d. Google Calendar

Guidance: level 1

:: Automatic identification and data capture ::

_____ uses electromagnetic fields to automatically identify and track tags attached to objects. The tags contain electronically stored information. Passive tags collect energy from a nearby RFID reader`s interrogating radio waves. Active tags have a local power source and may operate hundreds of meters from the RFID reader. Unlike a barcode, the tag need not be within the line of sight of the reader, so it may be embedded in the tracked object. RFID is one method of automatic identification and data capture .

Exam Probability: **Low**

22. *Answer choices:*

(see index for correct answer)

- a. Psion Teklogix
- b. Smart label
- c. Facial recognition system
- d. High-frequency direction finding

:: Ethically disputed business practices ::

_____ is the use of messaging systems to send an unsolicited message , especially advertising, as well as sending messages repeatedly on the same site. While the most widely recognized form of spam is email spam, the term is applied to similar abuses in other media: instant messaging spam, Usenet newsgroup spam, Web search engine spam, spam in blogs, wiki spam, online classified ads spam, mobile phone messaging spam, Internet forum spam, junk fax transmissions, social spam, spam mobile apps, television advertising and file sharing spam. It is named after Spam, a luncheon meat, by way of a Monty Python sketch about a restaurant that has Spam in every dish and where patrons annoyingly chant "Spam!" over and over again.

Exam Probability: **High**

23. *Answer choices:*

(see index for correct answer)

- a. Creative accounting
- b. Patent troll
- c. Unfair labor practice
- d. Spamming

:: ::

In linguistics, a _____ is the smallest element that can be uttered in isolation with objective or practical meaning.

Exam Probability: **Low**

24. *Answer choices:*

(see index for correct answer)

- a. functional perspective
- b. levels of analysis
- c. Sarbanes-Oxley act of 2002
- d. interpersonal communication

Guidance: level 1

:: ::

_____ consists of tailoring a service or a product to accommodate specific individuals, sometimes tied to groups or segments of individuals. A wide variety of organizations use _____ to improve customer satisfaction, digital sales conversion, marketing results, branding, and improved website metrics as well as for advertising. _____ is a key element in social media and recommender systems.

Exam Probability: **Medium**

25. *Answer choices:*

(see index for correct answer)

- a. Personalization
- b. levels of analysis
- c. corporate values
- d. interpersonal communication

Guidance: level 1

:: Information technology management ::

B2B is often contrasted with business-to-consumer . In B2B commerce, it is often the case that the parties to the relationship have comparable negotiating power, and even when they do not, each party typically involves professional staff and legal counsel in the negotiation of terms, whereas B2C is shaped to a far greater degree by economic implications of information asymmetry. However, within a B2B context, large companies may have many commercial, resource and information advantages over smaller businesses. The United Kingdom government, for example, created the post of Small Business Commissioner under the Enterprise Act 2016 to "enable small businesses to resolve disputes" and "consider complaints by small business suppliers about payment issues with larger businesses that they supply."

Exam Probability: **Medium**

26. *Answer choices:*

(see index for correct answer)

- a. Runbook

- b. Software asset management
- c. Enterprise portal
- d. Automic

Guidance: level 1

:: Market research ::

_____ s are many different distantly related animals that typically have a long cylindrical tube-like body and no limbs. _____ s vary in size from microscopic to over 1 metre in length for marine polychaete _____ s , 6.7 metres for the African giant earth _____ , Microchaetus rappi, and 58 metres for the marine nemertean _____ , Lineus longissimus. Various types of _____ occupy a small variety of parasitic niches, living inside the bodies of other animals. Free-living _____ species do not live on land, but instead, live in marine or freshwater environments, or underground by burrowing.In biology, " _____ " refers to an obsolete taxon, vermes, used by Carolus Linnaeus and Jean-Baptiste Lamarck for all non-arthropod invertebrate animals, now seen to be paraphyletic. The name stems from the Old English word wyrm. Most animals called " _____ s" are invertebrates, but the term is also used for the amphibian caecilians and the slow _____ Anguis, a legless burrowing lizard. Invertebrate animals commonly called " _____ s" include annelids , nematodes , platyhelminthes , marine nemertean _____ s , marine Chaetognatha , priapulid _____ s, and insect larvae such as grubs and maggots.

Exam Probability: **Medium**

27. *Answer choices:*

(see index for correct answer)

- a. Demographic marketer
- b. Mall-intercept personal interview
- c. News ratings in Australia
- d. Worm

Guidance: level 1

:: Data management ::

_____ , or IG, is the management of information at an organization. _____ balances the use and security of information. _____ helps with legal compliance, operational transparency, and reducing expenditures associated with legal discovery. An organization can establish a consistent and logical framework for employees to handle data through their _____ policies and procedures. These policies guide proper behavior regarding how organizations and their employees handle electronically stored information .

Exam Probability: **High**

28. *Answer choices:*
(see index for correct answer)

- a. National Information Governance Board for Health and Social Care
- b. Data aggregator
- c. Storage block
- d. Sales intelligence

Guidance: level 1

:: Data security ::

_____ , sometimes shortened to InfoSec, is the practice of preventing unauthorized access, use, disclosure, disruption, modification, inspection, recording or destruction of information. The information or data may take any form, e.g. electronic or physical. _____ `s primary focus is the balanced protection of the confidentiality, integrity and availability of data while maintaining a focus on efficient policy implementation, all without hampering organization productivity. This is largely achieved through a multi-step risk management process that identifies assets, threat sources, vulnerabilities, potential impacts, and possible controls, followed by assessment of the effectiveness of the risk management plan.

Exam Probability: **Medium**

29. *Answer choices:*

(see index for correct answer)

- a. Signed and Encrypted Email Over The Internet
- b. Information security
- c. Airbackup
- d. Security controls

Guidance: level 1

:: Critical thinking ::

In psychology, _____ is regarded as the cognitive process resulting in the selection of a belief or a course of action among several alternative possibilities. Every _____ process produces a final choice, which may or may not prompt action.

Exam Probability: **High**

30. *Answer choices:*

(see index for correct answer)

- a. Theory of justification
- b. Ad hoc hypothesis
- c. Source credibility
- d. Decision-making

Guidance: level 1

:: Network analyzers ::

A _____ , meaning "meat eater" , is an organism that derives its energy and nutrient requirements from a diet consisting mainly or exclusively of animal tissue, whether through predation or scavenging. Animals that depend solely on animal flesh for their nutrient requirements are called obligate _____ s while those that also consume non-animal food are called facultative _____ s. Omnivores also consume both animal and non-animal food, and, apart from the more general definition, there is no clearly defined ratio of plant to animal material that would distinguish a facultative _____ from an omnivore. A _____ at the top of the food chain, not preyed upon by other animals, is termed an apex predator.

31. *Answer choices:*

(see index for correct answer)

- a. PathPing
- b. Carnivore
- c. OpenVAS
- d. Nessus

Guidance: level 1

:: Virtual reality ::

_____ is an experience taking place within simulated and immersive environments that can be similar to or completely different from the real world. Applications of _____ can include entertainment and educational purposes . Other, distinct types of VR style technology include augmented reality and mixed reality.

Exam Probability: **High**

32. *Answer choices:*

(see index for correct answer)

- a. Digital environment
- b. Virtual reality

- c. Sega VR
- d. AGX Multiphysics

Guidance: level 1

:: Data management ::

" _____ " is a field that treats ways to analyze, systematically extract information from, or otherwise deal with data sets that are too large or complex to be dealt with by traditional data-processing application software. Data with many cases offer greater statistical power, while data with higher complexity may lead to a higher false discovery rate. _____ challenges include capturing data, data storage, data analysis, search, sharing, transfer, visualization, querying, updating, information privacy and data source. _____ was originally associated with three key concepts: volume, variety, and velocity. Other concepts later attributed with _____ are veracity and value.

Exam Probability: **Low**

33. *Answer choices:*

(see index for correct answer)

- a. Meta-data management
- b. Data conditioning
- c. Big data
- d. Linear medium

Guidance: level 1

A _____ is a published declaration of the intentions, motives, or views of the issuer, be it an individual, group, political party or government. A _____ usually accepts a previously published opinion or public consensus or promotes a new idea with prescriptive notions for carrying out changes the author believes should be made. It often is political or artistic in nature, but may present an individual's life stance. _____ s relating to religious belief are generally referred to as creeds.

Exam Probability: **High**

34. *Answer choices:*

(see index for correct answer)

- a. personal values
- b. Sarbanes-Oxley act of 2002
- c. empathy
- d. levels of analysis

Guidance: level 1

:: Cloud storage ::

_____ was an online backup service for both Windows and macOS users. Linux support was made available in Q3, 2014. In 2007 _____ was acquired by EMC, and in 2013 _____ was included in the EMC Backup Recovery Systems division's product list.On September 7, 2016, Dell Inc. acquired EMC Corporation to form Dell Technologies, restructuring the original Dell Inc. as a subsidiary of Dell Technologies.. On March 19, 2018 Carbonite acquired _____ from Dell for $148.5 million in cash and in 2019 shut down the service, incorporating _____ 's clients into its own online backup service programs.

Exam Probability: **High**

35. *Answer choices:*

(see index for correct answer)

- a. Mozy
- b. Tahoe-LAFS
- c. GreenQloud
- d. Udini

Guidance: level 1

:: Security compliance ::

_____ refers to the inability to withstand the effects of a hostile environment. A window of _____ is a time frame within which defensive measures are diminished, compromised or lacking.

36. *Answer choices:*

(see index for correct answer)

- a. Vulnerability
- b. Month of bugs
- c. North American Electric Reliability Corporation
- d. Vulnerability management

Guidance: level 1

:: Outsourcing ::

A service-level agreement is a commitment between a service provider and a client. Particular aspects of the service – quality, availability, responsibilities – are agreed between the service provider and the service user. The most common component of SLA is that the services should be provided to the customer as agreed upon in the contract. As an example, Internet service providers and telcos will commonly include _____ s within the terms of their contracts with customers to define the level of service being sold in plain language terms. In this case the SLA will typically have a technical definition in mean time between failures , mean time to repair or mean time to recovery ; identifying which party is responsible for reporting faults or paying fees; responsibility for various data rates; throughput; jitter; or similar measurable details.

37. *Answer choices:*

(see index for correct answer)

- a. Service level agreement
- b. Strategic sourcing
- c. Divestiture
- d. LEO

Guidance: level 1

:: Management ::

A _____ defines or constrains some aspect of business and always resolves to either true or false. _____ s are intended to assert business structure or to control or influence the behavior of the business. _____ s describe the operations, definitions and constraints that apply to an organization. _____ s can apply to people, processes, corporate behavior and computing systems in an organization, and are put in place to help the organization achieve its goals.

Exam Probability: **Low**

38. *Answer choices:*

(see index for correct answer)

- a. Scenario planning
- b. Quality control
- c. Project management

- d. Business rule

Guidance: level 1

:: Computer networking ::

A backbone is a part of computer network that interconnects various pieces of network, providing a path for the exchange of information between different LANs or subnetworks. A backbone can tie together diverse networks in the same building, in different buildings in a campus environment, or over wide areas. Normally, the backbone's capacity is greater than the networks connected to it.

Exam Probability: **Medium**

39. *Answer choices:*

(see index for correct answer)

- a. Softwire
- b. Traffic flow
- c. Backbone network
- d. Eirpac

Guidance: level 1

:: Supply chain management terms ::

In business and finance, _____ is a system of organizations, people, activities, information, and resources involved inmoving a product or service from supplier to customer. _____ activities involve the transformation of natural resources, raw materials, and components into a finished product that is delivered to the end customer. In sophisticated _____ systems, used products may re-enter the _____ at any point where residual value is recyclable. _____ s link value chains.

Exam Probability: **Medium**

40. *Answer choices:*

(see index for correct answer)

- a. Overstock
- b. inventory management
- c. Cool Chain Quality Indicator
- d. Supply-chain management

Guidance: level 1

:: Data interchange standards ::

_____ is the concept of businesses electronically communicating information that was traditionally communicated on paper, such as purchase orders and invoices. Technical standards for EDI exist to facilitate parties transacting such instruments without having to make special arrangements.

Exam Probability: **Low**

41. *Answer choices:*

(see index for correct answer)

- a. ASC X12
- b. Data Interchange Standards Association
- c. Uniform Communication Standard
- d. Electronic data interchange

Guidance: level 1

:: E-commerce ::

_____ , cybersecurity or information technology security is the protection of computer systems from theft or damage to their hardware, software or electronic data, as well as from disruption or misdirection of the services they provide.

Exam Probability: **Medium**

42. *Answer choices:*

(see index for correct answer)

- a. TXT402
- b. Customer Access and Retrieval System
- c. Postback
- d. Location-based commerce

:: Management ::

_____ is the kind of knowledge that is difficult to transfer to another person by means of writing it down or verbalizing it. For example, that London is in the United Kingdom is a piece of explicit knowledge that can be written down, transmitted, and understood by a recipient. However, the ability to speak a language, ride a bicycle, knead dough, play a musical instrument, or design and use complex equipment requires all sorts of knowledge that is not always known explicitly, even by expert practitioners, and which is difficult or impossible to explicitly transfer to other people.

Exam Probability: **High**

43. *Answer choices:*

(see index for correct answer)

- a. Production flow analysis
- b. Stakeholder
- c. Failure demand
- d. Tacit knowledge

:: Google services ::

_____ is a web mapping service developed by Google. It offers satellite imagery, aerial photography, street maps, 360° panoramic views of streets , real-time traffic conditions, and route planning for traveling by foot, car, bicycle and air , or public transportation.

Exam Probability: **Low**

44. *Answer choices:*

(see index for correct answer)

- a. Google APIs
- b. AdSense
- c. Google Web History
- d. Google Calendar

Guidance: level 1

:: Survey methodology ::

An _____ is a conversation where questions are asked and answers are given. In common parlance, the word " _____ " refers to a one-on-one conversation between an _____ er and an _____ ee. The _____ er asks questions to which the _____ ee responds, usually so information may be transferred from _____ ee to _____ er . Sometimes, information can be transferred in both directions. It is a communication, unlike a speech, which produces a one-way flow of information.

Exam Probability: **Low**

45. *Answer choices:*

(see index for correct answer)

- a. National Health Interview Survey
- b. Interview
- c. Census
- d. Enterprise feedback management

Guidance: level 1

:: Big data ::

_____ is the discovery, interpretation, and communication of meaningful patterns in data; and the process of applying those patterns towards effective decision making. In other words, _____ can be understood as the connective tissue between data and effective decision making, within an organization. Especially valuable in areas rich with recorded information, _____ relies on the simultaneous application of statistics, computer programming and operations research to quantify performance.

Exam Probability: **High**

46. *Answer choices:*

(see index for correct answer)

- a. Sessionization
- b. Analytics
- c. Datameer

- d. Sumo Logic

Guidance: level 1

:: Marketing by medium ::

_____ , also called online marketing or Internet advertising or web advertising, is a form of marketing and advertising which uses the Internet to deliver promotional marketing messages to consumers. Many consumers find _____ disruptive and have increasingly turned to ad blocking for a variety of reasons. When software is used to do the purchasing, it is known as programmatic advertising.

Exam Probability: **Medium**

47. *Answer choices:*
(see index for correct answer)

- a. Online advertising
- b. Social intelligence architect
- c. New media marketing
- d. Viral marketing

Guidance: level 1

:: Advertising techniques ::

The _____ is a story from the Trojan War about the subterfuge that the Greeks used to enter the independent city of Troy and win the war. In the canonical version, after a fruitless 10-year siege, the Greeks constructed a huge wooden horse, and hid a select force of men inside including Odysseus. The Greeks pretended to sail away, and the Trojans pulled the horse into their city as a victory trophy. That night the Greek force crept out of the horse and opened the gates for the rest of the Greek army, which had sailed back under cover of night. The Greeks entered and destroyed the city of Troy, ending the war.

Exam Probability: **Low**

48. *Answer choices:*

(see index for correct answer)

- a. Transpromotional
- b. Repetition variation
- c. Trojan horse
- d. Below the line

Guidance: level 1

:: Digital rights management ::

_____ tools or technological protection measures are a set of access control technologies for restricting the use of proprietary hardware and copyrighted works. DRM technologies try to control the use, modification, and distribution of copyrighted works , as well as systems within devices that enforce these policies.

Exam Probability: **Medium**

49. *Answer choices:*

(see index for correct answer)

- a. Aladdin Knowledge Systems
- b. Digital rights management
- c. Conax
- d. Trace vector decoder

Guidance: level 1

:: Commerce ::

_____ , Inc. is an American media-services provider headquartered in Los Gatos, California, founded in 1997 by Reed Hastings and Marc Randolph in Scotts Valley, California. The company's primary business is its subscription-based streaming OTT service which offers online streaming of a library of films and television programs, including those produced in-house. As of April 2019, _____ had over 148 million paid subscriptions worldwide, including 60 million in the United States, and over 154 million subscriptions total including free trials. It is available almost worldwide except in mainland China as well as Syria, North Korea, and Crimea . The company also has offices in the Netherlands, Brazil, India, Japan, and South Korea. _____ is a member of the Motion Picture Association of America .

Exam Probability: **Medium**

50. *Answer choices:*

(see index for correct answer)

- a. Netflix
- b. PIN pad
- c. Oxygen bar
- d. Church sale

Guidance: level 1

:: Data collection ::

_____ is information that either does not have a pre-defined data model or is not organized in a pre-defined manner. Unstructured information is typically text-heavy, but may contain data such as dates, numbers, and facts as well. This results in irregularities and ambiguities that make it difficult to understand using traditional programs as compared to data stored in fielded form in databases or annotated in documents.

Exam Probability: **Medium**

51. *Answer choices:*
(see index for correct answer)

- a. Unstructured data
- b. Relational data mining
- c. Synthetic Environment for Analysis and Simulations
- d. Interpellation

:: Asset ::

In financial accounting, an _____ is any resource owned by the business. Anything tangible or intangible that can be owned or controlled to produce value and that is held by a company to produce positive economic value is an _____ . Simply stated, _____ s represent value of ownership that can be converted into cash . The balance sheet of a firm records the monetary value of the _____ s owned by that firm. It covers money and other valuables belonging to an individual or to a business.

Exam Probability: **Medium**

52. *Answer choices:*

(see index for correct answer)

- a. Asset
- b. Current asset

:: Types of marketing ::

In microeconomics and management, _____ is an arrangement in which the supply chain of a company is owned by that company. Usually each member of the supply chain produces a different product or service, and the products combine to satisfy a common need. It is contrasted with horizontal integration, wherein a company produces several items which are related to one another. _____ has also described management styles that bring large portions of the supply chain not only under a common ownership, but also into one corporation .

Exam Probability: **Low**

53. *Answer choices:*

(see index for correct answer)

- a. Menu engineering
- b. Customerization
- c. Project SCUM
- d. Vertical integration

Guidance: level 1

:: Identity management ::

_____ is the ability of an individual or group to seclude themselves, or information about themselves, and thereby express themselves selectively. The boundaries and content of what is considered private differ among cultures and individuals, but share common themes. When something is private to a person, it usually means that something is inherently special or sensitive to them. The domain of _____ partially overlaps with security , which can include the concepts of appropriate use, as well as protection of information. _____ may also take the form of bodily integrity.

Exam Probability: **Low**

54. *Answer choices:*
(see index for correct answer)

- a. Privacy
- b. Identity assurance
- c. Identity verification service
- d. Mobile signature

Guidance: level 1

:: Supply chain management ::

ERP is usually referred to as a category of business management software — typically a suite of integrated applications—that an organization can use to collect, store, manage, and interpret data from these many business activities.

Exam Probability: **High**

55. *Answer choices:*

(see index for correct answer)

- a. Enterprise resource planning
- b. Enterprise carbon accounting
- c. Murphy Warehouse Company
- d. Irancode

Guidance: level 1

:: Data privacy ::

_____ is the relationship between the collection and dissemination of data, technology, the public expectation of privacy, legal and political issues surrounding them. It is also known as data privacy or data protection,

Exam Probability: **Medium**

56. *Answer choices:*

(see index for correct answer)

- a. Information privacy
- b. Statewatch
- c. Article 29 Working Party
- d. Data Privacy Day

Guidance: level 1

:: Data management ::

A _____, or metadata repository, as defined in the IBM Dictionary of Computing, is a "centralized repository of information about data such as meaning, relationships to other data, origin, usage, and format". Oracle defines it as a collection of tables with metadata. The term can have one of several closely related meanings pertaining to databases and database management systems .

Exam Probability: **Low**

57. *Answer choices:*

(see index for correct answer)

- a. Operational system
- b. Data discovery
- c. Data dictionary
- d. Enterprise bus matrix

Guidance: level 1

:: Payment systems ::

_____ s are part of a payment system issued by financial institutions, such as a bank, to a customer that enables its owner to access the funds in the customer's designated bank accounts, or through a credit account and make payments by electronic funds transfer and access automated teller machines . Such cards are known by a variety of names including bank cards, ATM cards, MAC , client cards, key cards or cash cards.

Exam Probability: **Medium**

58. *Answer choices:*

(see index for correct answer)

- a. Payment card
- b. Cheque truncation system
- c. CashU
- d. PA-DSS

Guidance: level 1

:: Business models ::

_____ , or The Computer Utility, is a service provisioning model in which a service provider makes computing resources and infrastructure management available to the customer as needed, and charges them for specific usage rather than a flat rate. Like other types of on-demand computing , the utility model seeks to maximize the efficient use of resources and/or minimize associated costs. Utility is the packaging of system resources, such as computation, storage and services, as a metered service. This model has the advantage of a low or no initial cost to acquire computer resources; instead, resources are essentially rented.

Exam Probability: **High**

59. *Answer choices:*

(see index for correct answer)

- a. Lawyers on Demand
- b. Business networking
- c. Copy to China
- d. Utility computing

Guidance: level 1

Marketing

Marketing is the study and management of exchange relationships. Marketing is the business process of creating relationships with and satisfying customers. With its focus on the customer, marketing is one of the premier components of business management.

Marketing is defined by the American Marketing Association as "the activity, set of institutions, and processes for creating, communicating, delivering, and exchanging offerings that have value for customers, clients, partners, and society at large."

:: ::

Retail is the process of selling consumer goods or services to customers through multiple channels of distribution to earn a profit. Retailers satisfy demand identified through a supply chain. The term "retailer" is typically applied where a service provider fills the small orders of a large number of individuals, who are end-users, rather than large orders of a small number of wholesale, corporate or government clientele. Shopping generally refers to the act of buying products. Sometimes this is done to obtain final goods, including necessities such as food and clothing; sometimes it takes place as a recreational activity. Recreational shopping often involves window shopping and browsing: it does not always result in a purchase.

Exam Probability: **High**

1. *Answer choices:*

(see index for correct answer)

- a. personal values
- b. deep-level diversity
- c. Retailing
- d. information systems assessment

Guidance: level 1

:: ::

_____ is the practice of deliberately managing the spread of information between an individual or an organization and the public. _____ may include an organization or individual gaining exposure to their audiences using topics of public interest and news items that do not require direct payment. This differentiates it from advertising as a form of marketing communications. _____ is the idea of creating coverage for clients for free, rather than marketing or advertising. But now, advertising is also a part of greater PR Activities. An example of good _____ would be generating an article featuring a client, rather than paying for the client to be advertised next to the article. The aim of _____ is to inform the public, prospective customers, investors, partners, employees, and other stakeholders and ultimately persuade them to maintain a positive or favorable view about the organization, its leadership, products, or political decisions. _____ professionals typically work for PR and marketing firms, businesses and companies, government, and public officials as PIOs and nongovernmental organizations, and nonprofit organizations. Jobs central to _____ include account coordinator, account executive, account supervisor, and media relations manager.

Exam Probability: **Low**

2. *Answer choices:*

(see index for correct answer)

- a. hierarchical
- b. information systems assessment
- c. Public relations
- d. open system

Guidance: level 1

:: Direct marketing ::

_____ is a form of direct marketing using databases of customers or potential customers to generate personalized communications in order to promote a product or service for marketing purposes. The method of communication can be any addressable medium, as in direct marketing.

Exam Probability: **Low**

3. *Answer choices:*

(see index for correct answer)

- a. Direct Marketing Association
- b. Flyer
- c. Specialty catalogs
- d. Database marketing

Guidance: level 1

:: Marketing ::

_____ is the marketing of products that are presumed to be environmentally safe. It incorporates a broad range of activities, including product modification, changes to the production process, sustainable packaging, as well as modifying advertising. Yet defining _____ is not a simple task where several meanings intersect and contradict each other; an example of this will be the existence of varying social, environmental and retail definitions attached to this term. Other similar terms used are environmental marketing and ecological marketing.

Exam Probability: **Medium**

4. *Answer choices:*

(see index for correct answer)

- a. Immersion marketing
- b. Green marketing
- c. Postmodern branding
- d. Private-label

Guidance: level 1

:: Income ::

In business and accounting, net income is an entity's income minus cost of goods sold, expenses and taxes for an accounting period. It is computed as the residual of all revenues and gains over all expenses and losses for the period, and has also been defined as the net increase in shareholders' equity that results from a company's operations. In the context of the presentation of financial statements, the IFRS Foundation defines net income as synonymous with profit and loss. The difference between revenue and the cost of making a product or providing a service, before deducting overheads, payroll, taxation, and interest payments. This is different from operating income .

Exam Probability: **Medium**

5. *Answer choices:*

(see index for correct answer)

- a. Private income
- b. Pay grade
- c. Signing bonus
- d. Per capita income

Guidance: level 1

:: Marketing ::

_____ is a growth strategy that identifies and develops new market segments for current products. A _____ strategy targets non-buying customers in currently targeted segments. It also targets new customers in new segments.

6. *Answer choices:*

(see index for correct answer)

- a. Net idol
- b. Market development
- c. Product bundling
- d. Ayelet Gneezy

Guidance: level 1

:: ::

Competition arises whenever at least two parties strive for a goal which cannot be shared: where one's gain is the other's loss .

Exam Probability: **Medium**

7. *Answer choices:*

(see index for correct answer)

- a. process perspective
- b. corporate values
- c. hierarchical
- d. Competitor

:: ::

_____ Corporation is an American multinational technology company with headquarters in Redmond, Washington. It develops, manufactures, licenses, supports and sells computer software, consumer electronics, personal computers, and related services. Its best known software products are the _____ Windows line of operating systems, the _____ Office suite, and the Internet Explorer and Edge Web browsers. Its flagship hardware products are the Xbox video game consoles and the _____ Surface lineup of touchscreen personal computers. As of 2016, it is the world's largest software maker by revenue, and one of the world's most valuable companies. The word "_____" is a portmanteau of "microcomputer" and "software". _____ is ranked No. 30 in the 2018 Fortune 500 rankings of the largest United States corporations by total revenue.

Exam Probability: **Low**

8. *Answer choices:*

(see index for correct answer)

- a. empathy
- b. Microsoft
- c. levels of analysis
- d. corporate values

:: Information technology management ::

B2B is often contrasted with business-to-consumer . In B2B commerce, it is often the case that the parties to the relationship have comparable negotiating power, and even when they do not, each party typically involves professional staff and legal counsel in the negotiation of terms, whereas B2C is shaped to a far greater degree by economic implications of information asymmetry. However, within a B2B context, large companies may have many commercial, resource and information advantages over smaller businesses. The United Kingdom government, for example, created the post of Small Business Commissioner under the Enterprise Act 2016 to "enable small businesses to resolve disputes" and "consider complaints by small business suppliers about payment issues with larger businesses that they supply."

Exam Probability: **Medium**

9. *Answer choices:*

(see index for correct answer)

- a. Business Information Services Library
- b. CatDV
- c. Virtual filing cabinet
- d. Intelligent device management

Guidance: level 1

:: Project management ::

A _____ is a source or supply from which a benefit is produced and it has some utility. _____ s can broadly be classified upon their availability—they are classified into renewable and non-renewable _____ s.Examples of non renewable _____ s are coal ,crude oil natural gas nuclear energy etc. Examples of renewable _____ s are air,water,wind,solar energy etc. They can also be classified as actual and potential on the basis of level of development and use, on the basis of origin they can be classified as biotic and abiotic, and on the basis of their distribution, as ubiquitous and localized . An item becomes a _____ with time and developing technology. Typically, _____ s are materials, energy, services, staff, knowledge, or other assets that are transformed to produce benefit and in the process may be consumed or made unavailable. Benefits of _____ utilization may include increased wealth, proper functioning of a system, or enhanced well-being. From a human perspective a natural _____ is anything obtained from the environment to satisfy human needs and wants. From a broader biological or ecological perspective a _____ satisfies the needs of a living organism .

Exam Probability: **Low**

10. *Answer choices:*

- a. Research program
- b. Drag cost
- c. Soft Costs
- d. Resource

Guidance: level 1

:: Advertising ::

A _____ is a large outdoor advertising structure, typically found in high-traffic areas such as alongside busy roads. _____ s present large advertisements to passing pedestrians and drivers. Typically showing witty slogans and distinctive visuals, _____ s are highly visible in the top designated market areas.

Exam Probability: **Medium**

11. *Answer choices:*

(see index for correct answer)

- a. Driven media
- b. Contingency sponsorship
- c. Ad-ID
- d. Flurry

Guidance: level 1

:: Competition (economics) ::

_____ arises whenever at least two parties strive for a goal which cannot be shared: where one's gain is the other's loss.

Exam Probability: **Medium**

12. *Answer choices:*

(see index for correct answer)

- a. Competition
- b. Currency competition
- c. Regulatory competition
- d. Transfer pricing

Guidance: level 1

:: Reputation management ::

A _____ is an astronomical object consisting of a luminous spheroid of plasma held together by its own gravity. The nearest _____ to Earth is the Sun. Many other _____ s are visible to the naked eye from Earth during the night, appearing as a multitude of fixed luminous points in the sky due to their immense distance from Earth. Historically, the most prominent _____ s were grouped into constellations and asterisms, the brightest of which gained proper names. Astronomers have assembled _____ catalogues that identify the known _____ s and provide standardized stellar designations. However, most of the estimated 300 sextillion _____ s in the Universe are invisible to the naked eye from Earth, including all _____ s outside our galaxy, the Milky Way.

Exam Probability: **High**

13. *Answer choices:*

(see index for correct answer)

- a. Star
- b. Reputation system

- c. Yasni
- d. TrustRank

Guidance: level 1

:: ::

_____ are interactive computer-mediated technologies that facilitate the creation and sharing of information, ideas, career interests and other forms of expression via virtual communities and networks. The variety of stand-alone and built-in _____ services currently available introduces challenges of definition; however, there are some common features.

Exam Probability: **Low**

14. *Answer choices:*

(see index for correct answer)

- a. Social media
- b. empathy
- c. corporate values
- d. cultural

Guidance: level 1

:: Data analysis ::

_____ is a process of inspecting, cleansing, transforming, and modeling data with the goal of discovering useful information, informing conclusions, and supporting decision-making. _____ has multiple facets and approaches, encompassing diverse techniques under a variety of names, and is used in different business, science, and social science domains. In today's business world, _____ plays a role in making decisions more scientific and helping businesses operate more effectively.

Exam Probability: **Medium**

15. *Answer choices:*
(see index for correct answer)

- a. Natural Language Toolkit
- b. Boolean analysis
- c. Missing data
- d. Data analysis

Guidance: level 1

:: International trade ::

In finance, an _____ is the rate at which one currency will be exchanged for another. It is also regarded as the value of one country's currency in relation to another currency. For example, an interbank _____ of 114 Japanese yen to the United States dollar means that ¥114 will be exchanged for each US$1 or that US$1 will be exchanged for each ¥114. In this case it is said that the price of a dollar in relation to yen is ¥114, or equivalently that the price of a yen in relation to dollars is $1/114.

16. *Answer choices:*

(see index for correct answer)

- a. Northwest Cattle Project
- b. Market price support
- c. New International Economic Order
- d. International Trade Awards

Guidance: level 1

:: Product development ::

In business and engineering, _____ covers the complete process of bringing a new product to market. A central aspect of NPD is product design, along with various business considerations. _____ is described broadly as the transformation of a market opportunity into a product available for sale. The product can be tangible or intangible , though sometimes services and other processes are distinguished from "products." NPD requires an understanding of customer needs and wants, the competitive environment, and the nature of the market.Cost, time and quality are the main variables that drive customer needs. Aiming at these three variables, innovative companies develop continuous practices and strategies to better satisfy customer requirements and to increase their own market share by a regular development of new products. There are many uncertainties and challenges which companies must face throughout the process. The use of best practices and the elimination of barriers to communication are the main concerns for the management of the NPD .

17. *Answer choices:*

(see index for correct answer)

- a. Brief
- b. New product development
- c. Product concept
- d. Collaborative product development

Guidance: level 1

:: Marketing techniques ::

The _____ or unique selling point is a marketing concept first
proposed as a theory to explain a pattern in successful advertising campaigns
of the early 1940s. The USP states that such campaigns made unique propositions
to customers that convinced them to switch brands. The term was developed by
television advertising pioneer Rosser Reeves of Ted Bates & Company.
Theodore Levitt, a professor at Harvard Business School, suggested that,
"Differentiation is one of the most important strategic and tactical activities
in which companies must constantly engage." The term has been used to describe
one`s "personal brand" in the marketplace. Today, the term is used in other
fields or just casually to refer to any aspect of an object that differentiates
it from similar objects.

Exam Probability: **Medium**

18. *Answer choices:*

(see index for correct answer)

- a. Unique selling proposition
- b. Blackout dates
- c. Microsegment
- d. unique selling point

Guidance: level 1

:: Investment ::

In finance, the benefit from an _____ is called a return. The return may consist of a gain realised from the sale of property or an _____, unrealised capital appreciation , or _____ income such as dividends, interest, rental income etc., or a combination of capital gain and income. The return may also include currency gains or losses due to changes in foreign currency exchange rates.

Exam Probability: **High**

19. *Answer choices:*

(see index for correct answer)

- a. Quality investing
- b. Investment
- c. Superannuation in Australia
- d. Search fund

Guidance: level 1

:: ::

A _____ is a person who trades in commodities produced by other people. Historically, a _____ is anyone who is involved in business or trade. _____ s have operated for as long as industry, commerce, and trade have existed. During the 16th-century, in Europe, two different terms for _____ s emerged: One term, meerseniers, described local traders such as bakers, grocers, etc.; while a new term, koopman (Dutch: koopman, described _____ s who operated on a global stage, importing and exporting goods over vast distances, and offering added-value services such as credit and finance.

Exam Probability: **Low**

20. *Answer choices:*

(see index for correct answer)

- a. Character
- b. process perspective
- c. interpersonal communication
- d. Merchant

Guidance: level 1

:: ::

A _____ is an organized collection of data, generally stored and accessed electronically from a computer system. Where _____ s are more complex they are often developed using formal design and modeling techniques.

21. *Answer choices:*

(see index for correct answer)

- a. deep-level diversity
- b. Sarbanes-Oxley act of 2002
- c. hierarchical perspective
- d. Database

Guidance: level 1

:: ::

According to the philosopher Piyush Mathur , "Tangibility is the property that a phenomenon exhibits if it has and/or transports mass and/or energy and/or momentum".

Exam Probability: **High**

22. *Answer choices:*

(see index for correct answer)

- a. hierarchical perspective
- b. empathy
- c. surface-level diversity
- d. cultural

:: ::

An _____ is an area of the production, distribution, or trade, and consumption of goods and services by different agents. Understood in its broadest sense, `The _____ is defined as a social domain that emphasize the practices, discourses, and material expressions associated with the production, use, and management of resources`. Economic agents can be individuals, businesses, organizations, or governments. Economic transactions occur when two parties agree to the value or price of the transacted good or service, commonly expressed in a certain currency. However, monetary transactions only account for a small part of the economic domain.

Exam Probability: **Medium**

23. *Answer choices:*

(see index for correct answer)

- a. surface-level diversity
- b. Sarbanes-Oxley act of 2002
- c. levels of analysis
- d. Character

:: ::

Advertising is a marketing communication that employs an openly sponsored, non-personal message to promote or sell a product, service or idea. Sponsors of advertising are typically businesses wishing to promote their products or services. Advertising is differentiated from public relations in that an advertiser pays for and has control over the message. It differs from personal selling in that the message is non-personal, i.e., not directed to a particular individual. Advertising is communicated through various mass media, including traditional media such as newspapers, magazines, television, radio, outdoor advertising or direct mail; and new media such as search results, blogs, social media, websites or text messages. The actual presentation of the message in a medium is referred to as an _____ , or "ad" or advert for short.

Exam Probability: **Medium**

24. *Answer choices:*

(see index for correct answer)

- a. imperative
- b. cultural
- c. levels of analysis
- d. surface-level diversity

Guidance: level 1

:: ::

_____ is change in the heritable characteristics of biological populations over successive generations. These characteristics are the expressions of genes that are passed on from parent to offspring during reproduction. Different characteristics tend to exist within any given population as a result of mutation, genetic recombination and other sources of genetic variation. _____ occurs when _____ ary processes such as natural selection and genetic drift act on this variation, resulting in certain characteristics becoming more common or rare within a population. It is this process of _____ that has given rise to biodiversity at every level of biological organisation, including the levels of species, individual organisms and molecules.

Exam Probability: **Medium**

25. *Answer choices:*

(see index for correct answer)

- a. hierarchical perspective
- b. co-culture
- c. similarity-attraction theory
- d. corporate values

Guidance: level 1

:: ::

A _____ is any person who contracts to acquire an asset in return for some form of consideration.

Exam Probability: **High**

26. *Answer choices:*

(see index for correct answer)

- a. empathy
- b. open system
- c. imperative
- d. Buyer

Guidance: level 1

:: Costs ::

In economics, _____ is the total economic cost of production and is made up of variable cost, which varies according to the quantity of a good produced and includes inputs such as labour and raw materials, plus fixed cost, which is independent of the quantity of a good produced and includes inputs that cannot be varied in the short term: fixed costs such as buildings and machinery, including sunk costs if any. Since cost is measured per unit of time, it is a flow variable.

Exam Probability: **Low**

27. *Answer choices:*

(see index for correct answer)

- a. Total cost

- b. Implicit cost
- c. Sliding scale fees
- d. Repugnancy costs

Guidance: level 1

:: ::

_____ is a concept of English common law and is a necessity for simple contracts but not for special contracts . The concept has been adopted by other common law jurisdictions, including the US.

Exam Probability: **Medium**

28. *Answer choices:*

(see index for correct answer)

- a. empathy
- b. information systems assessment
- c. hierarchical perspective
- d. Consideration

Guidance: level 1

:: Consumer theory ::

A _____ is a technical term in psychology, economics and philosophy usually used in relation to choosing between alternatives. For example, someone prefers A over B if they would rather choose A than B.

Exam Probability: **High**

29. *Answer choices:*

(see index for correct answer)

- a. Time-based pricing
- b. Business contract hire
- c. Convex preferences
- d. Consumer sovereignty

Guidance: level 1

:: Marketing ::

_____ is a market strategy in which a firm decides to ignore market segment differences and appeal the whole market with one offer or one strategy, which supports the idea of broadcasting a message that will reach the largest number of people possible. Traditionally _____ has focused on radio, television and newspapers as the media used to reach this broad audience. By reaching the largest audience possible, exposure to the product is maximized, and in theory this would directly correlate with a larger number of sales or buys into the product.

Exam Probability: **Low**

30. *Answer choices:*

(see index for correct answer)

- a. Bayesian inference in marketing
- b. Customer acquisition management
- c. Mass marketing
- d. Democratized transactional giving

Guidance: level 1

:: Evaluation methods ::

_____ is a scientific method of observation to gather non-numerical data. This type of research "refers to the meanings, concepts definitions, characteristics, metaphors, symbols, and description of things" and not to their "counts or measures." This research answers why and how a certain phenomenon may occur rather than how often. _____ approaches are employed across many academic disciplines, focusing particularly on the human elements of the social and natural sciences; in less academic contexts, areas of application include qualitative market research, business, service demonstrations by non-profits, and journalism.

Exam Probability: **High**

31. *Answer choices:*

(see index for correct answer)

- a. Analog observation
- b. Qualitative research

- c. quasi-experimental
- d. Transformative assessment

Guidance: level 1

:: Consumer theory ::

_____ is the quantity of a good that consumers are willing and able to purchase at various prices during a given period of time.

Exam Probability: **Medium**

32. *Answer choices:*

(see index for correct answer)

- a. Quality bias
- b. Delayed gratification
- c. Demand
- d. Slutsky equation

Guidance: level 1

:: Supply chain management terms ::

In business and finance, _____ is a system of organizations, people, activities, information, and resources involved in moving a product or service from supplier to customer. _____ activities involve the transformation of natural resources, raw materials, and components into a finished product that is delivered to the end customer. In sophisticated _____ systems, used products may re-enter the _____ at any point where residual value is recyclable. _____ s link value chains.

Exam Probability: **Low**

33. *Answer choices:*

(see index for correct answer)

- a. Will call
- b. Final assembly schedule
- c. Supply chain
- d. Capital spare

Guidance: level 1

:: ::

An _____ is a systematic and independent examination of books, accounts, statutory records, documents and vouchers of an organization to ascertain how far the financial statements as well as non-financial disclosures present a true and fair view of the concern. It also attempts to ensure that the books of accounts are properly maintained by the concern as required by law. _____ ing has become such a ubiquitous phenomenon in the corporate and the public sector that academics started identifying an " _____ Society". The _____ or perceives and recognises the propositions before them for examination, obtains evidence, evaluates the same and formulates an opinion on the basis of his judgement which is communicated through their _____ ing report.

Exam Probability: **Medium**

34. *Answer choices:*

(see index for correct answer)

- a. open system
- b. personal values
- c. corporate values
- d. Audit

Guidance: level 1

:: Business ::

The seller, or the provider of the goods or services, completes a sale in response to an acquisition, appropriation, requisition or a direct interaction with the buyer at the point of sale. There is a passing of title of the item, and the settlement of a price, in which agreement is reached on a price for which transfer of ownership of the item will occur. The seller, not the purchaser typically executes the sale and it may be completed prior to the obligation of payment. In the case of indirect interaction, a person who sells goods or service on behalf of the owner is known as a salesman or saleswoman or salesperson, but this often refers to someone _____ goods in a store/shop, in which case other terms are also common, including salesclerk, shop assistant, and retail clerk.

Exam Probability: **High**

35. *Answer choices:*

(see index for correct answer)

- a. Business development
- b. Closure
- c. EPG Model
- d. Professional conference organiser

Guidance: level 1

:: Survey methodology ::

A _____ is the procedure of systematically acquiring and recording information about the members of a given population. The term is used mostly in connection with national population and housing _____ es; other common _____ es include agriculture, business, and traffic _____ es. The United Nations defines the essential features of population and housing _____ es as "individual enumeration, universality within a defined territory, simultaneity and defined periodicity", and recommends that population _____ es be taken at least every 10 years. United Nations recommendations also cover _____ topics to be collected, official definitions, classifications and other useful information to co-ordinate international practice.

Exam Probability: **High**

36. *Answer choices:*

(see index for correct answer)

- a. Scale analysis
- b. National Health Interview Survey
- c. Self-report study
- d. Census

Guidance: level 1

:: Decision theory ::

A _____ is a deliberate system of principles to guide decisions and achieve rational outcomes. A _____ is a statement of intent, and is implemented as a procedure or protocol. Policies are generally adopted by a governance body within an organization. Policies can assist in both subjective and objective decision making. Policies to assist in subjective decision making usually assist senior management with decisions that must be based on the relative merits of a number of factors, and as a result are often hard to test objectively, e.g. work-life balance _____ . In contrast policies to assist in objective decision making are usually operational in nature and can be objectively tested, e.g. password _____ .

Exam Probability: **Low**

37. *Answer choices:*

(see index for correct answer)

- a. Linear partial information
- b. Statistical murder
- c. Distinction bias
- d. Ulysses pact

Guidance: level 1

:: Belief ::

_____ is an umbrella term of influence. _____ can attempt to influence a person's beliefs, attitudes, intentions, motivations, or behaviors. In business, _____ is a process aimed at changing a person's attitude or behavior toward some event, idea, object, or other person, by using written, spoken words or visual tools to convey information, feelings, or reasoning, or a combination thereof. _____ is also an often used tool in the pursuit of personal gain, such as election campaigning, giving a sales pitch, or in trial advocacy. _____ can also be interpreted as using one's personal or positional resources to change people's behaviors or attitudes.Systematic _____ is the process through which attitudes or beliefs are leveraged by appeals to logic and reason. Heuristic _____ on the other hand is the process through which attitudes or beliefs are leveraged by appeals to habit or emotion.

Exam Probability: **Low**

38. *Answer choices:*

(see index for correct answer)

- a. Epistemic closure
- b. Reality tunnel
- c. Blind men and an elephant
- d. Belief in luck

Guidance: level 1

:: ::

_____ is the act of conveying meanings from one entity or group to another through the use of mutually understood signs, symbols, and semiotic rules.

39. *Answer choices:*

(see index for correct answer)

- a. co-culture
- b. cultural
- c. Communication
- d. empathy

Guidance: level 1

:: Marketing analytics ::

_____ is a long-term, forward-looking approach to planning with the fundamental goal of achieving a sustainable competitive advantage. Strategic planning involves an analysis of the company's strategic initial situation prior to the formulation, evaluation and selection of market-oriented competitive position that contributes to the company's goals and marketing objectives.

40. *Answer choices:*

(see index for correct answer)

- a. marketing dashboard
- b. Advertising adstock
- c. Marketing resource management
- d. Marketing strategy

Guidance: level 1

:: Marketing ::

A _____ is the quantity of payment or compensation given by one party to another in return for one unit of goods or services.. A _____ is influenced by both production costs and demand for the product. A _____ may be determined by a monopolist or may be imposed on the firm by market conditions.

Exam Probability: **Medium**

41. *Answer choices:*

(see index for correct answer)

- a. Advertising media selection
- b. Earned media
- c. Aftersales
- d. Cultural consumer

:: Contract law ::

A _____ is a legally-binding agreement which recognises and governs the rights and duties of the parties to the agreement. A _____ is legally enforceable because it meets the requirements and approval of the law. An agreement typically involves the exchange of goods, services, money, or promises of any of those. In the event of breach of _____ , the law awards the injured party access to legal remedies such as damages and cancellation.

Exam Probability: **Medium**

42. *Answer choices:*

(see index for correct answer)

- a. Scots contract law
- b. Interconnect agreement
- c. Contract
- d. Implied warranty

:: Product management ::

A _____ is a professional role which is responsible for the development of products for an organization, known as the practice of product management. _____ s own the business strategy behind a product , specify its functional requirements and generally manage the launch of features. They coordinate work done by many other functions and are ultimately responsible for the business success of the product.

43. *Answer choices:*

(see index for correct answer)

- a. Requirement prioritization
- b. Obsolescence
- c. Tipping point
- d. Product manager

Guidance: level 1

:: Data interchange standards ::

_____ is the concept of businesses electronically communicating information that was traditionally communicated on paper, such as purchase orders and invoices. Technical standards for EDI exist to facilitate parties transacting such instruments without having to make special arrangements.

44. *Answer choices:*

(see index for correct answer)

- a. Common Alerting Protocol
- b. Electronic data interchange
- c. Data Interchange Standards Association
- d. Interaction protocol

Guidance: level 1

:: Marketing terminology ::

_____ is used in marketing to describe the inability to assess the value gained from engaging in an activity using any tangible evidence. It is often used to describe services where there is no tangible product that the customer can purchase, that can be seen or touched.

Exam Probability: **High**

45. *Answer choices:*

(see index for correct answer)

- a. Intangibility
- b. All commodity volume
- c. Factory-to-consumer
- d. Aspirational age

:: International trade ::

_____ or globalisation is the process of interaction and integration among people, companies, and governments worldwide. As a complex and multifaceted phenomenon, _____ is considered by some as a form of capitalist expansion which entails the integration of local and national economies into a global, unregulated market economy. _____ has grown due to advances in transportation and communication technology. With the increased global interactions comes the growth of international trade, ideas, and culture. _____ is primarily an economic process of interaction and integration that's associated with social and cultural aspects. However, conflicts and diplomacy are also large parts of the history of _____ , and modern _____ .

Exam Probability: **Low**

46. *Answer choices:*

(see index for correct answer)

- a. Oriental Development Company
- b. Trade finance
- c. Globalization
- d. Endaka

:: Business models ::

A _____ , _____ company or daughter company is a company that is owned or controlled by another company, which is called the parent company, parent, or holding company. The _____ can be a company, corporation, or limited liability company. In some cases it is a government or state-owned enterprise. In some cases, particularly in the music and book publishing industries, subsidiaries are referred to as imprints.

Exam Probability: **Medium**

47. *Answer choices:*

(see index for correct answer)

- a. Parent company
- b. Inclusive business model
- c. Subsidiary
- d. Legacy carrier

Guidance: level 1

:: bad_topic ::

Sponsoring something is the act of supporting an event, activity, person, or organization financially or through the provision of products or services. The individual or group that provides the support, similar to a benefactor, is known as sponsor.

48. *Answer choices:*

(see index for correct answer)

- a. Larry Flax
- b. set model
- c. incorrect
- d. CVS Corporation

Guidance: level 1

:: ::

_____ , known in Europe as research and technological development , refers to innovative activities undertaken by corporations or governments in developing new services or products, or improving existing services or products. _____ constitutes the first stage of development of a potential new service or the production process.

49. *Answer choices:*

(see index for correct answer)

- a. hierarchical
- b. interpersonal communication

- c. information systems assessment
- d. co-culture

:: Legal terms ::

A _____ is a person who is called upon to issue a response to a communication made by another. The term is used in legal contexts, in survey methodology, and in psychological conditioning.

Exam Probability: **High**

50. *Answer choices:*

(see index for correct answer)

- a. Appropriation
- b. Respondent
- c. Arbitration
- d. Motion for leave

:: ::

_____ LLC is an American multinational technology company that specializes in Internet-related services and products, which include online advertising technologies, search engine, cloud computing, software, and hardware. It is considered one of the Big Four technology companies, alongside Amazon, Apple and Facebook.

Exam Probability: **Medium**

51. *Answer choices:*

(see index for correct answer)

- a. cultural
- b. hierarchical
- c. levels of analysis
- d. personal values

Guidance: level 1

:: Brand management ::

In marketing, _____ is the analysis and planning on how a brand is perceived in the market. Developing a good relationship with the target market is essential for _____ . Tangible elements of _____ include the product itself; its look, price, and packaging, etc. The intangible elements are the experiences that the consumers share with the brand, and also the relationships they have with the brand. A brand manager would oversee all aspects of the consumer's brand association as well as relationships with members of the supply chain.

52. *Answer choices:*

(see index for correct answer)

- a. Brand management
- b. co-brand
- c. Brand Finance
- d. Marlboro Friday

Guidance: level 1

:: Monopoly (economics) ::

A _____ exists when a specific person or enterprise is the only supplier of a particular commodity. This contrasts with a monopsony which relates to a single entity's control of a market to purchase a good or service, and with oligopoly which consists of a few sellers dominating a market. Monopolies are thus characterized by a lack of economic competition to produce the good or service, a lack of viable substitute goods, and the possibility of a high _____ price well above the seller's marginal cost that leads to a high _____ profit. The verb monopolise or monopolize refers to the process by which a company gains the ability to raise prices or exclude competitors. In economics, a _____ is a single seller. In law, a _____ is a business entity that has significant market power, that is, the power to charge overly high prices. Although monopolies may be big businesses, size is not a characteristic of a _____ . A small business may still have the power to raise prices in a small industry .

53. *Answer choices:*

(see index for correct answer)

- a. Demonopolization
- b. Monopoly
- c. Contestable market
- d. Legal monopoly

Guidance: level 1

:: Production economics ::

In microeconomics, _____ are the cost advantages that enterprises obtain due to their scale of operation , with cost per unit of output decreasing with increasing scale.

Exam Probability: **Medium**

54. *Answer choices:*

(see index for correct answer)

- a. Diseconomies of scale
- b. Marginal cost of capital schedule
- c. Marginal rate of technical substitution
- d. Economies of scale

Guidance: level 1

:: Management ::

_____ is the process of thinking about the activities required to achieve a desired goal. It is the first and foremost activity to achieve desired results. It involves the creation and maintenance of a plan, such as psychological aspects that require conceptual skills. There are even a couple of tests to measure someone's capability of _____ well. As such, _____ is a fundamental property of intelligent behavior. An important further meaning, often just called " _____ " is the legal context of permitted building developments.

Exam Probability: **High**

55. *Answer choices:*

(see index for correct answer)

- a. Technology scouting
- b. Modes of leadership
- c. Hierarchical organization
- d. Planning

Guidance: level 1

:: Marketing ::

_____ is "commercial competition characterized by the repeated cutting of prices below those of competitors". One competitor will lower its price, then others will lower their prices to match. If one of them reduces their price again, a new round of reductions starts. In the short term, _____ s are good for buyers, who can take advantage of lower prices. Often they are not good for the companies involved because the lower prices reduce profit margins and can threaten their survival.

Exam Probability: **Medium**

56. *Answer choices:*

(see index for correct answer)

- a. Discoverability
- b. Market intelligence
- c. Price war
- d. Enterprise relationship management

Guidance: level 1

:: ::

_____ is a means of protection from financial loss. It is a form of risk management, primarily used to hedge against the risk of a contingent or uncertain loss

Exam Probability: **Low**

57. *Answer choices:*

(see index for correct answer)

- a. hierarchical
- b. cultural
- c. co-culture
- d. Insurance

Guidance: level 1

:: Marketing ::

_____ is the percentage of a market accounted for by a specific entity. In a survey of nearly 200 senior marketing managers, 67% responded that they found the revenue- "dollar _____ " metric very useful, while 61% found "unit _____ " very useful.

Exam Probability: **Low**

58. *Answer choices:*

(see index for correct answer)

- a. Generic trademark
- b. Market share
- c. Pricing objectives
- d. Customer equity

:: Retailing ::

A _____ is a retail establishment offering a wide range of consumer goods in different product categories known as "departments". In modern major cities, the _____ made a dramatic appearance in the middle of the 19th century, and permanently reshaped shopping habits, and the definition of service and luxury. Similar developments were under way in London , in Paris and in New York .

Exam Probability: **Medium**

59. *Answer choices:*

(see index for correct answer)

- a. Department store
- b. Bastyr Dispensary
- c. Catalog merchant
- d. Home shopping

Manufacturing

Manufacturing is the production of merchandise for use or sale using labor and machines, tools, chemical and biological processing, or formulation. The term may refer to a range of human activity, from handicraft to high tech, but is most commonly applied to industrial design , in which raw materials are transformed into finished goods on a large scale. Such finished goods may be sold to other manufacturers for the production of other, more complex products, such as aircraft, household appliances, furniture, sports equipment or automobiles, or sold to wholesalers, who in turn sell them to retailers, who then sell them to end users and consumers.

:: Metal forming ::

_____ is a type of motion that combines rotation and translation of that object with respect to a surface , such that, if ideal conditions exist, the two are in contact with each other without sliding.

Exam Probability: **Low**

1. *Answer choices:*

(see index for correct answer)

- a. Forming limit diagram
- b. Rolling
- c. Deep drawing
- d. Structural shape rolling

Guidance: level 1

:: Metrics ::

_____ is a computer model developed by the University of Idaho, that uses Landsat satellite data to compute and map evapotranspiration . _____ calculates ET as a residual of the surface energy balance, where ET is estimated by keeping account of total net short wave and long wave radiation at the vegetation or soil surface, the amount of heat conducted into soil, and the amount of heat convected into the air above the surface. The difference in these three terms represents the amount of energy absorbed during the conversion of liquid water to vapor, which is ET. _____ expresses near-surface temperature gradients used in heat convection as indexed functions of radio _____ surface temperature, thereby eliminating the need for absolutely accurate surface temperature and the need for air-temperature measurements.

Exam Probability: **Medium**

2. *Answer choices:*

(see index for correct answer)

- a. Cleanroom suitability
- b. Parts-per notation
- c. METRIC
- d. Accommodation index

Guidance: level 1

:: ::

_____ refers to the confirmation of certain characteristics of an object, person, or organization. This confirmation is often, but not always, provided by some form of external review, education, assessment, or audit. Accreditation is a specific organization's process of _____ . According to the National Council on Measurement in Education, a _____ test is a credentialing test used to determine whether individuals are knowledgeable enough in a given occupational area to be labeled "competent to practice" in that area.

Exam Probability: **Low**

3. *Answer choices:*

(see index for correct answer)

- a. corporate values
- b. personal values
- c. co-culture
- d. Certification

Guidance: level 1

:: Project management ::

In economics, _____ is the assignment of available resources to various uses. In the context of an entire economy, resources can be allocated by various means, such as markets or central planning.

Exam Probability: **Medium**

4. *Answer choices:*

(see index for correct answer)

- a. Scrumedge
- b. Resource allocation
- c. Budgeted cost of work performed
- d. Lean project management

Guidance: level 1

:: Insulators ::

A _____ is a piece of soft cloth large enough either to cover or to enfold a great portion of the user's body, usually when sleeping or otherwise at rest, thereby trapping radiant bodily heat that otherwise would be lost through convection, and so keeping the body warm.

Exam Probability: **High**

5. *Answer choices:*

(see index for correct answer)

- a. Pentafluoropropane
- b. Dynamic insulation
- c. Sleeping bag
- d. Malter effect

:: Costs ::

In economics, _____ is the total economic cost of production and is made up of variable cost, which varies according to the quantity of a good produced and includes inputs such as labour and raw materials, plus fixed cost, which is independent of the quantity of a good produced and includes inputs that cannot be varied in the short term: fixed costs such as buildings and machinery, including sunk costs if any. Since cost is measured per unit of time, it is a flow variable.

Exam Probability: **High**

6. *Answer choices:*

(see index for correct answer)

- a. Direct labor cost
- b. Total cost
- c. Psychic cost
- d. Cost curve

:: Manufacturing ::

_____ or lean production, often simply "lean", is a systematic method for the minimization of waste within a manufacturing system without sacrificing productivity, which can cause problems. Lean also takes into account waste created through overburden and waste created through unevenness in work loads . Working from the perspective of the client who consumes a product or service, "value" is any action or process that a customer would be willing to pay for.

Exam Probability: **Low**

7. *Answer choices:*

(see index for correct answer)

- a. Axiomatic product development lifecycle
- b. manufacturer
- c. Lean manufacturing
- d. Axiomatic design

Guidance: level 1

:: Commercial item transport and distribution ::

In commerce, supply-chain management , the management of the flow of goods and services, involves the movement and storage of raw materials, of work-in-process inventory, and of finished goods from point of origin to point of consumption. Interconnected or interlinked networks, channels and node businesses combine in the provision of products and services required by end customers in a supply chain. Supply-chain management has been defined as the "design, planning, execution, control, and monitoring of supply-chain activities with the objective of creating net value, building a competitive infrastructure, leveraging worldwide logistics, synchronizing supply with demand and measuring performance globally."SCM practice draws heavily from the areas of industrial engineering, systems engineering, operations management, logistics, procurement, information technology, and marketing and strives for an integrated approach. Marketing channels play an important role in supply-chain management. Current research in supply-chain management is concerned with topics related to sustainability and risk management, among others. Some suggest that the "people dimension" of SCM, ethical issues, internal integration, transparency/visibility, and human capital/talent management are topics that have, so far, been underrepresented on the research agenda.

Exam Probability: **High**

8. *Answer choices:*

(see index for correct answer)

- a. Swap body
- b. Dautel
- c. Supply chain management
- d. Standard Carrier Alpha Code

Guidance: level 1

:: Production and manufacturing ::

_____ is a set of techniques and tools for process improvement. Though as a shortened form it may be found written as 6S, it should not be confused with the methodology known as 6S .

Exam Probability: **High**

9. *Answer choices:*

(see index for correct answer)

- a. Shop foreman
- b. Six Sigma
- c. IBM RFID Information Center
- d. Digital materialization

Guidance: level 1

:: Data management ::

_____ is an object-oriented program and library developed by CERN. It was originally designed for particle physics data analysis and contains several features specific to this field, but it is also used in other applications such as astronomy and data mining. The latest release is 6.16.00, as of 2018-11-14.

Exam Probability: **Medium**

10. *Answer choices:*

- a. Two-phase commit protocol
- b. Document-oriented database
- c. ROOT
- d. Tagsistant

Guidance: level 1

:: Project management ::

_____ s can take many forms depending on the type of project being implemented and the nature of the organization. The _____ details the project deliverables and describes the major objectives. The objectives should include measurable success criteria for the project.

Exam Probability: **Medium**

11. *Answer choices:*

- a. Indian Institute of Project Management
- b. Scope statement
- c. Project appraisal
- d. Akihabara syndrome

:: Data management ::

_____ refers to a data-driven improvement cycle used for improving, optimizing and stabilizing business processes and designs. The _____ improvement cycle is the core tool used to drive Six Sigma projects. However, _____ is not exclusive to Six Sigma and can be used as the framework for other improvement applications.

Exam Probability: **Medium**

12. *Answer choices:*

(see index for correct answer)

- a. DMAIC
- b. Chunked transfer encoding
- c. Reference data
- d. Holistic Data Management

:: Costs ::

In microeconomic theory, the _____ , or alternative cost, of making a particular choice is the value of the most valuable choice out of those that were not taken. In other words, opportunity that will require sacrifices.

Exam Probability: **High**

13. *Answer choices:*

(see index for correct answer)

- a. Cost of poor quality
- b. Opportunity cost
- c. Average cost
- d. Direct materials cost

Guidance: level 1

:: Management ::

_____ is the identification, evaluation, and prioritization of risks followed by coordinated and economical application of resources to minimize, monitor, and control the probability or impact of unfortunate events or to maximize the realization of opportunities.

Exam Probability: **High**

14. *Answer choices:*

(see index for correct answer)

- a. Mushroom management
- b. Peer pressure
- c. Action item
- d. Topple rate

Guidance: level 1

:: Commercial item transport and distribution ::

_____ in logistics and supply chain management is an organization's use of third-party businesses to outsource elements of its distribution, warehousing, and fulfillment services.

Exam Probability: **High**

15. *Answer choices:*

(see index for correct answer)

- a. Tail lift
- b. Container crane
- c. Third-party logistics
- d. Dock

Guidance: level 1

:: Elementary mathematics ::

In mathematics, a _____ is an enumerated collection of objects in which repetitions are allowed. Like a set, it contains members . The number of elements is called the length of the _____ . Unlike a set, the same elements can appear multiple times at different positions in a _____ , and order matters. Formally, a _____ can be defined as a function whose domain is either the set of the natural numbers or the set of the first n natural numbers . The position of an element in a _____ is its rank or index; it is the natural number from which the element is the image. It depends on the context or a specific convention, if the first element has index 0 or 1.
When a symbol has been chosen for denoting a _____ , the nth element of the _____ is denoted by this symbol with n as subscript; for example, the nth element of the Fibonacci _____ is generally denoted Fn.

Exam Probability: **Medium**

16. *Answer choices:*

(see index for correct answer)

- a. Ordinate
- b. Sequence
- c. Versor
- d. Slope

Guidance: level 1

:: Project management ::

A _____ is a team whose members usually belong to different groups, functions and are assigned to activities for the same project. A team can be divided into sub-teams according to need. Usually _____ s are only used for a defined period of time. They are disbanded after the project is deemed complete. Due to the nature of the specific formation and disbandment, _____ s are usually in organizations.

Exam Probability: **Low**

17. *Answer choices:*

(see index for correct answer)

- a. Collaborative planning software
- b. Theory Z of Ouchi
- c. Karol Adamiecki
- d. Project team

Guidance: level 1

:: Product management ::

_____ s, also known as Shewhart charts or process-behavior charts, are a statistical process control tool used to determine if a manufacturing or business process is in a state of control.

Exam Probability: **Low**

18. *Answer choices:*

(see index for correct answer)

- a. Control chart
- b. Trademark
- c. Discontinuation
- d. Dwinell-Wright Company

Guidance: level 1

:: Procurement ::

A _____ is a standard business process whose purpose is to invite suppliers into a bidding process to bid on specific products or services. RfQ generally means the same thing as Call for bids and Invitation for bid .

Exam Probability: **Medium**

19. *Answer choices:*

(see index for correct answer)

- a. Request for quotation
- b. Request for tender
- c. Inverted Sourcing
- d. Proposal theme statement

Guidance: level 1

:: Project management ::

Contemporary business and science treat as a _____ any undertaking, carried out individually or collaboratively and possibly involving research or design, that is carefully planned to achieve a particular aim.

Exam Probability: **High**

20. *Answer choices:*

(see index for correct answer)

- a. Mandated lead arranger
- b. ISO 31000
- c. A Guide to the Project Management Body of Knowledge
- d. Critical path drag

Guidance: level 1

:: Management ::

_____ is a category of business activity made possible by software tools that aim to provide customers with both independence from vendors and better means for engaging with vendors. These same tools can also apply to individuals' relations with other institutions and organizations.

Exam Probability: **Medium**

21. *Answer choices:*

(see index for correct answer)

- a. Enterprise smart grid
- b. Facilitator
- c. Vendor relationship management
- d. Power to the edge

Guidance: level 1

:: Semiconductor companies ::

_____ Corporation is a Japanese multinational conglomerate corporation headquartered in Konan, Minato, Tokyo. Its diversified business includes consumer and professional electronics, gaming, entertainment and financial services. The company owns the largest music entertainment business in the world, the largest video game console business and one of the largest video game publishing businesses, and is one of the leading manufacturers of electronic products for the consumer and professional markets, and a leading player in the film and television entertainment industry. _____ was ranked 97th on the 2018 Fortune Global 500 list.

Exam Probability: **Low**

22. *Answer choices:*

(see index for correct answer)

- a. Sony
- b. Nuvoton
- c. GreenChip
- d. Sharp Corporation

Guidance: level 1

:: Quality ::

The _____ , formerly the _____ Control , is a knowledge-based global community of quality professionals, with nearly 80,000 members dedicated to promoting and advancing quality tools, principles, and practices in their workplaces and communities.

Exam Probability: **Low**

23. *Answer choices:*

(see index for correct answer)

- a. American Society for Quality
- b. European Organization for Quality
- c. OptiY
- d. The Partnership for Excellence

Guidance: level 1

:: Chemical reactions ::

A _____ is a process that leads to the chemical transformation of one set of chemical substances to another. Classically, _____ s encompass changes that only involve the positions of electrons in the forming and breaking of chemical bonds between atoms, with no change to the nuclei , and can often be described by a chemical equation. Nuclear chemistry is a sub-discipline of chemistry that involves the _____ s of unstable and radioactive elements where both electronic and nuclear changes can occur.

Exam Probability: **Low**

24. *Answer choices:*

(see index for correct answer)

- a. Hydrogen atom abstraction
- b. Adduct purification
- c. Associative substitution
- d. Jacobi coordinates

Guidance: level 1

:: ::

An _____ is, most an organized examination or formal evaluation exercise. In engineering activities _____ involves the measurements, tests, and gauges applied to certain characteristics in regard to an object or activity. The results are usually compared to specified requirements and standards for determining whether the item or activity is in line with these targets, often with a Standard _____ Procedure in place to ensure consistent checking. _____ s are usually non-destructive.

Exam Probability: **Medium**

25. *Answer choices:*

(see index for correct answer)

- a. Inspection
- b. open system
- c. imperative
- d. Sarbanes-Oxley act of 2002

Guidance: level 1

:: Process management ::

A _____ is a diagram commonly used in chemical and process engineering to indicate the general flow of plant processes and equipment. The PFD displays the relationship between major equipment of a plant facility and does not show minor details such as piping details and designations. Another commonly used term for a PFD is a flowsheet.

26. *Answer choices:*

(see index for correct answer)

- a. Six Sigma for ROI
- b. Process flow diagram
- c. Artifact-centric business process model
- d. Ideal tasks

Guidance: level 1

:: Chemical processes ::

_____ is the understanding and application of the fundamental principles and laws of nature that allow us to transform raw material and energy into products that are useful to society, at an industrial level. By taking advantage of the driving forces of nature such as pressure, temperature and concentration gradients, as well as the law of conservation of mass, process engineers can develop methods to synthesize and purify large quantities of desired chemical products. _____ focuses on the design, operation, control, optimization and intensification of chemical, physical, and biological processes. _____ encompasses a vast range of industries, such as agriculture, automotive, biotechnical, chemical, food, material development, mining, nuclear, petrochemical, pharmaceutical, and software development. The application of systematic computer-based methods to _____ is "process systems engineering".

27. *Answer choices:*

(see index for correct answer)

- a. Process engineering
- b. Integrated gasification combined cycle
- c. Asymmetric hydrogenation
- d. Derivatization

Guidance: level 1

:: Project management ::

A _____ is a professional in the field of project management. _____ s have the responsibility of the planning, procurement and execution of a project, in any undertaking that has a defined scope, defined start and a defined finish; regardless of industry. _____ s are first point of contact for any issues or discrepancies arising from within the heads of various departments in an organization before the problem escalates to higher authorities. Project management is the responsibility of a _____ . This individual seldom participates directly in the activities that produce the end result, but rather strives to maintain the progress, mutual interaction and tasks of various parties in such a way that reduces the risk of overall failure, maximizes benefits, and minimizes costs.

Exam Probability: **High**

28. *Answer choices:*

(see index for correct answer)

- a. Scope statement
- b. Project manager
- c. Logical framework approach
- d. Time horizon

Guidance: level 1

:: Occupational safety and health ::

_____ is a chemical element with symbol Pb and atomic number 82. It is a heavy metal that is denser than most common materials. _____ is soft and malleable, and also has a relatively low melting point. When freshly cut, _____ is silvery with a hint of blue; it tarnishes to a dull gray color when exposed to air. _____ has the highest atomic number of any stable element and three of its isotopes are endpoints of major nuclear decay chains of heavier elements.

Exam Probability: **Low**

29. *Answer choices:*
(see index for correct answer)

- a. Defensible space
- b. Occupational health nursing
- c. American College of Occupational and Environmental Medicine
- d. Wildfire

Guidance: level 1

:: Management ::

A _____ is an idea of the future or desired result that a person or a group of people envisions, plans and commits to achieve. People endeavor to reach _____ s within a finite time by setting deadlines.

Exam Probability: **Medium**

30. *Answer choices:*

(see index for correct answer)

- a. Meeting system
- b. Goal
- c. Records manager
- d. Vorstand

Guidance: level 1

:: Materials science ::

An _____ is a polymer with viscoelasticity and very weak intermolecular forces, and generally low Young's modulus and high failure strain compared with other materials. The term, a portmanteau of elastic polymer, is often used interchangeably with rubber, although the latter is preferred when referring to vulcanisates. Each of the monomers which link to form the polymer is usually a compound of several elements among carbon, hydrogen, oxygen and silicon. _____ s are amorphous polymers maintained above their glass transition temperature, so that considerable molecular reconformation, without breaking of covalent bonds, is feasible. At ambient temperatures, such rubbers are thus relatively soft and deformable. Their primary uses are for seals, adhesives and molded flexible parts. Application areas for different types of rubber are manifold and cover segments as diverse as tires, soles for shoes, and damping and insulating elements. The importance of these rubbers can be judged from the fact that global revenues are forecast to rise to US$56 billion in 2020.

Exam Probability: **Medium**

31. *Answer choices:*

(see index for correct answer)

- a. NASLA
- b. Coulomb explosion
- c. Elastomer
- d. Materials science in science fiction

Guidance: level 1

:: Natural materials ::

_____ is a finely-grained natural rock or soil material that combines one or more _____ minerals with possible traces of quartz, metal oxides and organic matter. Geologic _____ deposits are mostly composed of phyllosilicate minerals containing variable amounts of water trapped in the mineral structure. _____ s are plastic due to particle size and geometry as well as water content, and become hard, brittle and non–plastic upon drying or firing. Depending on the soil's content in which it is found, _____ can appear in various colours from white to dull grey or brown to deep orange-red.

Exam Probability: **High**

32. *Answer choices:*

(see index for correct answer)

- a. Levant bole
- b. Crushed stone
- c. Clay
- d. Light clay

Guidance: level 1

:: Sensitivity analysis ::

_____ is the study of how the uncertainty in the output of a mathematical model or system can be divided and allocated to different sources of uncertainty in its inputs. A related practice is uncertainty analysis, which has a greater focus on uncertainty quantification and propagation of uncertainty; ideally, uncertainty and _____ should be run in tandem.

33. *Answer choices:*

(see index for correct answer)

- a. Tornado diagram
- b. Fourier amplitude sensitivity testing
- c. Elementary effects method
- d. Sensitivity analysis

Guidance: level 1

:: Project management ::

A _____ is a type of bar chart that illustrates a project schedule, named after its inventor, Henry Gantt , who designed such a chart around the years 1910–1915. Modern _____ s also show the dependency relationships between activities and current schedule status.

Exam Probability: **Low**

34. *Answer choices:*

(see index for correct answer)

- a. Gantt chart
- b. The Practice Standard for Scheduling
- c. TargetProcess

- d. Time limit

Guidance: level 1

:: Project management ::

In political science, an _____ is a means by which a petition signed by a certain minimum number of registered voters can force a government to choose to either enact a law or hold a public vote in parliament in what is called indirect _____ , or under direct _____ , the proposition is immediately put to a plebiscite or referendum, in what is called a Popular initiated Referendum or citizen-initiated referendum).

Exam Probability: **High**

35. *Answer choices:*

(see index for correct answer)

- a. PRINCE2
- b. Initiative
- c. Constructability
- d. Project plan

Guidance: level 1

:: Production economics ::

In economics and related disciplines, a _____ is a cost in making any economic trade when participating in a market.

Exam Probability: **Low**

36. *Answer choices:*

(see index for correct answer)

- a. Diseconomies of scale
- b. Transaction cost
- c. Constant elasticity of transformation
- d. Foundations of Economic Analysis

Guidance: level 1

:: Management ::

_____ is a process by which entities review the quality of all factors involved in production. ISO 9000 defines _____ as "A part of quality management focused on fulfilling quality requirements".

Exam Probability: **Medium**

37. *Answer choices:*

(see index for correct answer)

- a. Preparation
- b. Earned value management
- c. SimulTrain
- d. Marketing plan

Guidance: level 1

:: Waste ::

_____ are unwanted or unusable materials. _____ is any substance which is discarded after primary use, or is worthless, defective and of no use. A by-product by contrast is a joint product of relatively minor economic value. A _____ product may become a by-product, joint product or resource through an invention that raises a _____ product's value above zero.

Exam Probability: **High**

38. *Answer choices:*
(see index for correct answer)

- a. Biodegradable waste
- b. Waste
- c. Sharps waste
- d. Metabolic waste

Guidance: level 1

:: Supply chain management ::

_____ is the process of finding and agreeing to terms, and acquiring goods, services, or works from an external source, often via a tendering or competitive bidding process. _____ is used to ensure the buyer receives goods, services, or works at the best possible price when aspects such as quality, quantity, time, and location are compared. Corporations and public bodies often define processes intended to promote fair and open competition for their business while minimizing risks such as exposure to fraud and collusion.

Exam Probability: **High**

39. *Answer choices:*

(see index for correct answer)

- a. Procurement
- b. Logistics Bureau
- c. Transportation management system
- d. Vendor-managed inventory

Guidance: level 1

:: Project management ::

Rolling-wave planning is the process of project planning in waves as the project proceeds and later details become clearer; similar to the techniques used in agile software development approaches like Scrum..

40. *Answer choices:*

(see index for correct answer)

- a. Rolling Wave planning
- b. Punch list
- c. Theory Z
- d. NetPoint

Guidance: level 1

:: Finance ::

_____ is a financial estimate intended to help buyers and owners determine the direct and indirect costs of a product or system. It is a management accounting concept that can be used in full cost accounting or even ecological economics where it includes social costs.

Exam Probability: **High**

41. *Answer choices:*

(see index for correct answer)

- a. Asset-backed commercial paper program
- b. Farm
- c. Debt-for-nature swap

- d. Total cost of ownership

Guidance: level 1

:: Risk analysis ::

Supply-chain risk management is "the implementation of strategies to manage both everyday and exceptional risks along the supply chain based on continuous risk assessment with the objective of reducing vulnerability and ensuring continuity".

Exam Probability: **Low**

42. *Answer choices:*

(see index for correct answer)

- a. Supply chain risk management
- b. Risk analysis
- c. Precautionary principle
- d. Unintended consequences

Guidance: level 1

:: Commerce ::

A _____ is an employee within a company, business or other organization who is responsible at some level for buying or approving the acquisition of goods and services needed by the company. Responsible for buying the best quality products, goods and services for their company at the most competitive prices, _____ s work in a wide range of sectors for many different organizations. The position responsibilities may be the same as that of a buyer or purchasing agent, or may include wider supervisory or managerial responsibilities. A _____ may oversee the acquisition of materials needed for production, general supplies for offices and facilities, equipment, or construction contracts. A _____ often supervises purchasing agents and buyers, but in small companies the _____ may also be the purchasing agent or buyer. The _____ position may also carry the title "Procurement Manager" or in the public sector, "Procurement Officer". He or she can come from both an Engineering or Economics background.

Exam Probability: **High**

43. *Answer choices:*

(see index for correct answer)

- a. Fixed price
- b. Purchasing manager
- c. Staple right
- d. Dumping

Guidance: level 1

:: Project management ::

A _____ is the approximation of the cost of a program, project, or operation. The _____ is the product of the cost estimating process. The _____ has a single total value and may have identifiable component values. A problem with a cost overrun can be avoided with a credible, reliable, and accurate _____ . A cost estimator is the professional who prepares _____ s. There are different types of cost estimators, whose title may be preceded by a modifier, such as building estimator, or electrical estimator, or chief estimator. Other professionals such as quantity surveyors and cost engineers may also prepare _____ s or contribute to _____ s. In the US, according to the Bureau of Labor Statistics, there were 185,400 cost estimators in 2010. There are around 75,000 professional quantity surveyors working in the UK.

Exam Probability: **Low**

44. *Answer choices:*

(see index for correct answer)

- a. Deployment Plan
- b. TimeTac
- c. Theory Z
- d. Cost estimate

Guidance: level 1

:: Project management ::

_____ is the right to exercise power, which can be formalized by a state and exercised by way of judges, appointed executives of government, or the ecclesiastical or priestly appointed representatives of a God or other deities.

Exam Probability: **Medium**

45. *Answer choices:*

(see index for correct answer)

- a. Authority
- b. Project management process
- c. Pre-mortem
- d. Mandated lead arranger

Guidance: level 1

:: Distribution, retailing, and wholesaling ::

The _____ is a distribution channel phenomenon in which forecasts yield supply chain inefficiencies. It refers to increasing swings in inventory in response to shifts in customer demand as one moves further up the supply chain. The concept first appeared in Jay Forrester's Industrial Dynamics and thus it is also known as the Forrester effect. The _____ was named for the way the amplitude of a whip increases down its length. The further from the originating signal, the greater the distortion of the wave pattern. In a similar manner, forecast accuracy decreases as one moves upstream along the supply chain. For example, many consumer goods have fairly consistent consumption at retail but this signal becomes more chaotic and unpredictable as the focus moves away from consumer purchasing behavior.

Exam Probability: **High**

46. *Answer choices:*

(see index for correct answer)

- a. Bullwhip effect
- b. Cash and carry
- c. Plataforma Europa
- d. Independent News

Guidance: level 1

:: Project management ::

Some scenarios associate "this kind of planning" with learning "life skills". _____ s are necessary, or at least useful, in situations where individuals need to know what time they must be at a specific location to receive a specific service, and where people need to accomplish a set of goals within a set time period.

Exam Probability: **Low**

47. *Answer choices:*

(see index for correct answer)

- a. Project Management South Africa
- b. Association for Project Management
- c. Schedule
- d. Commissioning management systems

Guidance: level 1

:: Promotion and marketing communications ::

The _____ of American Manufacturers, now ThomasNet, is an online platform for supplier discovery and product sourcing in the US and Canada. It was once known as the "big green books" and "Thomas Registry", and was a multi-volume directory of industrial product information covering 650,000 distributors, manufacturers and service companies within 67,000-plus industrial categories that is now published on ThomasNet.

Exam Probability: **High**

48. *Answer choices:*

- a. Slasher Sale
- b. Street team
- c. Thomas Register
- d. London International Awards

Guidance: level 1

:: Information technology management ::

The term _____ is used to refer to periods when a system is unavailable. _____ or outage duration refers to a period of time that a system fails to provide or perform its primary function. Reliability, availability, recovery, and unavailability are related concepts. The unavailability is the proportion of a time-span that a system is unavailable or offline. This is usually a result of the system failing to function because of an unplanned event, or because of routine maintenance .

Exam Probability: **Low**

49. *Answer choices:*

- a. IT Interaction Model
- b. Change management
- c. Downtime

- d. Information model

:: Data interchange standards ::

_____ is the concept of businesses electronically communicating information that was traditionally communicated on paper, such as purchase orders and invoices. Technical standards for EDI exist to facilitate parties transacting such instruments without having to make special arrangements.

Exam Probability: **Medium**

50. *Answer choices:*
(see index for correct answer)

- a. Uniform Communication Standard
- b. Electronic data interchange
- c. Domain Application Protocol
- d. Data Interchange Standards Association

:: Management ::

_____ , also known as natural process limits, are horizontal lines drawn on a statistical process control chart, usually at a distance of ±3 standard deviations of the plotted statistic from the statistic's mean.

Exam Probability: **Medium**

51. *Answer choices:*

(see index for correct answer)

- a. Profitable growth
- b. Board of governors
- c. Automated decision support
- d. Control limits

Guidance: level 1

:: Lean manufacturing ::

_____ is a scheduling system for lean manufacturing and just-in-time manufacturing . Taiichi Ohno, an industrial engineer at Toyota, developed _____ to improve manufacturing efficiency. _____ is one method to achieve JIT. The system takes its name from the cards that track production within a factory. For many in the automotive sector, _____ is known as the "Toyota nameplate system" and as such the term is not used by some other automakers.

Exam Probability: **Low**

52. *Answer choices:*

(see index for correct answer)

- a. Kanban
- b. Autonomation
- c. Lean laboratory
- d. JobShopLean

Guidance: level 1

:: Goods ::

In most contexts, the concept of _____ denotes the conduct that should be preferred when posed with a choice between possible actions. _____ is generally considered to be the opposite of evil, and is of interest in the study of morality, ethics, religion and philosophy. The specific meaning and etymology of the term and its associated translations among ancient and contemporary languages show substantial variation in its inflection and meaning depending on circumstances of place, history, religious, or philosophical context.

Exam Probability: **High**

53. *Answer choices:*

(see index for correct answer)

- a. Good
- b. Veblen good

- c. Club good
- d. Speciality goods

Guidance: level 1

:: Project management ::

A _____ is one of a series of numbered markers placed along a road or boundary at intervals of one mile or occasionally, parts of a mile. They are typically located at the side of the road or in a median or central reservation. They are alternatively known as mile markers, mileposts or mile posts . Mileage is the distance along the road from a fixed commencement point. Commonly the term " _____ " may also refer to markers placed at other distances, such as every kilometre.

Exam Probability: **Medium**

54. *Answer choices:*

(see index for correct answer)

- a. Elemental cost planning
- b. Project management office
- c. Milestone
- d. PRINCE2

Guidance: level 1

:: Information technology management ::

_____ is a collective term for all approaches to prepare , support and help individuals, teams, and organizations in making organizational change. The most common change drivers include: technological evolution, process reviews, crisis, and consumer habit changes; pressure from new business entrants, acquisitions, mergers, and organizational restructuring. It includes methods that redirect or redefine the use of resources, business process, budget allocations, or other modes of operation that significantly change a company or organization. Organizational _____ considers the full organization and what needs to change, while _____ may be used solely to refer to how people and teams are affected by such organizational transition. It deals with many different disciplines, from behavioral and social sciences to information technology and business solutions.

Exam Probability: **High**

55. *Answer choices:*

(see index for correct answer)

- a. Acceptable use policy
- b. Change management
- c. Data warehouse appliance
- d. Software license server

Guidance: level 1

:: Knowledge representation ::

_____ s are causal diagrams created by Kaoru Ishikawa that show the causes of a specific event.

Exam Probability: **Medium**

56. *Answer choices:*

(see index for correct answer)

- a. Scripts
- b. National Library of Medicine classification
- c. General Architecture for Text Engineering
- d. Ishikawa diagram

Guidance: level 1

:: Process management ::

_____ is a statistics package developed at the Pennsylvania State University by researchers Barbara F. Ryan, Thomas A. Ryan, Jr., and Brian L. Joiner in 1972. It began as a light version of OMNITAB 80, a statistical analysis program by NIST. Statistical analysis software such as _____ automates calculations and the creation of graphs, allowing the user to focus more on the analysis of data and the interpretation of results. It is compatible with other _____ , Inc. software.

Exam Probability: **High**

57. *Answer choices:*

(see index for correct answer)

- a. Minitab
- b. Process
- c. Artifact-centric business process model
- d. Process specification

Guidance: level 1

:: Industrial engineering ::

The _____ is the design of any task that aims to describe or explain the variation of information under conditions that are hypothesized to reflect the variation. The term is generally associated with experiments in which the design introduces conditions that directly affect the variation, but may also refer to the design of quasi-experiments, in which natural conditions that influence the variation are selected for observation.

Exam Probability: **High**

58. *Answer choices:*

(see index for correct answer)

- a. Inspection in manufacturing
- b. Service quality
- c. Blend time
- d. Work Measurement

:: Product management ::

_____ is the state of being which occurs when an object, service, or practice is no longer wanted even though it may still be in good working order; however, the international standard EN62402 _____ Management - Application Guide defines _____ as being the "transition from availability of products by the original manufacturer or supplier to unavailability". _____ frequently occurs because a replacement has become available that has, in sum, more advantages compared to the disadvantages incurred by maintaining or repairing the original. Obsolete also refers to something that is already disused or discarded, or antiquated. Typically, _____ is preceded by a gradual decline in popularity.

Exam Probability: **Medium**

59. *Answer choices:*

(see index for correct answer)

- a. Rapid prototyping
- b. Trademark look
- c. Obsolescence
- d. Product information

Commerce

Commerce relates to "the exchange of goods and services, especially on a large scale." It includes legal, economic, political, social, cultural and technological systems that operate in any country or internationally.

:: E-commerce ::

A _____ is a hosted service offering that acts as an intermediary between business partners sharing standards based or proprietary data via shared business processes. The offered service is referred to as " _____ services".

Exam Probability: **High**

1. *Answer choices:*

(see index for correct answer)

- a. Electronic bill payment
- b. Silent commerce
- c. SAF-T
- d. TXT402

Guidance: level 1

:: Auctioneering ::

_____ are electronic auctions, which can be used by sellers to sell their items to many potential buyers. Sellers and buyers can be individuals, organizations etc.

Exam Probability: **Medium**

2. *Answer choices:*

(see index for correct answer)

- a. Call for bids
- b. Forward auction
- c. Japanese auction
- d. AntiqueWeek

Guidance: level 1

:: ::

In logic and philosophy, an _____ is a series of statements , called the premises or premisses , intended to determine the degree of truth of another statement, the conclusion. The logical form of an _____ in a natural language can be represented in a symbolic formal language, and independently of natural language formally defined " _____ s" can be made in math and computer science.

Exam Probability: **Low**

3. *Answer choices:*

(see index for correct answer)

- a. levels of analysis
- b. Argument
- c. deep-level diversity
- d. similarity-attraction theory

Guidance: level 1

:: Land value taxation ::

_____ , sometimes referred to as dry _____ , is the solid surface of Earth that is not permanently covered by water. The vast majority of human activity throughout history has occurred in _____ areas that support agriculture, habitat, and various natural resources. Some life forms have developed from predecessor species that lived in bodies of water.

Exam Probability: **Low**

4. *Answer choices:*

(see index for correct answer)

- a. Physiocracy
- b. Henry George
- c. Land
- d. Land value tax

Guidance: level 1

:: Business terms ::

The _____ or reception is an area where visitors arrive and first encounter a staff at a place of business. _____ staff will deal with whatever question the visitor has and put them in contact with a relevant person at the company. Broadly speaking, the _____ includes roles that affect the revenues of the business. The term _____ is in contrast to the term back office which refers to a company's operations, personnel, accounting, payroll and financial departments which do not interact directly with customers.

5. *Answer choices:*

(see index for correct answer)

- a. operating cost
- b. Strategic partner
- c. organizational capital
- d. back office

Guidance: level 1

:: Marketing ::

_____ is a concept introduced in a book of the same name in 1999 by marketing expert Seth Godin. _____ is a non-traditional marketing technique that advertises goods and services when advance consent is given.

Exam Probability: **Medium**

6. *Answer choices:*

(see index for correct answer)

- a. Permission marketing
- b. Lead generation
- c. Primary research
- d. Adobe Social

:: ::

An _____ is the production of goods or related services within an economy. The major source of revenue of a group or company is the indicator of its relevant _____. When a large group has multiple sources of revenue generation, it is considered to be working in different industries. Manufacturing _____ became a key sector of production and labour in European and North American countries during the Industrial Revolution, upsetting previous mercantile and feudal economies. This came through many successive rapid advances in technology, such as the production of steel and coal.

Exam Probability: **Medium**

7. *Answer choices:*

(see index for correct answer)

- a. process perspective
- b. similarity-attraction theory
- c. Character
- d. Industry

:: Accounting source documents ::

A _____ is a commercial document and first official offer issued by a buyer to a seller indicating types, quantities, and agreed prices for products or services. It is used to control the purchasing of products and services from external suppliers. _____ s can be an essential part of enterprise resource planning system orders.

Exam Probability: **High**

8. *Answer choices:*

(see index for correct answer)

- a. Purchase order
- b. Remittance advice
- c. Credit memorandum
- d. Invoice

Guidance: level 1

:: ::

_____ is the provision of service to customers before, during and after a purchase. The perception of success of such interactions is dependent on employees "who can adjust themselves to the personality of the guest". _____ concerns the priority an organization assigns to _____ relative to components such as product innovation and pricing. In this sense, an organization that values good _____ may spend more money in training employees than the average organization or may proactively interview customers for feedback.

9. *Answer choices:*

(see index for correct answer)

- a. corporate values
- b. cultural
- c. personal values
- d. Customer service

Guidance: level 1

:: Payments ::

A _____ or government incentive is a form of financial aid or support extended to an economic sector generally with the aim of promoting economic and social policy. Although commonly extended from government, the term _____ can relate to any type of support – for example from NGOs or as implicit subsidies. Subsidies come in various forms including: direct and indirect .

Exam Probability: **Medium**

10. *Answer choices:*

(see index for correct answer)

- a. County payments
- b. Subsidy

- c. Deficiency payments
- d. Tuition payments

Guidance: level 1

:: Economics terminology ::

_____ is the total receipts a seller can obtain from selling goods or services to buyers. It can be written as P × Q, which is the price of the goods multiplied by the quantity of the sold goods.

Exam Probability: **Medium**

11. *Answer choices:*

(see index for correct answer)

- a. Total revenue
- b. Physical capital
- c. Capital stock
- d. Normal profit

Guidance: level 1

:: Information technology management ::

_____s or pop-ups are forms of online advertising on the World Wide Web. A pop-up is a graphical user interface display area, usually a small window, that suddenly appears in the foreground of the visual interface. The pop-up window containing an advertisement is usually generated by JavaScript that uses cross-site scripting , sometimes with a secondary payload that uses Adobe Flash. They can also be generated by other vulnerabilities/security holes in browser security.

Exam Probability: **Low**

12. *Answer choices:*

(see index for correct answer)

- a. Business record
- b. Change control
- c. Pop-up ad
- d. Professional Petroleum Data Management Association

Guidance: level 1

:: Stock market ::

_____ is freedom from, or resilience against, potential harm caused by others. Beneficiaries of _____ may be of persons and social groups, objects and institutions, ecosystems or any other entity or phenomenon vulnerable to unwanted change by its environment.

Exam Probability: **High**

13. *Answer choices:*

(see index for correct answer)

- a. Sell side
- b. Trading turret
- c. Security
- d. High-frequency trading

Guidance: level 1

:: Marketing ::

A _____ is an overall experience of a customer that distinguishes an organization or product from its rivals in the eyes of the customer. _____ s are used in business, marketing, and advertising. Name _____ s are sometimes distinguished from generic or store _____ s.

Exam Probability: **Medium**

14. *Answer choices:*

(see index for correct answer)

- a. Market information systems
- b. Brand
- c. Corporate capabilities package
- d. Behance

:: Market research ::

_____ is an organized effort to gather information about target markets or customers. It is a very important component of business strategy. The term is commonly interchanged with marketing research; however, expert practitioners may wish to draw a distinction, in that marketing research is concerned specifically about marketing processes, while _____ is concerned specifically with markets.

Exam Probability: **Medium**

15. *Answer choices:*

(see index for correct answer)

- a. Sociomapping
- b. Nonprobability sampling
- c. IRI
- d. Market research

Guidance: level 1

:: Credit cards ::

A _____ is a payment card issued to users to enable the cardholder to pay a merchant for goods and services based on the cardholder's promise to the card issuer to pay them for the amounts plus the other agreed charges. The card issuer creates a revolving account and grants a line of credit to the cardholder, from which the cardholder can borrow money for payment to a merchant or as a cash advance.

Exam Probability: **High**

16. *Answer choices:*

(see index for correct answer)

- a. Barclaycard
- b. CardIt
- c. Netbanx
- d. Credit card

Guidance: level 1

:: Information technology management ::

B2B is often contrasted with business-to-consumer . In B2B commerce, it is often the case that the parties to the relationship have comparable negotiating power, and even when they do not, each party typically involves professional staff and legal counsel in the negotiation of terms, whereas B2C is shaped to a far greater degree by economic implications of information asymmetry. However, within a B2B context, large companies may have many commercial, resource and information advantages over smaller businesses. The United Kingdom government, for example, created the post of Small Business Commissioner under the Enterprise Act 2016 to "enable small businesses to resolve disputes" and "consider complaints by small business suppliers about payment issues with larger businesses that they supply."

Exam Probability: **Low**

17. *Answer choices:*

(see index for correct answer)

- a. Business-to-business
- b. Information protection policy
- c. Downtime
- d. Storage hypervisor

Guidance: level 1

:: Cash flow ::

_____ s are narrowly interconnected with the concepts of value, interest rate and liquidity. A _____ that shall happen on a future day tN can be transformed into a _____ of the same value in t0.

18. *Answer choices:*

- a. Cash flow
- b. Cash carrier
- c. Invoice discounting
- d. Discounted payback period

Guidance: level 1

:: Supply chain management terms ::

In business and finance, _____ is a system of organizations, people, activities, information, and resources involved in moving a product or service from supplier to customer. _____ activities involve the transformation of natural resources, raw materials, and components into a finished product that is delivered to the end customer. In sophisticated _____ systems, used products may re-enter the _____ at any point where residual value is recyclable. _____ s link value chains.

Exam Probability: **High**

19. *Answer choices:*

- a. Capital spare

- b. Supply chain
- c. Price look-up code
- d. Cool Chain Quality Indicator

Guidance: level 1

:: Marketing ::

_____ is the percentage of a market accounted for by a specific entity. In a survey of nearly 200 senior marketing managers, 67% responded that they found the revenue- "dollar _____ " metric very useful, while 61% found "unit _____ " very useful.

Exam Probability: **Low**

20. *Answer choices:*

(see index for correct answer)

- a. Market share
- b. Customer acquisition cost
- c. Keyword research
- d. Official statistics

Guidance: level 1

:: Price fixing convictions ::

_____ is the flag carrier airline of the United Kingdom, headquartered at Waterside, Harmondsworth. It is the second largest airline in the United Kingdom, based on fleet size and passengers carried, behind easyJet. The airline is based in Waterside near its main hub at London Heathrow Airport. In January 2011 BA merged with Iberia, creating the International Airlines Group , a holding company registered in Madrid, Spain. IAG is the world's third-largest airline group in terms of annual revenue and the second-largest in Europe. It is listed on the London Stock Exchange and in the FTSE 100 Index. _____ is the first passenger airline to have generated more than $1 billion on a single air route in a year .

Exam Probability: **Medium**

21. *Answer choices:*

(see index for correct answer)

- a. Siemens
- b. Grolsch Brewery
- c. Anheuser-Busch InBev
- d. British Airways

Guidance: level 1

:: Commercial item transport and distribution ::

Wholesaling or distributing is the sale of goods or merchandise to retailers; to industrial, commercial, institutional, or other professional business users; or to other _____ rs and related subordinated services. In general, it is the sale of goods to anyone other than a standard consumer.

22. *Answer choices:*

(see index for correct answer)

- a. Yacht transport
- b. Toll Global Logistics
- c. Food distribution
- d. Whiddy Island Disaster

Guidance: level 1

:: Production economics ::

In microeconomics, _____ are the cost advantages that enterprises obtain due to their scale of operation , with cost per unit of output decreasing with increasing scale.

Exam Probability: **High**

23. *Answer choices:*

(see index for correct answer)

- a. Average fixed cost
- b. Split-off point
- c. Foundations of Economic Analysis
- d. Economies of scale

:: ::

_____ is the production of products for use or sale using labour and machines, tools, chemical and biological processing, or formulation. The term may refer to a range of human activity, from handicraft to high tech, but is most commonly applied to industrial design, in which raw materials are transformed into finished goods on a large scale. Such finished goods may be sold to other manufacturers for the production of other, more complex products, such as aircraft, household appliances, furniture, sports equipment or automobiles, or sold to wholesalers, who in turn sell them to retailers, who then sell them to end users and consumers.

Exam Probability: **High**

24. *Answer choices:*

(see index for correct answer)

- a. co-culture
- b. Sarbanes-Oxley act of 2002
- c. hierarchical perspective
- d. similarity-attraction theory

:: Computer access control ::

_____ is the act of confirming the truth of an attribute of a single piece of data claimed true by an entity. In contrast with identification, which refers to the act of stating or otherwise indicating a claim purportedly attesting to a person or thing's identity, _____ is the process of actually confirming that identity. It might involve confirming the identity of a person by validating their identity documents, verifying the authenticity of a website with a digital certificate, determining the age of an artifact by carbon dating, or ensuring that a product is what its packaging and labeling claim to be. In other words, _____ often involves verifying the validity of at least one form of identification.

Exam Probability: **Medium**

25. *Answer choices:*

(see index for correct answer)

- a. Identity driven networking
- b. Authentication
- c. Access control list
- d. Hacking Team

Guidance: level 1

:: Industrial Revolution ::

The _____ , now also known as the First _____ , was the transition to new manufacturing processes in Europe and the US, in the period from about 1760 to sometime between 1820 and 1840. This transition included going from hand production methods to machines, new chemical manufacturing and iron production processes, the increasing use of steam power and water power, the development of machine tools and the rise of the mechanized factory system. The _____ also led to an unprecedented rise in the rate of population growth.

Exam Probability: Low

26. *Answer choices:*

(see index for correct answer)

- a. Sykes Bleaching Company
- b. The Making of the English Working Class
- c. Derby Silk Mill
- d. Thomas Walmsley and Sons

Guidance: level 1

:: ::

In economics _____ is a theoretical concept where all markets are in equilibrium, and all prices and quantities have fully adjusted and are in equilibrium. The _____ contrasts with the short run where there are some constraints and markets are not fully in equilibrium.

Exam Probability: Low

27. *Answer choices:*

(see index for correct answer)

- a. functional perspective
- b. Long run
- c. hierarchical perspective
- d. empathy

Guidance: level 1

:: ::

A trade union is an association of workers forming a legal unit or legal personhood, usually called a "bargaining unit", which acts as bargaining agent and legal representative for a unit of employees in all matters of law or right arising from or in the administration of a collective agreement. Labour unions typically fund the formal organisation, head office, and legal team functions of the labour union through regular fees or union dues. The delegate staff of the labour union representation in the workforce are made up of workplace volunteers who are appointed by members in democratic elections.

Exam Probability: **Low**

28. *Answer choices:*

(see index for correct answer)

- a. hierarchical
- b. surface-level diversity

- c. personal values
- d. deep-level diversity

Guidance: level 1

:: Workplace ::

_____ is asystematic determination of a subject's merit, worth and significance, using criteria governed by a set of standards. It can assist an organization, program, design, project or any other intervention or initiative to assess any aim, realisable concept/proposal, or any alternative, to help in decision-making; or to ascertain the degree of achievement or value in regard to the aim and objectives and results of any such action that has been completed. The primary purpose of _____ , in addition to gaining insight into prior or existing initiatives, is to enable reflection and assist in the identification of future change.

Exam Probability: **Low**

29. *Answer choices:*
(see index for correct answer)

- a. performance review
- b. Toxic workplace
- c. Workplace health surveillance
- d. Evaluation

Guidance: level 1

:: E-commerce ::

_____ is a method of e-commerce where shoppers' friends become involved in the shopping experience. _____ attempts to use technology to mimic the social interactions found in physical malls and stores. With the rise of mobile devices, _____ is now extending beyond the online world and into the offline world of shopping.

Exam Probability: **High**

30. *Answer choices:*

(see index for correct answer)

- a. KonaKart
- b. DVD-by-mail
- c. TRADACOMS
- d. Centricom

Guidance: level 1

:: Commercial item transport and distribution ::

In commerce, supply-chain management , the management of the flow of goods and services, involves the movement and storage of raw materials, of work-in-process inventory, and of finished goods from point of origin to point of consumption. Interconnected or interlinked networks, channels and node businesses combine in the provision of products and services required by end customers in a supply chain. Supply-chain management has been defined as the "design, planning, execution, control, and monitoring of supply-chain activities with the objective of creating net value, building a competitive infrastructure, leveraging worldwide logistics, synchronizing supply with demand and measuring performance globally."SCM practice draws heavily from the areas of industrial engineering, systems engineering, operations management, logistics, procurement, information technology, and marketing and strives for an integrated approach. Marketing channels play an important role in supply-chain management. Current research in supply-chain management is concerned with topics related to sustainability and risk management, among others. Some suggest that the "people dimension" of SCM, ethical issues, internal integration, transparency/visibility, and human capital/talent management are topics that have, so far, been underrepresented on the research agenda.

Exam Probability: **Medium**

31. *Answer choices:*

(see index for correct answer)

- a. Mid-stream operation
- b. Zeppelin
- c. Boat trailer
- d. Sealift

Guidance: level 1

_____ is "property consisting of land and the buildings on it, along with its natural resources such as crops, minerals or water; immovable property of this nature; an interest vested in this an item of real property, buildings or housing in general. Also: the business of _____ ; the profession of buying, selling, or renting land, buildings, or housing." It is a legal term used in jurisdictions whose legal system is derived from English common law, such as India, England, Wales, Northern Ireland, United States, Canada, Pakistan, Australia, and New Zealand.

Exam Probability: **Low**

32. *Answer choices:*

(see index for correct answer)

- a. open system
- b. Sarbanes-Oxley act of 2002
- c. Real estate
- d. cultural

Guidance: level 1

:: Marketing ::

_____ comes from the Latin neg and otsia referring to businessmen who, unlike the patricians, had no leisure time in their industriousness; it held the meaning of business until the 17th century when it took on the diplomatic connotation as a dialogue between two or more people or parties intended to reach a beneficial outcome over one or more issues where a conflict exists with respect to at least one of these issues. Thus, _____ is a process of combining divergent positions into a joint agreement under a decision rule of unanimity.

Exam Probability: **Low**

33. *Answer choices:*

(see index for correct answer)

- a. Negotiation
- b. Mass marketing
- c. Enterprise relationship management
- d. Bluetooth advertising

Guidance: level 1

:: E-commerce ::

Customer to customer markets provide an innovative way to allow customers to interact with each other. Traditional markets require business to customer relationships, in which a customer goes to the business in order to purchase a product or service. In customer to customer markets, the business facilitates an environment where customers can sell goods or services to each other. Other types of markets include business to business and business to customer .

Exam Probability: **Medium**

34. *Answer choices:*

(see index for correct answer)

- a. Consumer-to-consumer
- b. Allbiz
- c. MusicPass
- d. Online wallet

Guidance: level 1

:: Asset ::

In financial accounting, an _____ is any resource owned by the business. Anything tangible or intangible that can be owned or controlled to produce value and that is held by a company to produce positive economic value is an _____ . Simply stated, _____ s represent value of ownership that can be converted into cash . The balance sheet of a firm records the monetary value of the _____ s owned by that firm. It covers money and other valuables belonging to an individual or to a business.

Exam Probability: **Medium**

35. *Answer choices:*

(see index for correct answer)

- a. Current asset

- b. Fixed asset

Guidance: level 1

:: Free market ::

In economics, a _____ is a system in which the prices for goods and services are determined by the open market and by consumers. In a _____ , the laws and forces of supply and demand are free from any intervention by a government or other authority and from all forms of economic privilege, monopolies and artificial scarcities. Proponents of the concept of _____ contrast it with a regulated market in which a government intervenes in supply and demand through various methods, such as tariffs, used to restrict trade and to protect the local economy. In an idealized free-market economy, prices for goods and services are set freely by the forces of supply and demand and are allowed to reach their point of equilibrium without intervention by government policy.

Exam Probability: **Low**

36. *Answer choices:*

(see index for correct answer)

- a. Piece rate
- b. Regulated market

Guidance: level 1

:: Insolvency ::

_____ is the process in accounting by which a company is brought to an end in the United Kingdom, Republic of Ireland and United States. The assets and property of the company are redistributed. _____ is also sometimes referred to as winding-up or dissolution, although dissolution technically refers to the last stage of _____ . The process of _____ also arises when customs, an authority or agency in a country responsible for collecting and safeguarding customs duties, determines the final computation or ascertainment of the duties or drawback accruing on an entry.

Exam Probability: **Medium**

37. *Answer choices:*

(see index for correct answer)

- a. Liquidator
- b. Bankruptcy
- c. Insolvency law of Russia
- d. Liquidation

Guidance: level 1

:: International trade ::

_____ involves the transfer of goods or services from one person or entity to another, often in exchange for money. A system or network that allows _____ is called a market.

38. *Answer choices:*

- a. Import license
- b. Trade
- c. Export-led growth
- d. Technical barriers to trade

Guidance: level 1

:: Hospitality industry ::

_____ refers to the relationship between a guest and a host, wherein the host receives the guest with goodwill, including the reception and entertainment of guests, visitors, or strangers. Louis, chevalier de Jaucourt describes _____ in the Encyclopédie as the virtue of a great soul that cares for the whole universe through the ties of humanity.

Exam Probability: **Low**

39. *Answer choices:*

- a. Cover charge
- b. Hospitality industry

- c. Restaurant ware
- d. Hospitality

Guidance: level 1

:: Evaluation ::

_____ is a way of preventing mistakes and defects in manufactured products and avoiding problems when delivering products or services to customers; which ISO 9000 defines as "part of quality management focused on providing confidence that quality requirements will be fulfilled". This defect prevention in _____ differs subtly from defect detection and rejection in quality control and has been referred to as a shift left since it focuses on quality earlier in the process .

Exam Probability: **Low**

40. *Answer choices:*

(see index for correct answer)

- a. Knowledge survey
- b. Quality assurance
- c. Australian Drug Evaluation Committee
- d. Narrative evaluation

Guidance: level 1

:: Business law ::

A _____ is a group of people who jointly supervise the activities of an organization, which can be either a for-profit business, nonprofit organization, or a government agency. Such a board's powers, duties, and responsibilities are determined by government regulations and the organization's own constitution and bylaws. These authorities may specify the number of members of the board, how they are to be chosen, and how often they are to meet.

Exam Probability: **High**

41. *Answer choices:*

(see index for correct answer)

- a. Equity of redemption
- b. Chattel mortgage
- c. Lien
- d. Board of directors

Guidance: level 1

:: Accounting source documents ::

An _____ , bill or tab is a commercial document issued by a seller to a buyer, relating to a sale transaction and indicating the products, quantities, and agreed prices for products or services the seller had provided the buyer.

42. *Answer choices:*

(see index for correct answer)

- a. Invoice
- b. Parcel audit
- c. Air waybill
- d. Superbill

Guidance: level 1

:: Management ::

_____ is a process by which entities review the quality of all factors involved in production. ISO 9000 defines _____ as "A part of quality management focused on fulfilling quality requirements".

Exam Probability: **Low**

43. *Answer choices:*

(see index for correct answer)

- a. Quality control
- b. Enterprise smart grid
- c. Information excellence
- d. Shamrock Organization

:: E-commerce ::

E-commerce is the activity of buying or selling of products on online services or over the Internet. _____ draws on technologies such as mobile commerce, electronic funds transfer, supply chain management, Internet marketing, online transaction processing, electronic data interchange , inventory management systems, and automated data collection systems.

Exam Probability: **High**

44. *Answer choices:*

(see index for correct answer)

- a. Scriptlance
- b. EPages
- c. IDEAL
- d. Electronic commerce

:: Marketing ::

_____ or stock is the goods and materials that a business holds for the ultimate goal of resale .

Exam Probability: **Medium**

45. *Answer choices:*

(see index for correct answer)

- a. Inventory
- b. Cause-related loyalty marketing
- c. Servicescape
- d. Movie packaging

Guidance: level 1

:: Management ::

A _____ is an idea of the future or desired result that a person or a group of people envisions, plans and commits to achieve. People endeavor to reach _____ s within a finite time by setting deadlines.

Exam Probability: **Medium**

46. *Answer choices:*

(see index for correct answer)

- a. Scrum
- b. Business process interoperability
- c. Maryland StateStat
- d. Context analysis

Guidance: level 1

:: Marketing ::

_____ or stock control can be broadly defined as "the activity of checking a shop's stock." However, a more focused definition takes into account the more science-based, methodical practice of not only verifying a business' inventory but also focusing on the many related facets of inventory management "within an organisation to meet the demand placed upon that business economically." Other facets of _____ include supply chain management, production control, financial flexibility, and customer satisfaction. At the root of _____ , however, is the _____ problem, which involves determining when to order, how much to order, and the logistics of those decisions.

Exam Probability: **Low**

47. *Answer choices:*

(see index for correct answer)

- a. Inbound marketing automation
- b. Grey market
- c. Gold party
- d. Market development

:: Marketing ::

_____ —an information- and communication-based electronic exchange environment—is a relatively new concept in marketing. Since physical boundaries no longer interfere with buy/sell decisions, the world has grown into several industry specific _____ s which are integration of marketplaces through sophisticated computer and telecommunication technologies. The term _____ was introduced by Jeffrey Rayport and John Sviokla in 1994 in their article "Managing in the _____" that appeared in Harvard Business Review. In the article the authors distinguished between electronic and conventional markets. In a _____, information and/or physical goods are exchanged, and transactions take place through computers and networks. These networks consist of blogs, forum threads, and micro-blogging services like Twitter. Businesses and their customers are enabled to create conversations and two-way communications about products and services. These conversations may also happen outside the sphere of control of a given business, when a marketing campaign or customer-service issue captures the attention of web-savvy consumers.

Exam Probability: **High**

48. *Answer choices:*

(see index for correct answer)

- a. Macromarketing
- b. Marketing Week
- c. Marketspace
- d. Contact centre

:: ::

A _____ is an individual or institution that legally owns one or more shares of stock in a public or private corporation. _____ s may be referred to as members of a corporation. Legally, a person is not a _____ in a corporation until their name and other details are entered in the corporation's register of _____ s or members.

Exam Probability: **Low**

49. *Answer choices:*

(see index for correct answer)

- a. personal values
- b. Shareholder
- c. corporate values
- d. Character

:: Organizational structure ::

An _____ defines how activities such as task allocation, coordination, and supervision are directed toward the achievement of organizational aims.

Exam Probability: **Medium**

50. *Answer choices:*

(see index for correct answer)

- a. Followership
- b. Organizational structure
- c. Unorganisation
- d. Organization of the New York City Police Department

Guidance: level 1

:: Manufacturing ::

A _____ is a building for storing goods. _____ s are used by manufacturers, importers, exporters, wholesalers, transport businesses, customs, etc. They are usually large plain buildings in industrial parks on the outskirts of cities, towns or villages.

Exam Probability: **Low**

51. *Answer choices:*

(see index for correct answer)

- a. Computer appliance
- b. Warehouse
- c. Wearever Cookware
- d. Part number

Guidance: level 1

:: ::

Walter Elias Disney was an American entrepreneur, animator, voice actor and film producer. A pioneer of the American animation industry, he introduced several developments in the production of cartoons. As a film producer, Disney holds the record for most Academy Awards earned by an individual, having won 22 Oscars from 59 nominations. He was presented with two Golden Globe Special Achievement Awards and an Emmy Award, among other honors. Several of his films are included in the National Film Registry by the Library of Congress.

Exam Probability: **Medium**

52. *Answer choices:*

(see index for correct answer)

- a. deep-level diversity
- b. Walt Disney
- c. functional perspective
- d. imperative

Guidance: level 1

:: E-commerce ::

A _____ is a financial transaction involving a very small sum of money and usually one that occurs online. A number of _____ systems were proposed and developed in the mid-to-late 1990s, all of which were ultimately unsuccessful. A second generation of _____ systems emerged in the 2010s.

Exam Probability: **Medium**

53. *Answer choices:*

(see index for correct answer)

- a. Micropayment
- b. FastSpring
- c. ORCA
- d. Online marketplace

Guidance: level 1

:: Budgets ::

A _____ is a financial plan for a defined period, often one year. It may also include planned sales volumes and revenues, resource quantities, costs and expenses, assets, liabilities and cash flows. Companies, governments, families and other organizations use it to express strategic plans of activities or events in measurable terms.

54. *Answer choices:*

(see index for correct answer)

- a. Budgeted cost of work scheduled
- b. Budget
- c. Personal budget
- d. Zero deficit budget

Guidance: level 1

:: ::

_____ is both a research area and a practical skill encompassing the ability of an individual or organization to "lead" or guide other individuals, teams, or entire organizations. Specialist literature debates various viewpoints, contrasting Eastern and Western approaches to _____ , and also United States versus European approaches. U.S. academic environments define _____ as "a process of social influence in which a person can enlist the aid and support of others in the accomplishment of a common task".

Exam Probability: **Low**

55. *Answer choices:*

(see index for correct answer)

- a. hierarchical

- b. hierarchical perspective
- c. Leadership
- d. surface-level diversity

Guidance: level 1

:: Supply chain management ::

_____ is the process of finding and agreeing to terms, and acquiring goods, services, or works from an external source, often via a tendering or competitive bidding process. _____ is used to ensure the buyer receives goods, services, or works at the best possible price when aspects such as quality, quantity, time, and location are compared. Corporations and public bodies often define processes intended to promote fair and open competition for their business while minimizing risks such as exposure to fraud and collusion.

Exam Probability: **Medium**

56. *Answer choices:*

(see index for correct answer)

- a. Wave picking
- b. Procurement
- c. Scan-based trading
- d. Supply network operations

Guidance: level 1

:: E-commerce ::

IBM _____ also known as WCS is a software platform framework for e-commerce, including marketing, sales, customer and order processing functionality in a tailorable, integrated package. It is a single, unified platform which offers the ability to do business directly with consumers, with businesses, indirectly through channel partners, or all of these simultaneously. _____ is a customizable, scalable and high availability solution built on the Java - Java EE platform using open standards, such as XML, and Web services.

Exam Probability: **Medium**

57. *Answer choices:*

(see index for correct answer)

- a. Loppi
- b. PDQ terminal
- c. Presumed security
- d. Online auction tools

Guidance: level 1

:: Project management ::

_____ is the right to exercise power, which can be formalized by a state and exercised by way of judges, appointed executives of government, or the ecclesiastical or priestly appointed representatives of a God or other deities.

Exam Probability: **High**

58. *Answer choices:*

(see index for correct answer)

- a. Authority
- b. Sunk costs
- c. Initiative
- d. Organizational project management

Guidance: level 1

:: ::

In business, overhead or overhead expense refers to an ongoing expense of operating a business. Overheads are the expenditure which cannot be conveniently traced to or identified with any particular cost unit, unlike operating expenses such as raw material and labor. Therefore, overheads cannot be immediately associated with the products or services being offered, thus do not directly generate profits. However, overheads are still vital to business operations as they provide critical support for the business to carry out profit making activities. For example, _____ s such as the rent for a factory allows workers to manufacture products which can then be sold for a profit. Such expenses are incurred for output generally and not for particular work order; e.g., wages paid to watch and ward staff, heating and lighting expenses of factory, etc. Overheads are also very important cost element along with direct materials and direct labor.

Exam Probability: **High**

59. *Answer choices:*

(see index for correct answer)

- a. process perspective
- b. Sarbanes-Oxley act of 2002
- c. surface-level diversity
- d. Overhead cost

Guidance: level 1

Business ethics

Business ethics (also known as corporate ethics) is a form of applied ethics or professional ethics, that examines ethical principles and moral or ethical problems that can arise in a business environment. It applies to all aspects of business conduct and is relevant to the conduct of individuals and entire organizations. These ethics originate from individuals, organizational statements or from the legal system. These norms, values, ethical, and unethical practices are what is used to guide business. They help those businesses maintain a better connection with their stakeholders.

:: ::

Bernard Lawrence _____ is an American former market maker, investment advisor, financier, fraudster, and convicted felon, who is currently serving a federal prison sentence for offenses related to a massive Ponzi scheme. He is the former non-executive chairman of the NASDAQ stock market, the confessed operator of the largest Ponzi scheme in world history, and the largest financial fraud in U.S. history. Prosecutors estimated the fraud to be worth $64.8 billion based on the amounts in the accounts of _____ 's 4,800 clients as of November 30, 2008.

Exam Probability: **Low**

1. *Answer choices:*

(see index for correct answer)

- a. functional perspective
- b. imperative
- c. empathy
- d. information systems assessment

Guidance: level 1

:: Commercial crimes ::

_____ is an agreement between participants on the same side in a market to buy or sell a product, service, or commodity only at a fixed price, or maintain the market conditions such that the price is maintained at a given level by controlling supply and demand.

2. *Answer choices:*

(see index for correct answer)

- a. Warehouse bank
- b. Price fixing
- c. Cheque fraud
- d. Counterfeit

Guidance: level 1

:: ::

A _____ is a set of rules, often written, with regards to clothing. _____ s are created out of social perceptions and norms, and vary based on purpose, circumstances and occasions. Different societies and cultures are likely to have different _____ s.

Exam Probability: **Medium**

3. *Answer choices:*

(see index for correct answer)

- a. cultural
- b. Dress code
- c. similarity-attraction theory

- d. levels of analysis

Guidance: level 1

:: Leadership ::

_____ is a theory of leadership where a leader works with teams to identify needed change, creating a vision to guide the change through inspiration, and executing the change in tandem with committed members of a group; it is an integral part of the Full Range Leadership Model. _____ serves to enhance the motivation, morale, and job performance of followers through a variety of mechanisms; these include connecting the follower's sense of identity and self to a project and to the collective identity of the organization; being a role model for followers in order to inspire them and to raise their interest in the project; challenging followers to take greater ownership for their work, and understanding the strengths and weaknesses of followers, allowing the leader to align followers with tasks that enhance their performance.

Exam Probability: **Low**

4. *Answer choices:*

(see index for correct answer)

- a. Transformational leadership
- b. The Leadership Council
- c. servant leader
- d. European Center for Leadership Development

Guidance: level 1

:: ::

MCI, Inc. was an American telecommunication corporation, currently a subsidiary of Verizon Communications, with its main office in Ashburn, Virginia. The corporation was formed originally as a result of the merger of _____ and MCI Communications corporations, and used the name MCI _____ , succeeded by _____ , before changing its name to the present version on April 12, 2003, as part of the corporation's ending of its bankruptcy status. The company traded on NASDAQ as WCOM and MCIP . The corporation was purchased by Verizon Communications with the deal finalizing on January 6, 2006, and is now identified as that company's Verizon Enterprise Solutions division with the local residential divisions being integrated slowly into local Verizon subsidiaries.

Exam Probability: **Low**

5. *Answer choices:*

(see index for correct answer)

- a. process perspective
- b. deep-level diversity
- c. imperative
- d. hierarchical perspective

Guidance: level 1

:: Criminal law ::

_____ is the body of law that relates to crime. It proscribes conduct perceived as threatening, harmful, or otherwise endangering to the property, health, safety, and moral welfare of people inclusive of one's self. Most _____ is established by statute, which is to say that the laws are enacted by a legislature. _____ includes the punishment and rehabilitation of people who violate such laws. _____ varies according to jurisdiction, and differs from civil law, where emphasis is more on dispute resolution and victim compensation, rather than on punishment or rehabilitation. Criminal procedure is a formalized official activity that authenticates the fact of commission of a crime and authorizes punitive or rehabilitative treatment of the offender.

Exam Probability: **High**

6. *Answer choices:*

(see index for correct answer)

- a. Mala in se
- b. Criminal law
- c. mitigating factor
- d. complicit

Guidance: level 1

:: ::

_____ is the means to see, hear, or become aware of something or someone through our fundamental senses. The term _____ derives from the Latin word perceptio, and is the organization, identification, and interpretation of sensory information in order to represent and understand the presented information, or the environment.

Exam Probability: **Medium**

7. *Answer choices:*

(see index for correct answer)

- a. co-culture
- b. open system
- c. Perception
- d. hierarchical perspective

Guidance: level 1

:: Social enterprise ::

Corporate social responsibility   is a type of international private business self-regulation. While once it was possible to describe CSR as an internal organisational policy or a corporate ethic strategy, that time has passed as various international laws have been developed and various organisations have used their authority to push it beyond individual or even industry-wide initiatives. While it has been considered a form of corporate self-regulation for some time, over the last decade or so it has moved considerably from voluntary decisions at the level of individual organisations, to mandatory schemes at regional, national and even transnational levels.

Exam Probability: **Medium**

8. *Answer choices:*

(see index for correct answer)

- a. Social enterprise
- b. Social venture

Guidance: level 1

:: Offshoring ::

A _____ is the temporary suspension or permanent termination of employment of an employee or, more commonly, a group of employees for business reasons, such as personnel management or downsizing an organization. Originally, _____ referred exclusively to a temporary interruption in work, or employment but this has evolved to a permanent elimination of a position in both British and US English, requiring the addition of "temporary" to specify the original meaning of the word. A _____ is not to be confused with wrongful termination. Laid off workers or displaced workers are workers who have lost or left their jobs because their employer has closed or moved, there was insufficient work for them to do, or their position or shift was abolished . Downsizing in a company is defined to involve the reduction of employees in a workforce. Downsizing in companies became a popular practice in the 1980s and early 1990s as it was seen as a way to deliver better shareholder value as it helps to reduce the costs of employers . Indeed, recent research on downsizing in the U.S., UK, and Japan suggests that downsizing is being regarded by management as one of the preferred routes to help declining organizations, cutting unnecessary costs, and improve organizational performance. Usually a _____ occurs as a cost cutting measure.

9. *Answer choices:*

(see index for correct answer)

- a. Advanced Contact Solutions
- b. Offshore custom software development
- c. Offshore company
- d. Sourcing advisory

Guidance: level 1

:: Social responsibility ::

The United Nations Global Compact is a non-binding United Nations pact to encourage businesses worldwide to adopt sustainable and socially responsible policies, and to report on their implementation. The _____ is a principle-based framework for businesses, stating ten principles in the areas of human rights, labor, the environment and anti-corruption. Under the Global Compact, companies are brought together with UN agencies, labor groups and civil society. Cities can join the Global Compact through the Cities Programme.

10. *Answer choices:*

(see index for correct answer)

- a. Clann Credo

- b. UN Global Compact
- c. Stakeholder engagement
- d. Strategic corporate social responsibility

Guidance: level 1

:: Progressive Era in the United States ::

The Clayton Antitrust Act of 1914 , was a part of United States antitrust law with the goal of adding further substance to the U.S. antitrust law regime; the _____ sought to prevent anticompetitive practices in their incipiency. That regime started with the Sherman Antitrust Act of 1890, the first Federal law outlawing practices considered harmful to consumers . The _____ specified particular prohibited conduct, the three-level enforcement scheme, the exemptions, and the remedial measures.

Exam Probability: **Low**

11. *Answer choices:*
(see index for correct answer)

- a. Clayton Antitrust Act
- b. Clayton Act
- c. pragmatism

Guidance: level 1

:: Anti-capitalism ::

_____ is a range of economic and social systems characterised by social ownership of the means of production and workers' self-management, as well as the political theories and movements associated with them. Social ownership can be public, collective or cooperative ownership, or citizen ownership of equity. There are many varieties of _____ and there is no single definition encapsulating all of them, with social ownership being the common element shared by its various forms.

Exam Probability: **High**

12. *Answer choices:*

(see index for correct answer)

- a. Socialism
- b. Derrick Jensen
- c. Situationist International
- d. Communitarianism

Guidance: level 1

:: Cognitive biases ::

In personality psychology, _____ is the degree to which people believe that they have control over the outcome of events in their lives, as opposed to external forces beyond their control. Understanding of the concept was developed by Julian B. Rotter in 1954, and has since become an aspect of personality studies. A person's "locus" is conceptualized as internal or external .

Exam Probability: **Low**

13. *Answer choices:*

(see index for correct answer)

- a. Outcome bias
- b. Self-defeating prophecy
- c. Locus of control
- d. Extension neglect

Guidance: level 1

:: ::

_____ is "property consisting of land and the buildings on it, along with its natural resources such as crops, minerals or water; immovable property of this nature; an interest vested in this an item of real property, buildings or housing in general. Also: the business of _____ ; the profession of buying, selling, or renting land, buildings, or housing." It is a legal term used in jurisdictions whose legal system is derived from English common law, such as India, England, Wales, Northern Ireland, United States, Canada, Pakistan, Australia, and New Zealand.

Exam Probability: **Medium**

14. *Answer choices:*

(see index for correct answer)

- a. process perspective
- b. cultural
- c. similarity-attraction theory
- d. surface-level diversity

Guidance: level 1

:: Public relations terminology ::

_____ , also called "green sheen", is a form of spin in which green PR or green marketing is deceptively used to promote the perception that an organization's products, aims or policies are environmentally friendly. Evidence that an organization is _____ often comes from pointing out the spending differences: when significantly more money or time has been spent advertising being "green" , than is actually spent on environmentally sound practices. _____ efforts can range from changing the name or label of a product to evoke the natural environment on a product that contains harmful chemicals to multimillion-dollar marketing campaigns portraying highly polluting energy companies as eco-friendly.Publicized accusations of _____ have contributed to the term's increasing use.

Exam Probability: **Medium**

15. *Answer choices:*

(see index for correct answer)

- a. PR Gallery
- b. Crisis communication
- c. Greenwashing
- d. Green PR

Guidance: level 1

:: ::

A _____ is a form of business network, for example, a local organization of businesses whose goal is to further the interests of businesses. Business owners in towns and cities form these local societies to advocate on behalf of the business community. Local businesses are members, and they elect a board of directors or executive council to set policy for the chamber. The board or council then hires a President, CEO or Executive Director, plus staffing appropriate to size, to run the organization.

Exam Probability: **Medium**

16. *Answer choices:*

(see index for correct answer)

- a. corporate values
- b. Chamber of Commerce
- c. empathy
- d. interpersonal communication

:: ::

Sustainability is the process of people maintaining change in a balanced environment, in which the exploitation of resources, the direction of investments, the orientation of technological development and institutional change are all in harmony and enhance both current and future potential to meet human needs and aspirations. For many in the field, sustainability is defined through the following interconnected domains or pillars: environment, economic and social, which according to Fritjof Capra is based on the principles of Systems Thinking. Sub-domains of _____ development have been considered also: cultural, technological and political. While _____ development may be the organizing principle for sustainability for some, for others, the two terms are paradoxical . _____ development is the development that meets the needs of the present without compromising the ability of future generations to meet their own needs. Brundtland Report for the World Commission on Environment and Development introduced the term of _____ development.

Exam Probability: **High**

17. *Answer choices:*

(see index for correct answer)

- a. Sustainable
- b. corporate values
- c. surface-level diversity
- d. hierarchical

:: ::

_____ is the study and management of exchange relationships. _____ is the business process of creating relationships with and satisfying customers. With its focus on the customer, _____ is one of the premier components of business management.

Exam Probability: **Low**

18. *Answer choices:*

(see index for correct answer)

- a. open system
- b. corporate values
- c. Character
- d. similarity-attraction theory

Guidance: level 1

:: International trade ::

_____ involves the transfer of goods or services from one person or entity to another, often in exchange for money. A system or network that allows _____ is called a market.

19. *Answer choices:*

(see index for correct answer)

- a. Silk Road
- b. Orderly marketing arrangement
- c. Reciprocity
- d. Trade

Guidance: level 1

:: United States federal trade legislation ::

The _____ of 1914 established the Federal Trade Commission. The Act, signed into law by Woodrow Wilson in 1914, outlaws unfair methods of competition and outlaws unfair acts or practices that affect commerce.

Exam Probability: **High**

20. *Answer choices:*

(see index for correct answer)

- a. Federal Trade Commission Act
- b. Tariff of 1824
- c. Bell Trade Act
- d. Cuban Democracy Act

:: ::

The _____ of 1977 is a United States federal law known primarily for two of its main provisions: one that addresses accounting transparency requirements under the Securities Exchange Act of 1934 and another concerning bribery of foreign officials. The Act was amended in 1988 and in 1998, and has been subject to continued congressional concerns, namely whether its enforcement discourages U.S. companies from investing abroad.

Exam Probability: **Low**

21. *Answer choices:*

(see index for correct answer)

- a. Foreign Corrupt Practices Act
- b. functional perspective
- c. levels of analysis
- d. open system

:: ::

A _____ is the ability to carry out a task with determined results often within a given amount of time, energy, or both. _____ s can often be divided into domain-general and domain-specific _____ s. For example, in the domain of work, some general _____ s would include time management, teamwork and leadership, self-motivation and others, whereas domain-specific _____ s would be used only for a certain job. _____ usually requires certain environmental stimuli and situations to assess the level of _____ being shown and used.

Exam Probability: **Medium**

22. *Answer choices:*

(see index for correct answer)

- a. deep-level diversity
- b. cultural
- c. imperative
- d. Character

Guidance: level 1

:: ::

A _____ is an organization, usually a group of people or a company, authorized to act as a single entity and recognized as such in law. Early incorporated entities were established by charter . Most jurisdictions now allow the creation of new _____ s through registration.

23. *Answer choices:*

(see index for correct answer)

- a. levels of analysis
- b. Corporation
- c. functional perspective
- d. cultural

Guidance: level 1

:: ::

The _____ , the Calvinist work ethic or the Puritan work ethic is a work ethic concept in theology, sociology, economics and history that emphasizes that hard work, discipline and frugality are a result of a person's subscription to the values espoused by the Protestant faith, particularly Calvinism. The phrase was initially coined in 1904–1905 by Max Weber in his book The Protestant Ethic and the Spirit of Capitalism.

Exam Probability: **Medium**

24. *Answer choices:*

(see index for correct answer)

- a. functional perspective
- b. hierarchical

- c. process perspective
- d. Protestant work ethic

Guidance: level 1

:: Production and manufacturing ::

_____ is a set of techniques and tools for process improvement. Though as a shortened form it may be found written as 6S, it should not be confused with the methodology known as 6S .

Exam Probability: **Medium**

25. *Answer choices:*
(see index for correct answer)

- a. Detailed division of labor
- b. Fieldbus Foundation
- c. Six Sigma
- d. Rolled throughput yield

Guidance: level 1

:: Corporate scandals ::

The _____ was a privately held international group of financial services companies controlled by Allen Stanford, until it was seized by United States authorities in early 2009. Headquartered in the Galleria Tower II in Uptown Houston, Texas, it had 50 offices in several countries, mainly in the Americas, included the Stanford International Bank, and said it managed US$8.5 billion of assets for more than 30,000 clients in 136 countries on six continents. On February 17, 2009, U.S. Federal agents placed the company into receivership due to charges of fraud. Ten days later, the U.S. Securities and Exchange Commission amended its complaint to accuse Stanford of turning the company into a "massive Ponzi scheme".

Exam Probability: **Low**

26. *Answer choices:*

(see index for correct answer)

- a. Harken Energy scandal
- b. China Aviation Oil
- c. Stanford Financial Group
- d. Lynn Brewer

Guidance: level 1

:: Corporations law ::

A normal _____ consists of various departments that contribute to the company's overall mission and goals. Common departments include Marketing, [Finance, [[Operations managementOperations, Human Resource, and IT. These five divisions represent the major departments within a publicly traded company, though there are often smaller departments within autonomous firms. There is typically a CEO, and Board of Directors composed of the directors of each department. There are also company presidents, vice presidents, and CFOs.There is a great diversity in corporate forms as enterprises may range from single company to multi-corporate conglomerate. The four main _____ s are Functional, Divisional, Geographic, and the Matrix.Realistically, most corporations tend to have a "hybrid" structure, which is a combination of different models with one dominant strategy.

Exam Probability: **Medium**

27. *Answer choices:*

(see index for correct answer)

- a. Legal personality
- b. Drag-along right
- c. Corporate law
- d. United Kingdom company law

Guidance: level 1

:: ::

The Federal National Mortgage Association , commonly known as _____ , is a United States government-sponsored enterprise and, since 1968, a publicly traded company. Founded in 1938 during the Great Depression as part of the New Deal, the corporation's purpose is to expand the secondary mortgage market by securitizing mortgage loans in the form of mortgage-backed securities , allowing lenders to reinvest their assets into more lending and in effect increasing the number of lenders in the mortgage market by reducing the reliance on locally based savings and loan associations . Its brother organization is the Federal Home Loan Mortgage Corporation , better known as Freddie Mac. As of 2018, _____ is ranked #21 on the Fortune 500 rankings of the largest United States corporations by total revenue.

Exam Probability: **High**

28. *Answer choices:*

(see index for correct answer)

- a. empathy
- b. information systems assessment
- c. process perspective
- d. Character

Guidance: level 1

:: Fraud ::

In law, _____ is intentional deception to secure unfair or unlawful gain, or to deprive a victim of a legal right. _____ can violate civil law, a criminal law, or it may cause no loss of money, property or legal right but still be an element of another civil or criminal wrong. The purpose of _____ may be monetary gain or other benefits, for example by obtaining a passport, travel document, or driver's license, or mortgage _____, where the perpetrator may attempt to qualify for a mortgage by way of false statements.

Exam Probability: **Medium**

29. *Answer choices:*

(see index for correct answer)

- a. Cheat sheet
- b. Secret profit
- c. Medicare fraud
- d. Fraud

Guidance: level 1

:: Private equity ::

In finance, a high-yield bond is a bond that is rated below investment grade. These bonds have a higher risk of default or other adverse credit events, but typically pay higher yields than better quality bonds in order to make them attractive to investors.

Exam Probability: **Low**

30. *Answer choices:*

(see index for correct answer)

- a. High-yield
- b. Earnout
- c. Junk bond
- d. Airwide Solutions

Guidance: level 1

:: Competition regulators ::

The _____ is an independent agency of the United States government, established in 1914 by the _____ Act. Its principal mission is the promotion of consumer protection and the elimination and prevention of anticompetitive business practices, such as coercive monopoly. It is headquartered in the _____ Building in Washington, D.C.

Exam Probability: **Medium**

31. *Answer choices:*

(see index for correct answer)

- a. Directorate-General for Competition
- b. Competition Commission of India

- c. Federal Trade Commission
- d. Competition Appeal Tribunal

Guidance: level 1

:: Business law ::

A _____ is an arrangement where parties, known as partners, agree to cooperate to advance their mutual interests. The partners in a _____ may be individuals, businesses, interest-based organizations, schools, governments or combinations. Organizations may partner to increase the likelihood of each achieving their mission and to amplify their reach. A _____ may result in issuing and holding equity or may be only governed by a contract.

Exam Probability: **Medium**

32. *Answer choices:*

(see index for correct answer)

- a. Jurisdictional strike
- b. Partnership
- c. Business license
- d. Inslaw

Guidance: level 1

:: Business ethics ::

_____ is a persistent pattern of mistreatment from others in the workplace that causes either physical or emotional harm. It can include such tactics as verbal, nonverbal, psychological, physical abuse and humiliation. This type of workplace aggression is particularly difficult because, unlike the typical school bully, workplace bullies often operate within the established rules and policies of their organization and their society. In the majority of cases, bullying in the workplace is reported as having been by someone who has authority over their victim. However, bullies can also be peers, and occasionally subordinates. Research has also investigated the impact of the larger organizational context on bullying as well as the group-level processes that impact on the incidence and maintenance of bullying behaviour. Bullying can be covert or overt. It may be missed by superiors; it may be known by many throughout the organization. Negative effects are not limited to the targeted individuals, and may lead to a decline in employee morale and a change in organizational culture. It can also take place as overbearing supervision, constant criticism, and blocking promotions.

Exam Probability: **Low**

33. *Answer choices:*

(see index for correct answer)

- a. Sexual harassment
- b. Workplace bullying
- c. Corruption of Foreign Public Officials Act
- d. Corporate sustainability

Guidance: level 1

:: Leadership ::

_____ is leadership that is directed by respect for ethical beliefs and values and for the dignity and rights of others. It is thus related to concepts such as trust, honesty, consideration, charisma, and fairness.

Exam Probability: **Low**

34. *Answer choices:*

(see index for correct answer)

- a. Situational leadership theory
- b. The Leadership Council
- c. Evolutionary leadership theory
- d. Moral example

Guidance: level 1

:: Workplace ::

In business management, _____ is a management style whereby a manager closely observes and/or controls the work of his/her subordinates or employees.

Exam Probability: **High**

35. *Answer choices:*

(see index for correct answer)

- a. Occupational stress
- b. Workplace conflict
- c. Counterproductive work behavior
- d. Workplace aggression

Guidance: level 1

:: Power (social and political) ::

_____ is a form of reverence gained by a leader who has strong interpersonal relationship skills. _____ , as an aspect of personal power, becomes particularly important as organizational leadership becomes increasingly about collaboration and influence, rather than command and control.

Exam Probability: **Low**

36. *Answer choices:*

(see index for correct answer)

- a. Referent power
- b. need for power
- c. Expert power

Guidance: level 1

:: Writs ::

In common law, a writ of _____ is a writ whereby a private individual who assists a prosecution can receive all or part of any penalty imposed. Its name is an abbreviation of the Latin phrase _____ pro domino rege quam pro se ipso in hac parte sequitur, meaning "[he] who sues in this matter for the king as well as for himself."

Exam Probability: **Low**

37. *Answer choices:*

(see index for correct answer)

- a. Writ of execution
- b. Qui tam

Guidance: level 1

:: Business ethics ::

A _____ is a person who exposes any kind of information or activity that is deemed illegal, unethical, or not correct within an organization that is either private or public. The information of alleged wrongdoing can be classified in many ways: violation of company policy/rules, law, regulation, or threat to public interest/national security, as well as fraud, and corruption. Those who become _____ s can choose to bring information or allegations to surface either internally or externally. Internally, a _____ can bring his/her accusations to the attention of other people within the accused organization such as an immediate supervisor. Externally, a _____ can bring allegations to light by contacting a third party outside of an accused organization such as the media, government, law enforcement, or those who are concerned. _____ s, however, take the risk of facing stiff reprisal and retaliation from those who are accused or alleged of wrongdoing.

Exam Probability: **Low**

38. *Answer choices:*

(see index for correct answer)

- a. Repugnant market
- b. Whistleblower
- c. Destructionism
- d. CUC International

Guidance: level 1

:: Business ethics ::

_____ is a type of international private business self-regulation. While once it was possible to describe CSR as an internal organisational policy or a corporate ethic strategy, that time has passed as various international laws have been developed and various organisations have used their authority to push it beyond individual or even industry-wide initiatives. While it has been considered a form of corporate self-regulation for some time, over the last decade or so it has moved considerably from voluntary decisions at the level of individual organisations, to mandatory schemes at regional, national and even transnational levels.

Exam Probability: **Low**

39. *Answer choices:*

(see index for correct answer)

- a. Altruistic corporate social responsibility
- b. Corporate social responsibility
- c. Minecode
- d. Business Ethics Quarterly

Guidance: level 1

:: ::

Oriental Nicety, formerly _____ , Exxon Mediterranean, SeaRiver Mediterranean, S/R Mediterranean, Mediterranean, and Dong Fang Ocean, was an oil tanker that gained notoriety after running aground in Prince William Sound spilling hundreds of thousands of barrels of crude oil in Alaska. On March 24, 1989, while owned by the former Exxon Shipping Company, and captained by Joseph Hazelwood and First Mate James Kunkel bound for Long Beach, California, the vessel ran aground on the Bligh Reef resulting in the second largest oil spill in United States history. The size of the spill is estimated to have been 40,900 to 120,000 m3 , or 257,000 to 750,000 barrels. In 1989, the _____ oil spill was listed as the 54th largest spill in history.

Exam Probability: **High**

40. *Answer choices:*

(see index for correct answer)

- a. similarity-attraction theory
- b. deep-level diversity
- c. interpersonal communication
- d. surface-level diversity

Guidance: level 1

:: ::

_____ , O.S.A. was a German professor of theology, composer, priest, monk, and a seminal figure in the Protestant Reformation.

41. *Answer choices:*

(see index for correct answer)

- a. similarity-attraction theory
- b. corporate values
- c. imperative
- d. Martin Luther

Guidance: level 1

:: ::

_____ is a region of India consisting of the Indian states of Bihar, Jharkhand, West Bengal, Odisha and also the union territory Andaman and Nicobar Islands. West Bengal`s capital Kolkata is the largest city of this region. The Kolkata Metropolitan Area is the country`s third largest.

Exam Probability: **Low**

42. *Answer choices:*

(see index for correct answer)

- a. corporate values
- b. similarity-attraction theory
- c. East India

- d. process perspective

Guidance: level 1

:: ::

A _____ is a problem offering two possibilities, neither of which is
unambiguously acceptable or preferable. The possibilities are termed the horns
of the _____ , a clichéd usage, but distinguishing the _____ from
other kinds of predicament as a matter of usage.

Exam Probability: **Low**

43. *Answer choices:*

(see index for correct answer)

- a. Dilemma
- b. levels of analysis
- c. personal values
- d. corporate values

Guidance: level 1

:: Auditing ::

_____ refers to the independence of the internal auditor or of the external auditor from parties that may have a financial interest in the business being audited. Independence requires integrity and an objective approach to the audit process. The concept requires the auditor to carry out his or her work freely and in an objective manner.

Exam Probability: **Low**

44. *Answer choices:*

(see index for correct answer)

- a. Negative assurance
- b. Auditor independence
- c. Internal control
- d. Management audit

Guidance: level 1

:: Social philosophy ::

The "_____" is a method of determining the morality of issues. It asks a decision-maker to make a choice about a social or moral issue, and assumes that they have enough information to know the consequences of their possible decisions for everyone but would not know, or would not take into account, which person he or she is. The theory contends that not knowing one`s ultimate position in society would lead to the creation of a just system, as the decision-maker would not want to make decisions which benefit a certain group at the expense of another, because the decision-maker could theoretically end up in either group. The idea has been present in moral philosophy at least since the eighteenth century. The _____ is part of a long tradition of thinking in terms of a social contract that includes the writings of Immanuel Kant, Thomas Hobbes, John Locke, Jean Jacques Rousseau, and Thomas Jefferson. Prominent modern names attached to it are John Harsanyi and John Rawls.

Exam Probability: **Medium**

45. *Answer choices:*

(see index for correct answer)

- a. Freedom to contract
- b. Invisible hand
- c. Veil of ignorance
- d. Societal attitudes towards abortion

Guidance: level 1

:: United Kingdom labour law ::

The _____ was a series of programs, public work projects, financial reforms, and regulations enacted by President Franklin D. Roosevelt in the United States between 1933 and 1936. It responded to needs for relief, reform, and recovery from the Great Depression. Major federal programs included the Civilian Conservation Corps , the Civil Works Administration , the Farm Security Administration , the National Industrial Recovery Act of 1933 and the Social Security Administration . They provided support for farmers, the unemployed, youth and the elderly. The _____ included new constraints and safeguards on the banking industry and efforts to re-inflate the economy after prices had fallen sharply. _____ programs included both laws passed by Congress as well as presidential executive orders during the first term of the presidency of Franklin D. Roosevelt.

Exam Probability: **Medium**

46. *Answer choices:*

(see index for correct answer)

- a. New Deal
- b. Mutual trust and confidence
- c. Employment Protection Act 1975
- d. Labour Exchanges Act 1909

Guidance: level 1

:: Price fixing convictions ::

_____ AG is a German multinational conglomerate company headquartered in Berlin and Munich and the largest industrial manufacturing company in Europe with branch offices abroad.

Exam Probability: **Medium**

47. *Answer choices:*

(see index for correct answer)

- a. ThyssenKrupp
- b. JJB Sports
- c. Asahi Glass Co.
- d. Siemens

Guidance: level 1

:: Globalization-related theories ::

_____ is an economic system based on the private ownership of the means of production and their operation for profit. Characteristics central to _____ include private property, capital accumulation, wage labor, voluntary exchange, a price system, and competitive markets. In a capitalist market economy, decision-making and investment are determined by every owner of wealth, property or production ability in financial and capital markets, whereas prices and the distribution of goods and services are mainly determined by competition in goods and services markets.

Exam Probability: **Low**

48. *Answer choices:*

(see index for correct answer)

- a. Capitalism
- b. post-industrial
- c. Economic Development

Guidance: level 1

:: Advertising techniques ::

The _____ is a story from the Trojan War about the subterfuge that the Greeks used to enter the independent city of Troy and win the war. In the canonical version, after a fruitless 10-year siege, the Greeks constructed a huge wooden horse, and hid a select force of men inside including Odysseus. The Greeks pretended to sail away, and the Trojans pulled the horse into their city as a victory trophy. That night the Greek force crept out of the horse and opened the gates for the rest of the Greek army, which had sailed back under cover of night. The Greeks entered and destroyed the city of Troy, ending the war.

Exam Probability: **High**

49. *Answer choices:*

(see index for correct answer)

- a. Trojan horse
- b. Incomplete comparison
- c. Hard sell

- d. Debranding

Guidance: level 1

:: Statutory law ::

_____ or statute law is written law set down by a body of legislature or by a singular legislator . This is as opposed to oral or customary law; or regulatory law promulgated by the executive or common law of the judiciary. Statutes may originate with national, state legislatures or local municipalities.

Exam Probability: **High**

50. *Answer choices:*

(see index for correct answer)

- a. incorporation by reference
- b. ratification
- c. statute law
- d. Statutory law

Guidance: level 1

:: Corporate crime ::

_____ LLP, based in Chicago, was an American holding company. Formerly one of the "Big Five" accounting firms , the firm had provided auditing, tax, and consulting services to large corporations. By 2001, it had become one of the world's largest multinational companies.

Exam Probability: **Medium**

51. *Answer choices:*

(see index for correct answer)

- a. NatWest Three
- b. John Peter Galanis
- c. FirstEnergy
- d. Arthur Andersen

Guidance: level 1

:: Anti-competitive behaviour ::

_____ is a secret cooperation or deceitful agreement in order to deceive others, although not necessarily illegal, as a conspiracy. A secret agreement between two or more parties to limit open competition by deceiving, misleading, or defrauding others of their legal rights, or to obtain an objective forbidden by law typically by defrauding or gaining an unfair market advantage is an example of _____ . It is an agreement among firms or individuals to divide a market, set prices, limit production or limit opportunities.It can involve "unions, wage fixing, kickbacks, or misrepresenting the independence of the relationship between the colluding parties". In legal terms, all acts effected by _____ are considered void.

Exam Probability: **Medium**

52. *Answer choices:*

(see index for correct answer)

- a. Restraint of trade
- b. Collusion
- c. Resale price maintenance
- d. Byrd Amendment

Guidance: level 1

:: ::

The _____ is an 1848 political pamphlet by the German philosophers Karl Marx and Friedrich Engels. Commissioned by the Communist League and originally published in London just as the Revolutions of 1848 began to erupt, the Manifesto was later recognised as one of the world's most influential political documents. It presents an analytical approach to the class struggle and the conflicts of capitalism and the capitalist mode of production, rather than a prediction of communism's potential future forms.

Exam Probability: **High**

53. *Answer choices:*

(see index for correct answer)

- a. functional perspective
- b. Communist Manifesto
- c. hierarchical perspective
- d. empathy

Guidance: level 1

:: ::

_____ is a product prepared from the leaves of the _____ plant by curing them. The plant is part of the genus Nicotiana and of the Solanaceae family. While more than 70 species of _____ are known, the chief commercial crop is N. tabacum. The more potent variant N. rustica is also used around the world.

Exam Probability: **Low**

54. *Answer choices:*

(see index for correct answer)

- a. empathy
- b. imperative
- c. Tobacco
- d. surface-level diversity

Guidance: level 1

:: Trade unions ::

A _____ was a group formed of private citizens to administer law and order where they considered governmental structures to be inadequate. The term is commonly associated with the frontier areas of the American West in the mid-19th century, where groups attacked cattle rustlers and gangs, and people at gold mining claims. As non-state organizations no functioning checks existed to protect against excessive force or safeguard due process from the committees. In the years prior to the Civil War, some committees worked to free slaves and transport them to freedom.

Exam Probability: **Medium**

55. *Answer choices:*

(see index for correct answer)

- a. Independent union
- b. Bump
- c. Union democracy
- d. Vigilance committee

Guidance: level 1

:: ::

The _____ is an American stock exchange located at 11 Wall Street, Lower Manhattan, New York City, New York. It is by far the world's largest stock exchange by market capitalization of its listed companies at US$30.1 trillion as of February 2018. The average daily trading value was approximately US$169 billion in 2013. The NYSE trading floor is located at 11 Wall Street and is composed of 21 rooms used for the facilitation of trading. A fifth trading room, located at 30 Broad Street, was closed in February 2007. The main building and the 11 Wall Street building were designated National Historic Landmarks in 1978.

Exam Probability: **Low**

56. *Answer choices:*

(see index for correct answer)

- a. deep-level diversity
- b. New York Stock Exchange
- c. personal values
- d. surface-level diversity

:: Business ethics ::

The _____ are the names of two corporate codes of conduct, developed by the African-American preacher Rev. Leon Sullivan, promoting corporate social responsibility.

Exam Probability: **High**

57. *Answer choices:*
(see index for correct answer)

- a. United Nations Global Compact
- b. Sullivan principles
- c. Proceedings of the International Association for Business and Society
- d. Contingent work

:: ::

_____ ism is a form of government characterized by strong central power and limited political freedoms. Individual freedoms are subordinate to the state and there is no constitutional accountability and rule of law under an _____ regime. _____ regimes can be autocratic with power concentrated in one person or it can be more spread out between multiple officials and government institutions. Juan Linz's influential 1964 description of _____ ism characterized _____ political systems by four qualities.

Exam Probability: **High**

58. *Answer choices:*

(see index for correct answer)

- a. Authoritarian
- b. surface-level diversity
- c. imperative
- d. co-culture

Guidance: level 1

:: Toxicology ::

_____ or lead-based paint is paint containing lead. As pigment, lead chromate , Lead oxide, , and lead carbonate are the most common forms. Lead is added to paint to accelerate drying, increase durability, maintain a fresh appearance, and resist moisture that causes corrosion. It is one of the main health and environmental hazards associated with paint. In some countries, lead continues to be added to paint intended for domestic use, whereas countries such as the U.S. and the UK have regulations prohibiting this, although _____ may still be found in older properties painted prior to the introduction of such regulations. Although lead has been banned from household paints in the United States since 1978, paint used in road markings may still contain it. Alternatives such as water-based, lead-free traffic paint are readily available, and many states and federal agencies have changed their purchasing contracts to buy these instead.

Exam Probability: **Low**

59. *Answer choices:*

(see index for correct answer)

- a. Lead paint
- b. Evidence-based toxicology
- c. Phytotreatment
- d. Toxicant

Guidance: level 1

Accounting

Accounting or accountancy is the measurement, processing, and communication of financial information about economic entities such as businesses and corporations. The modern field was established by the Italian mathematician Luca Pacioli in 1494. Accounting, which has been called the "language of business", measures the results of an organization's economic activities and conveys this information to a variety of users, including investors, creditors, management, and regulators.

:: Generally Accepted Accounting Principles ::

In accounting, _____ is the income that a business have from its normal business activities, usually from the sale of goods and services to customers. _____ is also referred to as sales or turnover. Some companies receive _____ from interest, royalties, or other fees. _____ may refer to business income in general, or it may refer to the amount, in a monetary unit, earned during a period of time, as in "Last year, Company X had _____ of $42 million". Profits or net income generally imply total _____ minus total expenses in a given period. In accounting, in the balance statement it is a subsection of the Equity section and _____ increases equity, it is often referred to as the "top line" due to its position on the income statement at the very top. This is to be contrasted with the "bottom line" which denotes net income .

Exam Probability: **Medium**

1. *Answer choices:*

(see index for correct answer)

- a. Matching principle
- b. Trial balance
- c. Cost pool
- d. Revenue

Guidance: level 1

:: Labor terms ::

_____ , often called DI or disability income insurance, or income protection, is a form of insurance that insures the beneficiary's earned income against the risk that a disability creates a barrier for a worker to complete the core functions of their work. For example, the worker may suffer from an inability to maintain composure in the case of psychological disorders or an injury, illness or condition that causes physical impairment or incapacity to work. It encompasses paid sick leave, short-term disability benefits , and long-term disability benefits . Statistics show that in the US a disabling accident occurs, on average, once every second. In fact, nearly 18.5% of Americans are currently living with a disability, and 1 out of every 4 persons in the US workforce will suffer a disabling injury before retirement.

Exam Probability: **High**

2. *Answer choices:*

(see index for correct answer)

- a. Civilian workers
- b. Disability insurance
- c. Capital services
- d. Strike action

Guidance: level 1

:: Taxation ::

_____ is an estimate of the market value of a property, based on what a knowledgeable, willing, and unpressured buyer would probably pay to a knowledgeable, willing, and unpressured seller in the market. An estimate of _____ may be founded either on precedent or extrapolation. _____ differs from the intrinsic value that an individual may place on the same asset based on their own preferences and circumstances.

Exam Probability: **Medium**

3. *Answer choices:*

(see index for correct answer)

- a. Kharaj
- b. Tax investigation
- c. Fair market value
- d. Tax rate

Guidance: level 1

:: Stock market ::

A _____ , equity market or share market is the aggregation of buyers and sellers of stocks , which represent ownership claims on businesses; these may include securities listed on a public stock exchange, as well as stock that is only traded privately. Examples of the latter include shares of private companies which are sold to investors through equity crowdfunding platforms. Stock exchanges list shares of common equity as well as other security types, e.g. corporate bonds and convertible bonds.

4. *Answer choices:*

(see index for correct answer)

- a. Preferred stock
- b. Penny stock
- c. Abnormal return
- d. Ticker tape

Guidance: level 1

:: Accounting terminology ::

_____ or capital expense is the money a company spends to buy, maintain, or improve its fixed assets, such as buildings, vehicles, equipment, or land. It is considered a _____ when the asset is newly purchased or when money is used towards extending the useful life of an existing asset, such as repairing the roof.

Exam Probability: **High**

5. *Answer choices:*

(see index for correct answer)

- a. Adjusting entries
- b. Accounting equation

- c. outstanding balance
- d. Capital expenditure

Guidance: level 1

:: Basic financial concepts ::

_____ is a sustained increase in the general price level of goods and services in an economy over a period of time. When the general price level rises, each unit of currency buys fewer goods and services; consequently, _____ reflects a reduction in the purchasing power per unit of money a loss of real value in the medium of exchange and unit of account within the economy. The measure of _____ is the _____ rate, the annualized percentage change in a general price index, usually the consumer price index, over time. The opposite of _____ is deflation.

Exam Probability: **High**

6. *Answer choices:*

(see index for correct answer)

- a. Maturity date
- b. Tax shield
- c. Lodgement
- d. Leverage cycle

Guidance: level 1

:: Financial regulatory authorities of the United States ::

The _____ is the revenue service of the United States federal government. The government agency is a bureau of the Department of the Treasury, and is under the immediate direction of the Commissioner of Internal Revenue, who is appointed to a five-year term by the President of the United States. The IRS is responsible for collecting taxes and administering the Internal Revenue Code, the main body of federal statutory tax law of the United States. The duties of the IRS include providing tax assistance to taxpayers and pursuing and resolving instances of erroneous or fraudulent tax filings. The IRS has also overseen various benefits programs, and enforces portions of the Affordable Care Act.

Exam Probability: **High**

7. *Answer choices:*

(see index for correct answer)

- a. Office of the Comptroller of the Currency
- b. Internal Revenue Service
- c. Commodity Futures Trading Commission
- d. Farm Credit Administration

Guidance: level 1

:: Taxation and efficiency ::

_____ is the legal usage of the tax regime in a single territory to one's own advantage to reduce the amount of tax that is payable by means that are within the law. Tax sheltering is very similar, although unlike _____ tax sheltering is not necessarily legal. Tax havens are jurisdictions which facilitate reduced taxes.

Exam Probability: **Low**

8. *Answer choices:*

(see index for correct answer)

- a. Tax exporting
- b. Tax avoidance
- c. Capital flight
- d. Fiscal illusion

Guidance: level 1

:: Generally Accepted Accounting Principles ::

A _____ , in accrual accounting, is any account where the asset or liability is not realized until a future date , e.g. annuities, charges, taxes, income, etc. The deferred item may be carried, dependent on type of _____ , as either an asset or liability. See also accrual.

Exam Probability: **Low**

9. *Answer choices:*

(see index for correct answer)

- a. Trial balance
- b. Fin 48
- c. Deferral
- d. Petty cash

Guidance: level 1

:: Business law ::

A _____ , also known as the sole trader, individual entrepreneurship or proprietorship, is a type of enterprise that is owned and run by one person and in which there is no legal distinction between the owner and the business entity. A sole trader does not necessarily work `alone`—it is possible for the sole trader to employ other people.

Exam Probability: **Medium**

10. *Answer choices:*

(see index for correct answer)

- a. Sole proprietorship
- b. Ease of doing business index
- c. Subordination
- d. Ordinary course of business

:: Inventory ::

_____ is the amount of inventory a company has in stock at the end of its fiscal year. It is closely related with _____ cost, which is the amount of money spent to get these goods in stock. It should be calculated at the lower of cost or market.

Exam Probability: **Medium**

11. *Answer choices:*

(see index for correct answer)

- a. LIFO
- b. Consignment stock
- c. Ending inventory
- d. Phantom inventory

:: Asset ::

_____ s, also known as tangible assets or property, plant and equipment , is a term used in accounting for assets and property that cannot easily be converted into cash. This can be compared with current assets such as cash or bank accounts, described as liquid assets. In most cases, only tangible assets are referred to as fixed. IAS 16 defines _____ s as assets whose future economic benefit is probable to flow into the entity, whose cost can be measured reliably. _____ s belong to one of 2 types:"Freehold Assets" – assets which are purchased with legal right of ownership and used,and "Leasehold Assets" – assets used by owner without legal right for a particular period of time.

Exam Probability: **Low**

12. *Answer choices:*
(see index for correct answer)

- a. Fixed asset
- b. Asset

Guidance: level 1

:: Ethically disputed business practices ::

_____ , in accounting, is the act of intentionally influencing the process of financial reporting to obtain some private gain. _____ involves the alteration of financial reports to mislead stakeholders about the organization's underlying performance, or to "influence contractual outcomes that depend on reported accounting numbers."

Exam Probability: **High**

13. *Answer choices:*

(see index for correct answer)

- a. Earnings management
- b. Operation Red Spider
- c. at-will
- d. Market saturation

Guidance: level 1

:: Free accounting software ::

A _____ is the principal book or computer file for recording and totaling economic transactions measured in terms of a monetary unit of account by account type, with debits and credits in separate columns and a beginning monetary balance and ending monetary balance for each account.

Exam Probability: **Low**

14. *Answer choices:*

(see index for correct answer)

- a. Ledger
- b. HomeBank
- c. GnuCash

- d. Grisbi

Guidance: level 1

:: Accounting in the United States ::

_____ refers to a Memorandum of Understanding signed in September 2002 between the Financial Accounting Standards Board , the US standard setter, and the International Accounting Standards Board . The agreement is so called as it was reached in Norwalk.

Exam Probability: **High**

15. *Answer choices:*
(see index for correct answer)

- a. Trueblood Committee
- b. Legal liability of certified public accountants
- c. Norwalk Agreement
- d. Other comprehensive basis of accounting

Guidance: level 1

:: Types of business entity ::

A sole _____ , also known as the sole trader, individual entrepreneurship or _____ , is a type of enterprise that is owned and run by one person and in which there is no legal distinction between the owner and the business entity. A sole trader does not necessarily work `alone`—it is possible for the sole trader to employ other people.

Exam Probability: **Medium**

16. *Answer choices:*

(see index for correct answer)

- a. Intermediary corporation
- b. Delaware General Corporation Law
- c. Proprietorship
- d. Dual-listed company

Guidance: level 1

:: ::

Generally speaking, a _____ begins on the New Year`s Day of the given calendar system and ends on the day before the following New Year`s Day, and thus consists of a whole number of days. A year can also be measured by starting on any other named day of the calendar, and ending on the day before this named day in the following year. This may be termed a "year`s time", but not a " _____ ". To reconcile the _____ with the astronomical cycle certain years contain extra days .

17. *Answer choices:*

(see index for correct answer)

- a. hierarchical
- b. Calendar year
- c. co-culture
- d. deep-level diversity

Guidance: level 1

:: Hazard analysis ::

Broadly speaking, a _____ is the combined effort of 1. identifying and analyzing potential events that may negatively impact individuals, assets, and/or the environment ; and 2. making judgments "on the tolerability of the risk on the basis of a risk analysis" while considering influencing factors . Put in simpler terms, a _____ analyzes what can go wrong, how likely it is to happen, what the potential consequences are, and how tolerable the identified risk is. As part of this process, the resulting determination of risk may be expressed in a quantitative or qualitative fashion. The _____ is an inherent part of an overall risk management strategy, which attempts to, after a _____ , "introduce control measures to eliminate or reduce" any potential risk-related consequences.

Exam Probability: **Medium**

18. *Answer choices:*

(see index for correct answer)

- a. Hazard
- b. Swiss cheese model
- c. Hazard identification
- d. Risk assessment

Guidance: level 1

:: ::

In accounting, the _____ is a measure of the number of times inventory is sold or used in a time period such as a year. It is calculated to see if a business has an excessive inventory in comparison to its sales level. The equation for _____ equals the cost of goods sold divided by the average inventory. _____ is also known as inventory turns, merchandise turnover, stockturn, stock turns, turns, and stock turnover.

Exam Probability: **Low**

19. *Answer choices:*

(see index for correct answer)

- a. imperative
- b. corporate values
- c. information systems assessment
- d. Character

:: Competition (economics) ::

In taxation and accounting, _____ refers to the rules and methods for pricing transactions within and between enterprises under common ownership or control. Because of the potential for cross-border controlled transactions to distort taxable income, tax authorities in many countries can adjust intragroup transfer prices that differ from what would have been charged by unrelated enterprises dealing at arm's length . The OECD and World Bank recommend intragroup pricing rules based on the arm's-length principle, and 19 of the 20 members of the G20 have adopted similar measures through bilateral treaties and domestic legislation, regulations, or administrative practice. Countries with _____ legislation generally follow the OECD _____ Guidelines for Multinational Enterprises and Tax Administrations in most respects, although their rules can differ on some important details.

Exam Probability: **Low**

20. *Answer choices:*

(see index for correct answer)

- a. Transfer pricing
- b. Regulatory competition
- c. Level playing field
- d. Competition

:: Value theory ::

Within philosophy, it can be known as ethics or axiology. Early philosophical investigations sought to understand good and evil and the concept of "the good". Today, much of _____ aspires to the scientifically empirical, recording what people do value and attempting to understand why they value it in the context of psychology, sociology, and economics.

Exam Probability: **High**

21. *Answer choices:*

(see index for correct answer)

- a. Intrinsic theory of value
- b. Theory of value
- c. Value theory
- d. Marginalism

Guidance: level 1

:: Inventory ::

Costs are associated with particular goods using one of the several formulas, including specific identification, first-in first-out , or average cost. Costs include all costs of purchase, costs of conversion and other costs that are incurred in bringing the inventories to their present location and condition. Costs of goods made by the businesses include material, labor, and allocated overhead. The costs of those goods which are not yet sold are deferred as costs of inventory until the inventory is sold or written down in value.

Exam Probability: **Medium**

22. *Answer choices:*

(see index for correct answer)

- a. Phantom inventory
- b. Stock keeping unit
- c. Cost of goods sold
- d. Order fulfillment

Guidance: level 1

:: Data security ::

_____ is the concept of having more than one person required to complete a task. In business the separation by sharing of more than one individual in one single task is an internal control intended to prevent fraud and error. The concept is alternatively called segregation of duties or, in the political realm, separation of powers. In democracies, the separation of legislation from administration serves a similar purpose. The concept is addressed in technical systems and in information technology equivalently and generally addressed as redundancy.

Exam Probability: **Medium**

23. *Answer choices:*

(see index for correct answer)

- a. Separation of duties
- b. Offline private key
- c. Biometric passport
- d. Self-destruct

Guidance: level 1

:: Management ::

The _____ is a strategy performance management tool – a semi-standard structured report, that can be used by managers to keep track of the execution of activities by the staff within their control and to monitor the consequences arising from these actions.

24. *Answer choices:*

(see index for correct answer)

- a. Balanced scorecard
- b. Just in time
- c. Mission critical
- d. Goals Breakdown Structure

Guidance: level 1

:: ::

An _____ is a contingent motivator. Traditional _____ s are extrinsic motivators which reward actions to yield a desired outcome. The effectiveness of traditional _____ s has changed as the needs of Western society have evolved. While the traditional _____ model is effective when there is a defined procedure and goal for a task, Western society started to require a higher volume of critical thinkers, so the traditional model became less effective. Institutions are now following a trend in implementing strategies that rely on intrinsic motivations rather than the extrinsic motivations that the traditional _____ s foster.

Exam Probability: **High**

25. *Answer choices:*

(see index for correct answer)

- a. interpersonal communication
- b. Sarbanes-Oxley act of 2002
- c. functional perspective
- d. hierarchical perspective

:: United States Generally Accepted Accounting Principles ::

In a companies' financial reporting, _____ "includes all changes in equity during a period except those resulting from investments by owners and distributions to owners". Because that use excludes the effects of changing ownership interest, an economic measure of _____ is necessary for financial analysis from the shareholders' point of view

Exam Probability: **High**

26. *Answer choices:*

(see index for correct answer)

- a. Comprehensive annual financial report
- b. FIN 46
- c. Available for sale
- d. Single Audit

:: Legal terms ::

An _____ is an action which is inaccurate or incorrect. In some usages, an _____ is synonymous with a mistake. In statistics, "_____" refers to the difference between the value which has been computed and the correct value. An _____ could result in failure or in a deviation from the intended performance or behaviour.

Exam Probability: **High**

27. *Answer choices:*
(see index for correct answer)

- a. Omnibus hearing
- b. Champerty and maintenance
- c. Affray
- d. Error

Guidance: level 1

:: Financial accounting ::

_____ refers to any one of several methods by which a company, for `financial accounting` or tax purposes, depreciates a fixed asset in such a way that the amount of depreciation taken each year is higher during the earlier years of an asset's life. For financial accounting purposes, _____ is expected to be much more productive during its early years, so that depreciation expense will more accurately represent how much of an asset's usefulness is being used up each year. For tax purposes, _____ provides a way of deferring corporate income taxes by reducing taxable income in current years, in exchange for increased taxable income in future years. This is a valuable tax incentive that encourages businesses to purchase new assets.

Exam Probability: **Low**

28. *Answer choices:*

(see index for correct answer)

- a. Net worth
- b. SEC filing
- c. Equity method
- d. Holding gains

Guidance: level 1

:: Commerce ::

Continuation of an entity as a _____ is presumed as the basis for financial reporting unless and until the entity's liquidation becomes imminent. Preparation of financial statements under this presumption is commonly referred to as the _____ basis of accounting. If and when an entity's liquidation becomes imminent, financial statements are prepared under the liquidation basis of accounting .

Exam Probability: **Medium**

29. *Answer choices:*

(see index for correct answer)

- a. Reseller
- b. Uttarapatha
- c. Going concern
- d. Church sale

Guidance: level 1

:: Financial ratios ::

A _____ or accounting ratio is a relative magnitude of two selected numerical values taken from an enterprise's financial statements. Often used in accounting, there are many standard ratios used to try to evaluate the overall financial condition of a corporation or other organization. _____ s may be used by managers within a firm, by current and potential shareholders of a firm, and by a firm's creditors. Financial analysts use _____ s to compare the strengths and weaknesses in various companies. If shares in a company are traded in a financial market, the market price of the shares is used in certain _____ s.

Exam Probability: **Medium**

30. *Answer choices:*

(see index for correct answer)

- a. Rate of return on a portfolio
- b. Net capital outflow
- c. Debt-to-income ratio
- d. Financial ratio

Guidance: level 1

:: Management accounting ::

_____ is the profit the firm makes from serving a customer or customer group over a specified period of time, specifically the difference between the revenues earned from and the costs associated with the customer relationship in a specified period. According to Philip Kotler,"a profitable customer is a person, household or a company that overtime, yields a revenue stream that exceeds by an acceptable amount the company`s cost stream of attracting, selling and servicing the customer."

Exam Probability: **Medium**

31. *Answer choices:*

(see index for correct answer)

- a. Fixed assets management
- b. Activity-based management
- c. Pre-determined overhead rate
- d. Customer profitability

Guidance: level 1

:: Corporate taxation in the United States ::

A _____ , under United States federal income tax law, refers to any corporation that is taxed separately from its owners. A _____ is distinguished from an S corporation, which generally is not taxed separately. Most major companies are treated as _____ s for U.S. federal income tax purposes. _____ s and S corporations both enjoy limited liability, but only _____ s are subject to corporate income taxation.

32. *Answer choices:*

(see index for correct answer)

- a. C corporation
- b. Franchise tax
- c. Taxation of cooperative corporations in the United States
- d. Low-profit limited liability company

Guidance: level 1

:: International taxation ::

_____ is the levying of tax by two or more jurisdictions on the same declared income , asset , or financial transaction . Double liability is mitigated in a number of ways, for example.

33. *Answer choices:*

(see index for correct answer)

- a. Expatriation tax
- b. Foreign personal holding company
- c. Currency transaction tax
- d. Double taxation

:: Real estate ::

Amortisation is paying off an amount owed over time by making planned, incremental payments of principal and interest. To amortise a loan means "to kill it off". In accounting, amortisation refers to charging or writing off an intangible asset's cost as an operational expense over its estimated useful life to reduce a company's taxable income.

Exam Probability: **Medium**

34. *Answer choices:*

(see index for correct answer)

- a. Amortization
- b. Real estate pricing
- c. Real estate transaction
- d. Overseas property

:: Inventory ::

_____ is the maximum amount of goods, or inventory, that a company can possibly sell during this fiscal year. It has the formula.

Exam Probability: **Low**

35. *Answer choices:*

(see index for correct answer)

- a. Cost of goods sold
- b. Cost of goods available for sale
- c. Periodic inventory
- d. Order picking

Guidance: level 1

:: Accounting ::

_____ examines how accounting is used by individuals, organizations and government as well as the consequences that these practices have. Starting from the assumption that accounting both measures and makes visible certain economic events, _____ has studied the roles of accounting in organizations and society and the consequences that these practices have for individuals, organizations, governments and capital markets. It encompasses a broad range of topics including financial _____ , management _____ , auditing research, capital market research, accountability research, social responsibility research and taxation research.

Exam Probability: **Medium**

36. *Answer choices:*

(see index for correct answer)

- a. Accounting research
- b. Part exchange
- c. Engineering Accounting
- d. Earnings surprise

Guidance: level 1

:: Password authentication ::

A _____ , or sometimes redundantly a PIN number, is a numeric or alpha-numeric password used in the process of authenticating a user accessing a system.

Exam Probability: **Low**

37. *Answer choices:*

(see index for correct answer)

- a. Password-authenticated key agreement
- b. Cognitive password
- c. Personal identification number
- d. S/KEY

Guidance: level 1

:: Generally Accepted Accounting Principles ::

A _____ or reacquired stock is stock which is bought back by the issuing company, reducing the amount of outstanding stock on the open market .

Exam Probability: **High**

38. *Answer choices:*

(see index for correct answer)

- a. Treasury stock
- b. deferred revenue
- c. Net profit
- d. Expense

Guidance: level 1

:: Money ::

In economics, _____ is money in the physical form of currency, such as banknotes and coins. In bookkeeping and finance, _____ is current assets comprising currency or currency equivalents that can be accessed immediately or near-immediately . _____ is seen either as a reserve for payments, in case of a structural or incidental negative _____ flow or as a way to avoid a downturn on financial markets.

Exam Probability: **Medium**

39. *Answer choices:*

(see index for correct answer)

- a. Money creation
- b. Sequin
- c. Cash
- d. World Money Fair

Guidance: level 1

:: Management accounting ::

_____ is a method of identifying and evaluating activities that a business performs, using activity-based costing to carry out a value chain analysis or a re-engineering initiative to improve strategic and operational decisions in an organization.

Exam Probability: **High**

40. *Answer choices:*

(see index for correct answer)

- a. Variable cost
- b. Variable Costing
- c. Activity-based management

- d. Certified Management Accountants of Canada

Guidance: level 1

:: Management accounting ::

_____ is a managerial accounting cost concept. Under this method, manufacturing overhead is incurred in the period that a product is produced. This addresses the issue of absorption costing that allows income to rise as production rises. Under an absorption cost method, management can push forward costs to the next period when products are sold. This artificially inflates profits in the period of production by incurring less cost than would be incurred under a _____ system. _____ is generally not used for external reporting purposes. Under the Tax Reform Act of 1986, income statements must use absorption costing to comply with GAAP.

Exam Probability: **Low**

41. *Answer choices:*

(see index for correct answer)

- a. Overhead
- b. Management control system
- c. Variance
- d. Variable Costing

Guidance: level 1

:: International taxation ::

A _____ tax, or a retention tax, is an income tax to be paid to the government by the payer of the income rather than by the recipient of the income. The tax is thus withheld or deducted from the income due to the recipient. In most jurisdictions, _____ tax applies to employment income. Many jurisdictions also require _____ tax on payments of interest or dividends. In most jurisdictions, there are additional _____ tax obligations if the recipient of the income is resident in a different jurisdiction, and in those circumstances _____ tax sometimes applies to royalties, rent or even the sale of real estate. Governments use _____ tax as a means to combat tax evasion, and sometimes impose additional _____ tax requirements if the recipient has been delinquent in filing tax returns, or in industries where tax evasion is perceived to be common.

Exam Probability: **High**

42. *Answer choices:*

(see index for correct answer)

- a. Withholding
- b. Tax information exchange agreement
- c. Passive foreign investment company
- d. Exchange of information

Guidance: level 1

:: ::

_____ is a costing method that identifies activities in an organization and assigns the cost of each activity to all products and services according to the actual consumption by each. This model assigns more indirect costs into direct costs compared to conventional costing.

Exam Probability: **High**

43. *Answer choices:*

(see index for correct answer)

- a. Activity-based costing
- b. process perspective
- c. hierarchical
- d. Sarbanes-Oxley act of 2002

Guidance: level 1

:: Asset ::

In accounting, a _____ is any asset which can reasonably be expected to be sold, consumed, or exhausted through the normal operations of a business within the current fiscal year or operating cycle . Typical _____ s include cash, cash equivalents, short-term investments , accounts receivable, stock inventory, supplies, and the portion of prepaid liabilities which will be paid within a year.In simple words, assets which are held for a short period are known as _____ s. Such assets are expected to be realised in cash or consumed during the normal operating cycle of the business.

44. *Answer choices:*

(see index for correct answer)

- a. Fixed asset
- b. Current asset

Guidance: level 1

:: Types of accounting ::

Various _____ systems are used by various public sector entities. In the United States, for instance, there are two levels of government which follow different accounting standards set forth by independent, private sector boards. At the federal level, the Federal Accounting Standards Advisory Board sets forth the accounting standards to follow. Similarly, there is the _____ Standards Board for state and local level government.

Exam Probability: **High**

45. *Answer choices:*

(see index for correct answer)

- a. Product control
- b. Sustainability accounting
- c. Governmental accounting

:: Finance ::

The _____ of a corporation is the accumulated net income of the corporation that is retained by the corporation at a particular point of time, such as at the end of the reporting period. At the end of that period, the net income at that point is transferred from the Profit and Loss Account to the _____ account. If the balance of the _____ account is negative it may be called accumulated losses, retained losses or accumulated deficit, or similar terminology.

Exam Probability: **Medium**

46. *Answer choices:*

(see index for correct answer)

- a. Rollover
- b. Cheyette Model
- c. Short
- d. Trend following

:: Business law ::

An _____ is a natural person, business, or corporation that provides goods or services to another entity under terms specified in a contract or within a verbal agreement. Unlike an employee, an _____ does not work regularly for an employer but works as and when required, during which time they may be subject to law of agency. _____ s are usually paid on a freelance basis. Contractors often work through a limited company or franchise, which they themselves own, or may work through an umbrella company.

Exam Probability: Medium

47. *Answer choices:*

(see index for correct answer)

- a. Apparent authority
- b. Ease of doing business index
- c. Participation
- d. Independent contractor

Guidance: level 1

:: Tax credits ::

A _____ is a tax incentive which allows certain taxpayers to subtract the amount of the credit they have accrued from the total they owe the state. It may also be a credit granted in recognition of taxes already paid or, as in the United Kingdom, a form of state support.

Exam Probability: High

48. *Answer choices:*

(see index for correct answer)

- a. Tax credit
- b. Hope credit
- c. Lifetime Learning Credit
- d. Adoption tax credit

Guidance: level 1

:: Business models ::

A _____ is a company that owns enough voting stock in another firm to control management and operation by influencing or electing its board of directors. The company is deemed a subsidiary of the _____ .

Exam Probability: **Low**

49. *Answer choices:*

(see index for correct answer)

- a. Parent company
- b. Subsidiary
- c. Premium business model
- d. Home business

Guidance: level 1

:: ::

In the field of analysis of algorithms in computer science, the _____ is a method of amortized analysis based on accounting. The _____ often gives a more intuitive account of the amortized cost of an operation than either aggregate analysis or the potential method. Note, however, that this does not guarantee such analysis will be immediately obvious; often, choosing the correct parameters for the _____ requires as much knowledge of the problem and the complexity bounds one is attempting to prove as the other two methods.

Exam Probability: **Low**

50. *Answer choices:*

(see index for correct answer)

- a. Accounting method
- b. hierarchical
- c. process perspective
- d. levels of analysis

Guidance: level 1

:: ::

The _____ is an American stock exchange located at 11 Wall Street, Lower Manhattan, New York City, New York. It is by far the world's largest stock exchange by market capitalization of its listed companies at US$30.1 trillion as of February 2018. The average daily trading value was approximately US$169 billion in 2013. The NYSE trading floor is located at 11 Wall Street and is composed of 21 rooms used for the facilitation of trading. A fifth trading room, located at 30 Broad Street, was closed in February 2007. The main building and the 11 Wall Street building were designated National Historic Landmarks in 1978.

Exam Probability: **Medium**

51. *Answer choices:*

(see index for correct answer)

- a. hierarchical perspective
- b. open system
- c. co-culture
- d. cultural

Guidance: level 1

:: E-commerce ::

_____ is an e-commerce payment system used in the Netherlands, based on online banking. Introduced in 2005, this payment method allows customers to buy on the Internet using direct online transfers from their bank account.

Exam Probability: **Low**

52. *Answer choices:*

(see index for correct answer)

- a. Interface Technologies
- b. E-commerce in Southeast Asia
- c. Global Location Number
- d. IDEAL

Guidance: level 1

:: Management accounting ::

_____ is a professional business study of Accounts and management in which we learn importance of accounts in our management system.

Exam Probability: **Medium**

53. *Answer choices:*

(see index for correct answer)

- a. Cost accounting
- b. Dual overhead rate
- c. Resource consumption accounting
- d. Accounting management

:: Management ::

_____ is the identification, evaluation, and prioritization of risks followed by coordinated and economical application of resources to minimize, monitor, and control the probability or impact of unfortunate events or to maximize the realization of opportunities.

Exam Probability: **Medium**

54. *Answer choices:*

(see index for correct answer)

- a. Director
- b. Reverse innovation
- c. Risk management
- d. Performance indicator

:: Pharmaceutical industry ::

A _____ is a document in which data collected for a clinical trial is first recorded. This data is usually later entered in the case report form. The International Conference on Harmonisation of Technical Requirements for Registration of Pharmaceuticals for Human Use guidelines define _____ s as "original documents, data, and records." _____ s contain source data, which is defined as "all information in original records and certified copies of original records of clinical findings, observations, or other activities in a clinical trial necessary for the reconstruction and evaluation of the trial."

Exam Probability: **Low**

55. *Answer choices:*

(see index for correct answer)

- a. Average Wholesale Price
- b. Norwegian Medicines Agency
- c. Innovative Medicines Initiative
- d. Source document

Guidance: level 1

:: ::

An _____ , for United States federal income tax, is a closely held corporation that makes a valid election to be taxed under Subchapter S of Chapter 1 of the Internal Revenue Code. In general, _____ s do not pay any income taxes. Instead, the corporation's income or losses are divided among and passed through to its shareholders. The shareholders must then report the income or loss on their own individual income tax returns.

56. *Answer choices:*

(see index for correct answer)

- a. hierarchical perspective
- b. open system
- c. S corporation
- d. corporate values

Guidance: level 1

:: Generally Accepted Accounting Principles ::

Paid-in capital is capital that is contributed to a corporation by investors
by purchase of stock from the corporation, the primary market, not by purchase
of stock in the open market from other stockholders . It includes share capital
as well as additional paid-in capital.

Exam Probability: **Medium**

57. *Answer choices:*

(see index for correct answer)

- a. Revenue
- b. Contributed capital
- c. Deprival value

- d. Gross profit

Guidance: level 1

:: Quality control tools ::

A _____ is a type of diagram that represents an algorithm, workflow or process. _____ can also be defined as a diagramatic representation of an algorithm .

Exam Probability: **High**

58. *Answer choices:*

(see index for correct answer)

- a. EVOP
- b. Regression control chart
- c. Flowchart
- d. CUSUM

Guidance: level 1

:: Marketing ::

_____ or stock is the goods and materials that a business holds for the ultimate goal of resale .

Exam Probability: **Medium**

59. *Answer choices:*

(see index for correct answer)

- a. Marketing in schools
- b. Meta marketing
- c. Inventory
- d. Category management

Guidance: level 1

INDEX: Correct Answers

Foundations of Business

1. a: Decision-making

2. c: Customs

3. a: Explanation

4. a: Fraud

5. b: Market share

6. b: Reputation

7. c: Strategic planning

8. : Audience

9. b: Building

10. b: Pattern

11. : Target market

12. b: Regulation

13. : Evaluation

14. b: Trademark

15. : Industrial Revolution

16. : Sexual harassment

17. : Marketing

18. d: Patent

19. a: Crisis

20. a: Balance sheet

21. : Percentage

22. : Buyer

23. d: Human resources

24. d: Frequency

25. d: Ownership

26. d: Productivity

27. : Image

28. b: Document

29. d: Globalization

30. a: Stock

31. c: Comparative advantage

32. d: Debt

33. c: Feedback

34. b: Cash flow

35. d: Protection

36. d: Sustainability

37. : Consumer Protection

38. c: Analysis

39. : Sony

40. : Diagram

41. c: Present value

42. b: Demand

43. b: Asset

44. a: Inflation

45. d: Limited liability

46. b: Information technology

47. : Arthur Andersen

48. b: Federal Trade Commission

49. a: Interview

50. d: Capital market

51. c: Question

52. a: Authority

53. d: Health

54. d: Policy

55. b: Risk

56. c: Land

57. d: Property

58. b: Resource management

59. d: Organizational culture

Management

1. a: Revenue

2. d: Organizational culture

3. a: Quality control

4. b: Customs

5. : Glass ceiling

6. : Fixed cost

7. : Contingency theory

8. a: Virtual team

9. d: Choice

10. c: Environmental protection

11. d: Analysis

12. : Procurement

13. a: Market research

14. a: Consultant

15. b: Cooperation

16. : Leadership style

17. c: Decision-making

18. a: Firm

19. a: Incentive

20. a: Protection

21. : Risk management

22. c: European Union

23. b: Goal

24. b: Accounting

25. a: Training

26. a: Customer

27. d: SWOT analysis

28. : Balanced scorecard

29. b: Collective bargaining

30. d: Meeting

31. : Bias

32. d: Property

33. a: Stereotype

34. c: General manager

35. b: Process control

36. c: Raw material

37. d: Project team

38. c: Policy

39. b: North American Free Trade Agreement

40. b: Efficiency

41. c: Committee

42. c: Size

43. d: Employee stock

44. : Management

45. : Statistical process control

46. : Myers-Briggs type

47. : Management by objectives

48. a: Leadership

49. d: Training and development

50. d: Total cost

51. : Frequency

52. a: Gantt chart

53. c: Time management

54. d: Hotel

55. c: Entrepreneurship

56. b: Theory X

57. c: Business plan

58. b: Insurance

59. : Board of directors

Business law

1. b: Employment discrimination

2. : Affidavit

3. a: Security

4. : Reasonable person

5. d: World Trade Organization

6. : Mirror image rule

7. c: Punitive

8. d: Misdemeanor

9. c: Income

10. c: Proximate cause

11. a: Charter

12. : Puffery

13. c: Consumer credit

14. b: Apparent authority

15. c: Fraud

16. b: Merchant

17. : Limited liability

18. c: Personnel

19. d: Categorical imperative

20. : Unconscionability

21. d: Clayton Act

22. : Forgery

23. c: Adverse possession

24. : Credit

25. c: Statute

26. c: Patent

27. : Void contract

28. d: Injunction

29. : Hearing

30. : Respondeat superior

31. d: Fiduciary

32. b: Arbitration clause

33. b: Economic Espionage Act

34. b: False imprisonment

35. : Judicial review

36. a: Independent contractor

37. : Appeal

38. d: Inventory

39. b: Corporate governance

40. c: Mortgage

41. c: Affirmative action

42. a: Lease

43. b: Berne Convention

44. : Advertisement

45. b: Lien

46. a: Plaintiff

47. d: Statutory Law

48. a: Disclaimer

49. a: Resource

50. a: Sole proprietorship

51. c: Joint venture

52. b: Advertising

53. : Welfare

54. : Surety

55. : Expense

56. c: Contributory negligence

57. c: Insurance

58. : Investment

59. b: Deed

Finance

1. a: Book value

2. a: Budget

3. c: Present value

4. a: Merger

5. : Cash management

6. a: INDEX

7. d: Secondary market

8. d: General ledger

9. : Periodic inventory

10. : Worksheet

11. d: Net profit

12. : Free cash flow

13. a: Liquidity

14. : Financial Accounting Standards Board

15. a: Credit risk

16. a: Government bond

17. : Cost of goods sold

18. d: Internal rate of return

19. : Payroll

20. d: Net income

21. d: Pension fund

22. a: Interest rate

23. a: Value Line

24. b: Return on assets

25. a: Cash equivalent

26. b: Accountant

27. b: Indenture

28. a: Promissory note

29. a: Firm

30. : Debt-to-equity ratio

31. c: Internal control

32. c: Market risk

33. c: Interest

34. : Current ratio

35. c: Capital structure

36. d: Presentation

37. b: Hedge

38. d: Accounts receivable

39. c: Industry

40. b: Generally accepted accounting principles

41. : Equity method

42. : Accounting

43. d: Dividend

44. : Normal balance

45. a: Expense

46. d: Technology

47. a: Capital stock

48. c: Rate risk

49. : Yield curve

50. d: Manufacturing

51. d: Corporation

52. b: Inflation

53. : Securities and Exchange Commission

54. d: Financial management

55. c: Stock split

56. a: Income

57. : Expected return

58. d: Risk premium

59. a: Issuer

Human resource management

1. b: Officer

2. b: Just cause

3. d: Price Waterhouse v. Hopkins

4. d: Profit sharing

5. b: Mediation

6. c: Pregnancy discrimination

7. : Empowerment

8. c: Job enrichment

9. d: Social networking

10. : Sick leave

11. a: Distance learning

12. : Job evaluation

13. c: Referent power

14. d: Resource management

15. c: Authoritarianism

16. d: Interview

17. b: Aptitude

18. c: Glass ceiling

19. c: Performance management

20. b: Local union

21. : Congress

22. a: Coaching

23. c: Business model

24. c: Compa-ratio

25. a: Wage curve

26. : Golden parachute

27. : Cost of living

28. d: Employee referral

29. c: Organizational justice

30. : Job design

31. c: Internal consistency

32. : Census

33. : Professional association

34. b: Career development

35. b: Licensure

36. c: American Federation of Government Employees

37. c: Interdependence

38. d: Committee

39. d: Scientific management

40. d: Perception

41. c: Retraining

42. c: Free agent

43. c: Business game

44. b: Strategy map

45. : Scanlon plan

46. : Free Trade

47. b: Six Sigma

48. a: Retirement

49. d: Flexible spending account

50. : Hazard

51. : Workplace violence

52. : Succession planning

53. : Occupational Safety and Health Act

54. a: Performance appraisal

55. d: 360-degree feedback

56. b: Impression management

57. a: Labor relations

58. b: Workforce

59. b: Evaluation

Information systems

1. d: Government-to-citizen

2. : Blog

3. a: Resource management

4. c: ITunes

5. a: Avatar

6. b: Downtime

7. c: User interface

8. c: Automated teller machine

9. : Consumerization

10. a: Change management

11. a: Extranet

12. a: Chief information officer

13. a: Commercial off-the-shelf

14. a: Crowdsourcing

15. : Operational system

16. c: Gmail

17. a: One Laptop per Child

18. d: Strategic planning

19. a: Disaster recovery plan

20. c: Wiki

21. d: Google Calendar

22. : Radio-frequency identification

23. d: Spamming

24. : Word

25. a: Personalization

26. : Business-to-business

27. d: Worm

28. : Information governance

29. b: Information security

30. d: Decision-making

31. b: Carnivore

32. b: Virtual reality

33. c: Big data

34. : Manifesto

35. a: Mozy

36. a: Vulnerability

37. a: Service level agreement

38. d: Business rule

39. c: Backbone network

40. : Supply chain

41. d: Electronic data interchange

42. : Computer security

43. d: Tacit knowledge

44. : Google Maps

45. b: Interview

46. b: Analytics

47. a: Online advertising

48. c: Trojan horse

49. b: Digital rights management

50. a: Netflix

51. a: Unstructured data

52. a: Asset

53. d: Vertical integration

54. a: Privacy

55. a: Enterprise resource planning

56. a: Information privacy

57. c: Data dictionary

58. a: Payment card

59. d: Utility computing

Marketing

1. c: Retailing

2. c: Public relations

3. d: Database marketing

4. b: Green marketing

5. : Bottom line

6. b: Market development

7. d: Competitor

8. b: Microsoft

9. : Business-to-business

10. d: Resource

11. : Billboard

12. a: Competition

13. a: Star

14. a: Social media

15. d: Data analysis

16. : Exchange rate

17. b: New product development

18. a: Unique selling proposition

19. b: Investment

20. d: Merchant

21. d: Database

22. : Tangible

23. : Economy

24. : Advertisement

25. : Evolution

26. d: Buyer

27. a: Total cost

28. d: Consideration

29. : Preference

30. c: Mass marketing

31. b: Qualitative research

32. c: Demand

33. c: Supply chain

34. d: Audit

35. : Selling

36. d: Census

37. : Policy

38. : Persuasion

39. c: Communication

40. d: Marketing strategy

41. : Price

42. c: Contract

43. d: Product manager

44. b: Electronic data interchange

45. a: Intangibility

46. c: Globalization

47. c: Subsidiary

48. : Sponsorship

49. : Research and development

50. b: Respondent

51. : Google

52. a: Brand management

53. b: Monopoly

54. d: Economies of scale

55. d: Planning

56. c: Price war

57. d: Insurance

58. b: Market share

59. a: Department store

Manufacturing

1. b: Rolling

2. c: METRIC

3. d: Certification

4. b: Resource allocation

5. : Blanket

6. b: Total cost

7. c: Lean manufacturing

8. c: Supply chain management

9. b: Six Sigma

10. c: ROOT

11. b: Scope statement

12. a: DMAIC

13. b: Opportunity cost

14. : Risk management

15. c: Third-party logistics

16. b: Sequence

17. d: Project team

18. a: Control chart

19. a: Request for quotation

20. : Project

21. c: Vendor relationship management

22. a: Sony

23. a: American Society for Quality

24. : Chemical reaction

25. a: Inspection

26. b: Process flow diagram

27. a: Process engineering

28. b: Project manager

29. : Lead

30. b: Goal

31. c: Elastomer

32. c: Clay

33. d: Sensitivity analysis

34. a: Gantt chart

35. b: Initiative

36. b: Transaction cost

37. : Quality control

38. b: Waste

39. a: Procurement

40. a: Rolling Wave planning

41. d: Total cost of ownership

42. a: Supply chain risk management

43. b: Purchasing manager

44. d: Cost estimate

45. a: Authority

46. a: Bullwhip effect

47. c: Schedule

48. c: Thomas Register

49. c: Downtime

50. b: Electronic data interchange

51. d: Control limits

52. a: Kanban

53. a: Good

54. c: Milestone

55. b: Change management

56. d: Ishikawa diagram

57. a: Minitab

58. : Design of experiments

59. c: Obsolescence

Commerce

1. : Value-added network

2. b: Forward auction

3. b: Argument

4. c: Land

5. : Front office

6. a: Permission marketing

7. d: Industry

8. a: Purchase order

9. d: Customer service

10. b: Subsidy

11. a: Total revenue

12. c: Pop-up ad

13. c: Security

14. b: Brand

15. d: Market research

16. d: Credit card

17. a: Business-to-business

18. a: Cash flow

19. b: Supply chain

20. a: Market share

21. d: British Airways

22. : Wholesale

23. d: Economies of scale

24. : Manufacturing

25. b: Authentication

26. : Industrial Revolution

27. b: Long run

28. : Labor union

29. d: Evaluation

30. : Social shopping

31. : Supply chain management

32. c: Real estate

33. a: Negotiation

34. a: Consumer-to-consumer

35. c: Asset

36. c: Free market

37. d: Liquidation

38. b: Trade

39. d: Hospitality

40. b: Quality assurance

41. d: Board of directors

42. a: Invoice

43. a: Quality control

44. d: Electronic commerce

45. a: Inventory

46. : Goal

47. : Inventory control

48. c: Marketspace

49. b: Shareholder

50. b: Organizational structure

51. b: Warehouse

52. b: Walt Disney

53. a: Micropayment

54. b: Budget

55. c: Leadership

56. b: Procurement

57. : WebSphere Commerce

58. a: Authority

59. d: Overhead cost

Business ethics

1. : Madoff

2. b: Price fixing

3. b: Dress code

4. a: Transformational leadership

5. : WorldCom

6. b: Criminal law

7. c: Perception

8. c: Corporate citizenship

9. : Layoff

10. b: UN Global Compact

11. b: Clayton Act

12. a: Socialism

13. c: Locus of control

14. : Real estate

15. c: Greenwashing

16. b: Chamber of Commerce

17. a: Sustainable

18. : Marketing

19. d: Trade

20. a: Federal Trade Commission Act

21. a: Foreign Corrupt Practices Act

22. : Skill

23. b: Corporation

24. d: Protestant work ethic

25. c: Six Sigma

26. c: Stanford Financial Group

27. : Corporate structure

28. : Fannie Mae

29. d: Fraud

30. c: Junk bond

31. c: Federal Trade Commission

32. b: Partnership

33. b: Workplace bullying

34. : Ethical leadership

35. : Micromanagement

36. a: Referent power

37. b: Qui tam

38. b: Whistleblower

39. b: Corporate social responsibility

40. : Exxon Valdez

41. d: Martin Luther

42. c: East India

43. a: Dilemma

44. b: Auditor independence

45. c: Veil of ignorance

46. a: New Deal

47. d: Siemens

48. a: Capitalism

49. a: Trojan horse

50. d: Statutory law

51. d: Arthur Andersen

52. b: Collusion

53. b: Communist Manifesto

54. c: Tobacco

55. d: Vigilance committee

56. b: New York Stock Exchange

57. b: Sullivan principles

58. a: Authoritarian

59. a: Lead paint

Accounting

1. d: Revenue

2. b: Disability insurance

3. c: Fair market value

4. : Stock Market

5. d: Capital expenditure

6. : Inflation

7. b: Internal Revenue Service

8. b: Tax avoidance

9. c: Deferral

10. a: Sole proprietorship

11. c: Ending inventory

12. a: Fixed asset

13. a: Earnings management

14. a: Ledger

15. c: Norwalk Agreement

16. c: Proprietorship

17. b: Calendar year

18. d: Risk assessment

19. : Inventory turnover

20. a: Transfer pricing

21. c: Value theory

22. c: Cost of goods sold

23. a: Separation of duties

24. a: Balanced scorecard

25. : Incentive

26. : Comprehensive income

27. d: Error

28. : Accelerated depreciation

29. c: Going concern

30. d: Financial ratio

31. d: Customer profitability

32. a: C corporation

33. d: Double taxation

34. a: Amortization

35. b: Cost of goods available for sale

36. a: Accounting research

37. c: Personal identification number

38. a: Treasury stock

39. c: Cash

40. c: Activity-based management

41. d: Variable Costing

42. a: Withholding

43. a: Activity-based costing

44. b: Current asset

45. c: Governmental accounting

46. : Retained earnings

47. d: Independent contractor

48. a: Tax credit

49. a: Parent company

50. a: Accounting method

51. : New York Stock Exchange

52. d: IDEAL

53. d: Accounting management

54. c: Risk management

55. d: Source document

56. c: S corporation

57. b: Contributed capital

58. c: Flowchart

59. c: Inventory

CPSIA information can be obtained
at www.ICGtesting.com
Printed in the USA
LVHW031107301019
635717LV00004B/368/P